My Year Before the Mast

My Year Before the Mast

Annette Brock Davis

HOUNSLOW PRESS
A MEMBER OF THE DUNDURN GROUP
TORONTO· OXFORD

Hounslow Press
A Member of the Dundurn Group

Publisher: Anthony Hawke
Co-ordinator: John Stratton
Editor: Helen Hatton
Copyeditor: Barry Jowett
Design: Scott Reid
Printer: Transcontinental Printing Inc.

Canadian Cataloguing in Publication Data

Davis, Annette Brock, 1912–
My year before the mast

Includes bibliographical references
ISBN 0-88882-207-3
1. Davis, Annette Brock, 1912– . 2. Women sailors — Canada — Biography.
3. Sex discrimination against women. I. Title

HD6073.S42C3 1999   387.5'092   C99-930911-0

1   2   3   4   5   03   02   01   00   99

THE CANADA COUNCIL | LE CONSEIL DES ARTS
FOR THE ARTS | DU CANADA
SINCE 1957 | DEPUIS 1957

We acknowledge the support of the **Canada Council for the Arts** for our publishing program. We also acknowledge the support of the **Ontario Arts Council** and the **Book Publishing Industry Development Program** of the **Department of Canadian Heritage**.

Care has been taken to trace the ownership of copyright material used in this book. The author and the publisher welcome any information enabling them to rectify any references or credit in subsequent editions.

Printed and bound in Canada.

Printed on recycled paper.

Hounslow Press
8 Market Street
Suite 200
Toronto, Canada
M5E 1M6

Hounslow Press
73 Lime Walk
Headington, Oxford,
England
OX3 7AD

Hounslow Press
2250 Military Road
Tonawanda NY
U.S.A 14150

Contents

Acknowledgements   7

Chapter 1: Getting Under Way   9
Chapter 2: *L'Avenir* and I Meet   25
Chapter 3: We Sail   35
Chapter 4: Shipmates   45
Chapter 5: Changing Sails   57
Chapter 6: Work and Music Aboard   61
Chapter 7: Crossing the Line   73
Chapter 8: Jumbo Proposes   77
Chapter 9: The Westerlies   83
Chapter 10: Port Germein   103
Chapter 11: *L'Avenir* Departs   125
Chapter 12: Stowaway   131
Chapter 13: Heavy Weather   143
Chapter 14: Airman Has Something to Say   149
Chapter 15: Otto   153
Chapter 16: I Turn the Ship Around   161
Chapter 17: Murder and Rape?   165
Chapter 18: Doldrums   173
Chapter 19: Spellbinding Trade Winds   179
Chapter 20: Anchored for Good   185

Epilogue   195
Appendix   199
Glossary   206
Bibliography   219

Acknowledgements

Nearly seventy years span my adventures on *L'Avenir* and their telling in this book. Over that period I have been indebted to many who encouraged me to write my story. In the present, I must first acknowledge the boundless assistance of Dr. John Stratton of Toronto, who has been the catalyst and guiding spirit in the publication of this book. It was he who told historian and editor Dr. Helen Hatton of my voyage and arranged for her to be given a copy of my manuscript. He then presented her professional comments and edited text to Tony Hawke of Dundurn Press. John gave generously of his expertise as a photographer and author in the exacting work necessary to select and prepare old snapshots and drawings for illustrations, and in the work of layout and proofing. Without Dr. Stratton's generous willingness to bring together the various components essential in taking this work to publication, my manuscript would still be in the drawer. He has my deepest gratitude.

To Dr. Helen Hatton, Department of History, University of Toronto, my thanks for her assessment of the possibilities of my story, and for polishing my prose, professionally and excellently, yet with remarkable understanding, so that my individual voice was not lost.

At Dundurn Press, the enthusiasm of Tony Hawke, Director of Publishing, brought me so much encouragement, enabling me to complete the additional work needed for publication.

From the past, so many figures stand out. Without the willingness of Gustaf Erikson, owner of the Erikson Line, to break untold centuries of tradition, I would never have set foot on *L'Avenir*, where Captain Nils Erikson assessed me fairly as a crew member. My companions on the voyage — crew, officers, and passengers — all made their own individual, indelible contributions, shaping and colouring my year before the mast.

During my many visits to her in Oxford, Barbara Strachey Halpern encouraged me to write my story, and made suggestions from her memories of the trip to Australia on *L'Avenir*.

Captain Eino Koivistoinen, author of *Billowing Sails*, with a chapter on our meeting at Port Germein, and Commander Alan Easton, author of *50° North*, both appear in the text, but I am grateful for many years of friendship. Thanks to Willa and David Walker, Mrs. Simpson of Knowlton, Kate Stout, Edward and Linda Novarro of Houston, and Prof. Arthur Motyer, who all gave much encouragement. Philip Hicken of the School of Practical Art in Boston and Nantucket pronounced, "Your painting is 99% better than your writing"!

Finally, heartfelt thanks to my dear daughter Ann Gale Natali, for her wonderful support and unstinting time in arranging for copies, specialty photographic work, and in acting as liaison between myself, John Stratton, Helen Hatton, and Tony Hawke.

Chapter I   *Getting Under Way*

She lay at anchor in Copenhagen roadstead, her name reflecting from her bows in odd distortions of the word *L'Avenir*. Mist wove through the rigging, hiding her topmasts and muffling the drumming inside the barque's steel hull. Down in her emptied coal hold, the knocking of hammers was deafening, and the coal dust was so heavy that the fog outside seemed clear by comparison. Two lanterns flickered, illuminating here a Slavic cheekbone and there a Viking jaw, but their smoke obscured so much that the form of a girl — me, that is — was indistinguishable among the dozen seamen chipping the rust.

For four hours the hammering had been striking through me as though it was the wave vibrations of the universe. Yet here in this black hell, I had found the world I had desired above all. Like the barque *L'Avenir*, I had been at anchor too long. Now we both awaited the wind that would sail us to Australia. For a moment, while realizing this, I let my weary arm relax so that it dropped to my side. Suddenly I felt a whack on my left hand.

"HA! You no goot. You stop verk." A big Finn, an able seaman, seized my wrist, then flung back the cuff of my fisherman's jersey to squint at the luminous dial of my Canadian watch. "Two hour *mera nu*," he bellowed in his Swedo-English.

The others did not hear his announcement of two more hours till knock-off time; all were isolated by oceans of racket on islands of their own thoughts.

How long was an hour to me? A moment, when reckoning the years in which I had endeavoured to sail in such a vessel. *L'Avenir*! Her very name meant "the future." Now it was the present, September 21, 1933 (my twenty-third birthday), and this four-masted barque was outward bound to Australia.

L'Avenir trailed at the end of a line of sailing ships which for two thousand years had opened up the world to man through the sea-borne trade, from the coasters of the iron age to the clippers of the 1800s. Her owner, Gustaf Erikson, lived in the far away Aland Islands, which lie between Sweden and Finland. This remarkable shipowner had built up a fleet of twenty-three great sailing vessels, which he made pay when no one else seemed able to do so. Shipmates told me "Erikson can afford to lose a ship a year and remain solvent, as he carries his own insurance." The ships, which had no means of propulsion other than wind power, carried grain, mostly from Australia to Europe. The long sailing voyage served to warehouse the grain, so that it arrived in time for the European markets.

What kind of a life was this going to prove, aboard for the many months it took to sail to Australia round the Cape of Good Hope, load up in Australia and return around the dreaded Cape Horn? In a few weeks we would be chasing the horizon across a lone and watery field of sea, with no wireless to use for communication and only signal flags in the rare chance of encountering another vessel. *L'Avenir* sailed outside of the lanes used by steam ships. If anyone fell ill aboard, the only chance of recovery might lie in the hands of the master and officers and the obscure contents of an old medicine chest. Unreal as such isolation sounds today, it was not too uncommon then. I faced this life aboard as the only woman in the crew, and a naive and inexperienced girl at that, brought up in a gentle and sheltered home.

From such a comparative life of ease, the work day at sea involved sixteen hours duty one day and eight the next. When not standing one's turn as lookout, "police," and wheel, one was employed in such heavy work as hauling on tackles, heaving up the anchor, or lifting tons of sail canvas as well as devoting long hours to chipping rust, coiling lines, and other piddling jobs. In addition, all hands might be called out in an emergency, and if required, work could continue for as long as three days and nights with only brief periods below for meals. After standing watches soaking wet, after hours of pulley hauly, one turned in too exhausted even to pull off sea boots.

As a young woman sixty-five years ago, I expected to endure pressures and prejudices stronger than those of today, as well as the normal hardships. Why did I choose such a seemingly unrewarding career, to be buffeted about not only by high seas, but by the unwelcoming attitudes of the crew? The urge to follow the sea had grown imperceptibly within me and I cannot recall the actual point at which I fell in love with it. My parents' families were travelled. My father's sister, when a hundred years old, related to me how as a three-year-old, I enjoyed looking at albums of travel postcards. The card I liked best, *Vesuvio in Eruzione,* showed the black volcano glowing brilliantly with lava. Aunt Lily asked me, "What would you like to do when you grow up?" She chuckled with glee, remembering how very solemnly and emphatically, for a three-year-old, I replied, "I am going to travel all over the world and I'm going to see the *BURNING MOUNTAIN!*"

Sea fever may have struck on a Canadian lake, when as child captain of a pirate crew in a rowboat with a window-blind sail, I dreamt of doughty deeds as a sea rover in West Indian islands. The story of the *Black Buccaneer* and also the true tales of pirates by Hyatt Verrill reinforced the vivid picture of a life of freedom and adventure.

The only block to such a good life was that I was a girl, but I soon tossed that disability off. I just became a boy in thought, word, deed, and dress, as far as I was allowed. If anyone asked, "Why do you behave like that?" I replied, "Why not?" with the simplicity of an overprotected child. This resolve to be a boy would be counted as superfluous today, when such a range of activities are open to girls, but I felt cheated, somehow, of the best that life held to make it meaningful. Surely, in the 1920s, it would not be impossible for girls to flout their restrictions and to break free like boys, at least for a time? My tales of eighteenth century sailors cited true cases of women disguising themselves as men and going to sea or to war as sailors or soldiers. There was

Mary Read, for instance, who duelled with another pirate to protect her husband's life, as he was not the swordsman that she was. I even planned to run away to sea, a plot discovered by my tearful mother, who mistakenly believed it was because I wanted to leave home, rather than because I wanted to become a worthwhile member of a ship's crew in the glamour of the deep.

My incomprehensible desire to follow the sea could not have been excused on account of having a sea captain for a father, as did many a child born on the ocean in Victorian times. Such an involvement with ships because of an upbringing at sea would have been understandable. No, my father was a merchant, a minor one of what used to be termed the "Merchant Princes," in the more picturesque earlier days of my native city, Montreal. Not that the term described my father in any way. He had dutifully followed the custom of those days and entered his father's business after a prospecting trip to the Yukon in the gold rush days of '98 and a spell farming in Manitoba. He also maintained his interest in the Duke of York's Royal Canadian Hussars — at the time a volunteer regiment — as their colonel. In World War I, he went overseas with the Sixty-sixth Battery. I believe he really preferred life as a farmer or soldier, or perhaps as a sailor, to life in an office.

The Brocks were collateral descendants of General Sir Isaac Brock, who commanded the British forces in Upper Canada in the war of 1812, gained the support of Tecumseh and the Indians for the British cause, and captured Detroit. At the cost of his own life, he repulsed the American invaders at Queenston Heights, now dominated by Brock's Monument, a Canadian version of Nelson's Column in Trafalgar Square, London.

My mother was an Englishwoman of the type that never seems able to settle well into an adopted country. Her father, Colonel Francis Dent of the Fifth Dragoon Guards, was such an excellent judge of horses that he had been commissioned by the British government to go to Canada as a remount officer during the Boer War. His wife and daughter, my mother Doreen, accompanied him on this trip. In Ontario, Doreen Dent met Reginald Arthur Brock, my father. His father, William Rees Brock, had been born in a log cabin, although a gentleman's son of "an ancient English family" as it was described in those days. Through hard work and tremendous ability, Grandpapa had built up a large wholesale dry goods house, with warehouses across Canada.

When the young people became engaged, both the Dent and Brock families were not very keen on the prospects of this marriage, although it was welcomed on the surface. Both families shared the principles of loyalty to Britain, admiration of the royal family, the belief that under the Union Jack, British law was the fairest in the world and that the British were the finest people to govern their empire. But in the undercurrents of assessment, the Dents considered the Brocks dubiously, as being "in business," rather than being landowners, or in the army or navy as was traditional. The Dents maintained this opinion, despite the provincial Canadian view that being a wholesaler held a greater cachet than being a retailer.

They concealed it, but the Brocks, a distinguished family, were irritated that a haughty, Indian Raj type of army family should consider them "common" because they were "colonials." They were indeed colonial, in that two generations had been born in Canada, and before them, three generations had lived in Jamaica, where, in an eighteenth-century Jamaican book, they were described as "Doctors of physik and landed proprietors."

Nevertheless, mutual aversion was curiously mixed with mutual admiration. Charmed by the elegance and personality of my grandfather, Colonel Dent, the Brocks found in him the ideal of the honourable Victorian officer. They admired the artistic talents of his wife, and the rare English beauty of their prospective daughter-in-law. And my father, who was ten years older than Doreen, was ready to settle down. But Doreen did not seem too sure of her mind, perhaps because of the family's doubts about the "suitability" of the marriage, By the standards of her generation, Doreen was considered to be "spoilt." What was called spoiled then compares mildly with today's indulged moppets. When we were children, Mother used to tell us that, "When I was a little girl, when out driving I used to feel dreadfully sick with the swaying of the carriage. But my mother told me, 'Never mind. Your father likes you to go out for afternoon drives with him. So you must stand that feeling of sickness, and do make sure you don't vomit'!"

Mother was a very shy, nervous young woman. Her eyesight was so poor that she had to wear glasses. When she was about to be presented at court, her mother insisted that she take them off, even though they were only pince-nez. "They look so ugly and you are so awkward anyway. You must not be seen like that." Poor Doreen had to fumble her way up to the throne to make her difficult curtsey to the Queen. Harsh as this may seem, it was in the interest of bringing mother up well, and making possible a "good" and presumably happy marriage. Grandma was doing her duty as it was seen in those days.

When Doreen became engaged to my father, she was taken on a trip out west to Banff to be given time to think about her forthcoming marriage. On the train returning to Toronto, Doreen nearly told her mother that she really did not want to marry. "But I was so afraid of my mother and all the arrangements having been made, I held back and never told her how I really felt," she told me later. Hardly the beginning for a blissful marriage. Its effect may have induced me to regard marriage as binding rather than freeing and turned me into a roving rebel. Who can say?

When they married, Reginald was given the warehouse in Montreal to manage, and the couple's three children were born there. My mother continued to fret for her English homeland all through her young married life. My father was very good to her in that respect, allowing her many trips "home" to England to visit her widower father. After his death during World War I, she continued to visit her sister in the west of England at Taunton in Somerset and to travel in Europe as well. I had been born a "blue baby" and proclaimed "delicate," and on this pretext, was taken on more of these travels than my older bother and sister, who attended boarding schools in Canada. Travelling was considered a fabulous luxury in pre-airplane days, but actually we lived on a shoestring. I attended local schools in France, Italy, and Switzerland, picking up a smattering of French and Italian, but missing much of my schooling in a Montreal girl's academy called "The Study." My brother and sister grew up more compatible with the Canadian life and viewpoints than I, with my heady experiences of continental travel and schools.

On my way to school on the Riviera, I was stimulated by the sight of barques, feluccas, and what I imagined were piratical craft moored to the old mole in the harbour. I sailed in cobbles on the Yorkshire coast and with fishermen in the tides of Bristol

Channel, becoming more than ever embroiled in fantasies of life
at sea. When sailing aboard liners, mostly the small "A" class
vessels of the Cunard Line in and out of the St. Lawrence, we
would be aboard for ten days or even two weeks in the event of
thick fog. These trips were filled with so much nautical interest
that my affinity for eighteenth-century pirates began to mature
into investigation of modern sea-going life. By age 14 I was well
into Reed's *Seamanship*, and by 15 had begun building accurately
detailed scale models, not miniatures, of square riggers such as
Sovereign of the Seas and *Sea Witch*, in order to learn about
rigging. I sold some of the models in the Canadian Handicrafts
Store, and put the money aside for the day when I might find an
opportunity to get to sea. At 19, my schooling was over, and I
was supposed to become a debutante, but my real life was in
reading and learning ship lore. If only *Frankie's Trade*, as
described by Kipling, had been open to me!

> I did not
> Old Horn to all Atlantic said
> (A-Hay O! To me O Now where did Frankie learn his
> trade?)
> For he ran me down with a three-reef mas'le
> (All round the Horn!)
> I did not favour him at all.
> I made him pull and I made him haul...
> And stand his trick with the common sailor
> (All round the sands)

I saved enough pocket money to take an international
correspondence school course in navigation, which went up to
the standard of Master Mariner. Because I was a woman, the
committee of the school had to have a meeting to see if they
could allow me to take the course. Even in those days that
seemed ridiculous and I wished more than ever that I was a boy
with a boy's fuller life. I was so discontented with the narrow
lives of girls in those days. Once, when staying with my mother's
sister, Aunt Frances, in her large and historic house near Taunton
in England, I overheard the women discussing their friends: "And
who did she marry?" was a favourite question among the ladies,
disregarding any other qualities the subject of their conversation

might possess, such as whether she had qualified as an airwoman, or doctor, or a ballet dancer, not to mention a master mariner ...

One autumn when I was 19, we were returning to Canada aboard the Cunarder *Alaunia*, where we were much at home. A young bridge boy had gone into *Alaunia*'s fo'castle, where "Bolshevik Bill," a lookout man, was holding forth.

"Old Brockie's aboard."

"Who's Old Brockie?" the bridge boy, Ben Davis, wanted to know.

"Why, she's an odd girl, a nautical passenger. She even climbed up inside the foremast, right up to where I was on lookout in that damned old nest."

Ben Davis was something of a maverick among the crew because he had done a lot of reading on his own, and learned to speak French. Mainly though, it was his habit of leaving his shipmates while ashore and going to museums, concerts or sightseeing which earned him the title of "La de da Cockney" among the crew. He decided to be bold enough to meet me, but didn't summon enough courage until *Alaunia* was so far up the St. Lawrence that she was due to dock in Montreal the next day.

"Bonjour Mam'selle," he began, hoping that I was French-Canadian, and he could show off his French.

"Hullo," I replied.

"Oh ... would you like to meet me on the foredeck at eight bells?" Nothing loath, I said "Sure," to the prospect of a sailor pal. When we talked on the fore deck, he told me that he lived in London, where his father was a lawyer. He also mentioned his "tutor." How dull, I thought, disappointed, this is not a real sailor earning his living at sea. He is educated and just going to sea for fun. This was very far from the admiration Ben hoped that his story would inspire. Nevertheless, I agreed to correspond with him. This could not have been pleasing, neither to Cunard, which prohibited fraternizing with passengers except for the pursers and captain, nor to my parents, for all their broad-mindedness. In those days they could not encourage their daughter to write to a deckhand, even a "la de da" one. I was delighted to learn, once Ben "took off the dog" that his father was really a "Bobby" and that Ben was at sea to earn his living. We continued to write for three years, then he disappeared for some months and I heard no more until he appeared in Montreal and we met again.

"I am never going to see you any more," he announced.

"For goodness sake, why not?"

"Because I am in love with you!"

This was an unexpected turn of events, for I had enjoyed what I thought was a platonic friendship. But it did make me feel my power as a woman. Perversely, I gave him to understand that if he found me a job at sea, I then might be obliged to him, like the princess who sent her suitor on a mission to find her a rare, impossible treasure. We were such romantics, despite our insignificant lives. We continued to correspond, even after Ben joined the *Bendigo* as quartermaster on numerous voyages to Australia.

Friends suggested that I join the Women's Naval Service, which I thought would make me a sort of navy nursemaid, a role that did not hold much appeal. Warships, it was held, existed for the protection of the merchant fleet, but in fact they are the Sivas, the destroyers, of the ship world. The Vishnus, the peaceful merchant vessels, had more spiritual appeal for me. My desire to take even a small part in the carriage of cargoes that build life and give joy to those that receive them may have been the feminine side of my nature, but I didn't really know.

Hope came when I read a news clipping about a Scots woman, Victoria Drummond, who had qualified as a ship's engineer, and was serving at sea on the Blue Funnel Line. Possibly there was a place for me at sea, perhaps even as an officer, if I qualified. I decided to try to attend one of the navigation schools for second mates which advertised in the *Nautical Magazine*. Only one among the many to which I applied, the King Edward VII in Limehouse, London, would allow me to attend classes when next we were in England. During this period I applied to many British shipowners for a berth as an apprentice seaman, but they slammed their doors in sheer horror at the mere mention of such a proposition.

Then in 1933, everything came together when doors which had been shut for a long time all opened at once. First, a family friend who knew how much I longed to go to sea sent me a clipping about an American girl named Betty Jacobsen, who had been signed on as an apprentice seaman in the barque *Parma* of Finland. Although Betty Jacobsen had been kept as a passenger on the ship (as she was a friend of Alan Villiers, famous for his writings about the sea), I wondered if this did not bode fair for the possibility of an opening as a real sailor for me, and wrote to Captain de Cloux, master of the *Parma*, then in port in England. I also wrote to Ben, whose ship happened to be there at the same time, and asked him if he could look up the captain and find out more about this opportunity. Ben saw Captain de Cloux, and wrote back to say that I must get in touch with Clarkson and Co., in London, agents of the Finnish owner. Ben went to see Clarkson's for me and put in a word so that when they received my inquiries they would have some idea of what I was seeking. After so many rebuffs from shipowners, I did not expect much, and did not discourage my father when his friends at the Royal St. Lawrence Yacht Club began urging him, "Reggie, you ought to get that daughter of yours a motorboat to sail the river. That might settle her down as she knows so much about boats." He bought a large motorboat — less for himself than to please me — at a Depression bargain price, though he would have preferred the simplicity of a smaller craft. Together with my sister we were off on a long trip when a telegram was forwarded to me from Clarkson's, saying that I could join one of Erikson's sailing vessels, provided that I filled the requirements of his contract of "Conditions on which apprentices are accepted on Finnish sailing vessels." The contract read as follows:

1. The applicant should not be less than 16 years of age and should be of strong constitution.
2. The application for apprenticeship should be accompanied by the following: (a) 2 Doctors' certificates, one of which should state that the work of a seaman will not be harmful to the applicant (b) Clergyman's certificate (c) Certificate from the parent or Guardian stating that the applicant is authorised to go to sea. In this certificate, the Guardian must also guarantee to reimburse the owner for all expenses to which he may be put through desertion abroad or any misconduct on the part of the apprentice. This certificate must be certified by a Notary Public, Magistrate or Government Official.
3. The premium for an apprentice is £50 and the apprentice will receive 100 Finnish Marks (approximately 10/-) per month in wages.

4. The Apprenticeship is for a period of one year or a round voyage. Apprentices are not taken on in extra-European ports.

5. After a fully completed period of apprenticeship, the Apprentice is fully entitled to take up a position as a deck boy or ordinary seaman, at current rate of wages, on the same or other vessel belonging to the owner, provided he has obtained from the Captain a certificate as to his suitability for the work of a seaman. In this case, he will be signed on afresh, and in exchange for the guarantee previously given he must leave a guarantee undertaking amounting to 5,000 Finnish Marks as security against desertion. This is what is required from and given by every other seaman in the owner's employ.

6. The owner does not bind himself to give any instruction other than practical seamanship, and neither does he demand any definite educational grounding for obtaining the different positions.

7. The pupils themselves pay for their journey to the vessel in a European port and their journey home when their service has expired. Also, if they leave the vessel in consequence of lack of interest in the work or through any disciplinary misdemeanors.

8. At the commencement of the service, the pupil should be supplied with the necessary seaman's clothes and other customary equipment, i.e. oilskins, sea boots, bunk clothes etc.

9. A Passport for foreign countries is to be taken out and sent with the premium at the time of taking up the service, or when asked for.

10. Should this one year's period of Apprenticeship not be completed on account of Death or Accident, the owner will make a pro-rated repayment of the amount of the premium.

11. In case of illness, accident or disability the members of the crew are protected according to Finnish Law and Custom, and should it be necessary to leave a man behind in a foreign port for these reasons, the cost of treatment for his illness and his passage home shall be

borne by the owner according to Finnish Law.

12. When the apprentice is signed off, the Owner binds himself to provide him, through the Captain, with an official certificate showing the length of service and the position reached. The cost of this certificate is, however, borne by the seaman himself.

In my case, however the premium had been raised to £100 rather than the £50 required of boys. My entitlement to employment after a year was deleted from the offer as well. I deserted the motorboat posthaste to be on the spot in Montreal to receive further instructions from Clarkson's.

Imagine my feeling, at twenty-three years of age, when I was requested to obtain a statement from my father, signed before a lawyer, saying that he allowed me to sign on as an apprentice in an Erikson sailing vessel. I was a lot older than candidates in the British navy, who could not join if they were more than thirteen years old, as the navy deemed that after that age, it was too late for a boy to really get the way of a ship at sea. I wrote to my father in fear and trembling, making the request for his permission. He gave it and accompanied the document with the following letter:

> Montreal, Que.
> July 24th, 1933
>
> Dear Annette,
> I return you enclosed your letters and in order that I may not be misquoted, I will try and make some comment. In the first place, there are two factors; one is the ship and all that goes with it, and the other is yourself. I know nothing of the ship or her people, but regret that she is not all British and under British law. As for yourself, it is possible that you may pass the doctor, having no outstanding physical defects, but it takes more than that to make an A.B. To begin with, you have light thin bones which do not make the framework upon which necessary muscles and sinew has to be added to endure hard work and staying power, nor have you the short thick hands with feet to match needful for the same purpose. On the other hand, God has been good to you physically as you

have long thin feet and hands, useful to an artistic mind, and you have the constitution by which you might be spared to live a long time if your are reasonable. Now your temperament is such that if I may be facetious, going over your past record, your eyes are a little too big and you are inclined to map out projects for yourself too onerous to accomplish, thereby causing yourself some disappointment. You have a wishbone that would do credit to an elephant, and a backbone of an average human. I am not going to stand in your way, but I must be truthful and just to all parties concerned, including the shipowners who will, to some extent be responsible. You could be very happy if your could induce yourself to live day by day, enjoying those pleasures which might come within your reach. The happiest part of our life, includes helping others who may be our inferiors physically, mentally and financially, or even morally; — to "give strong aid when trouble's night is near" is better than "the vaulting ambition which only over-leaps itself."

> [signed] Yours affectionately
> Dad
> RA Brock

I felt so pained also at having deserted my motorboat. It was like being the little mermaid (in reverse) who had wanted to live ashore and have legs, but when she was given them, found that they hurt far more than her tail.

Nevertheless, all was arranged and in September 1933, I took passage on a cattle ship of the Manchester Line bound for England. Arriving at the Clarkson office in London, I was met by Mr. Calder. First the orders were that I was to sail in *Parma*, then came a confused vetoing of directions. Finally, it appeared that I was to join *L'Avenir*, now lying in Copenhagen harbour. This was cancelled and then confirmed by a telegram from Erikson in the Aland Island, saying "*L'Avenir* is to wait." Mr. Calder said, "In that case you can be on time to join her if you leave at 7:00 p.m. tonight. Could you be ready?" I replied with one word, "Yes." But my Phileas Fogg alacrity belied my doubts. This "maybe and maybe not" had rasped a jangled tune on my sore nerves, however, I forced myself to sign with a steady hand and turned over the apprenticeship fee payment of $500. I had saved it from making and selling the large and accurately detailed models of *Flying Cloud*,[1] *Sovereign of the Seas*, and *Sea Witch* to have the money ready if opportunity knocked.

The cheapest way to get to Copenhagen was by steamer. Mr. Calder accompanied me to the ticket agents to ensure that I got the right tickets with all the complications of a train to Harwich, boat to Denmark, and another train to cross the Danish islands. They had the oddest names! That night, with some surprise, I found myself aboard a clean Danish steamer, in the third class, where the propeller vibrations shook everyone so violently that most of us whooped with seasickness all night. Like Nelson, I became seasick too, despite all my travels. Between bouts I managed to write letters home and to Ben, who was then at sea returning to India and unaware that his pleas with the shipowner's agents had had such marvelous effect. Was it poetic justice that he, whose incantations with the shipowner had opened the gates to the sea for me, later became the unwilling cause of my leaving my calling?

On early morning arrival in Copenhagen, I managed to use a Danish telephone to call Shierbeck, the ship's agent. Breathlessly, I met him in his doorway. He blocked it, hard eyes slithering over me and voice grating. "You cannot go on board *L'Avenir* till the captain comes in. That will not be till ten o'clock."

I tried to walk off some of my excited impatience by wandering through the gardens along the waterfront, and admired the "Little Mermaid," with whose painful state I had so recently sympathized. Returning to Shierbeck's, I passed through the marine hardware in the front to the stuffiness of the office in the rear to wait for the captain. Whimsically, I pictured my future ship master as a sort of Captain Kettle, goateed and agile as an eel, arriving alone to observe me with seahawk eyes. Instead, an apple-faced man stood before me, breathing heavily. I choked back my surprise. What lay ahead for me under the command of this shaven-headed giant? He resembled nothing so much as the Germans caricatured as the killers of Belgian babies on the World War I propaganda posters that had lined hallways in my childhood and terrified my infant mind with their impression of ruthlessness. A twinkle in the captain's eye reassured me.

"Soo ... we are going to make a sailor of you, eh?"

Then he passed on, with a number of other seafaring men in his wake, retiring to a back room where he proceeded to expound loudly, in Swedish, to the accompaniment of tinkling glasses, leaving me alone to ponder on some of my mother's injunctions. "Even if you ever get to sea, the officers would resent a woman in the mess," she had warned, using the precepts of her military family. This had startled me for a moment, but I continued to believe that fellow seafarers would be waiting with a welcome when I boarded a ship. When I actually signed on with a shipowner, Mother had protested anxiously.

"You have no first hand knowledge and we don't even know anyone who has had any contact with those people in that foreign ship. Suppose they treat you badly on board? Who on earth could you turn to?"

"Go to the consul at the first port, of course,"

"Bah! Those consuls are often drunk, or could be paid off by anybody who needed them on their side." She dismissed my airy attempt at reassurance.

I squirmed restlessly on the office chair, remembering the questions raised by authoritative people. Old Captain Triggs of the Shipping Federation asked, "What would you do if a bunch of angry stokers came swarming up on your bridge?"

"Shoot them!" I had replied recklessly.

How I wished to forget "the girl who wants to go to sea as a sailor," and just have been able to don my dungarees in the fo'castle of an outward-bound tramp steamer, as thousands of seamen were doing. How happy to sail without fuss, with the freedom that only obscurity allows.

My struggle with momentary ambivalence ended abruptly as the men in the back room came lumbering out of the office. As he passed me the captain muttered, "We go to consul now. Come."

Chapter 2

L'Avenir and I Meet

Two of *L'Avenir's* officers accompanied us to the Finnish consul's office, where the articles of agreement with the Master were read out to me before I signed on as apprentice seaman at the usual wage of ten shillings ($2.50) a month. A leather chair had been drawn up for the master, into which he sank, relaxing, his podgy hands clasped over his stomach. One of the mates sat, swinging his crossed leg back and forth, while the other stood in the background, cap in hand, staring stolidly. I sat, alert as a watchful prairie dog, aware that a sailor should listen intently to the ship's articles being read, to make sure that there were no conditions in them which might be unfair to himself. But as the official's dry voice droned out the articles in Swedish, how was I to know if I had signed up for a voyage to Guam or Yaccamatiddy?

Once more in the Copenhagen street we waddled along in an odd procession, headed by our portly captain, followed by the mates, awkward in their shore rigs, and trailed by a rather overcome girl, very British in her tweed suit. Back again at Shierbeck's, we left with a farewell from the office staff. One man seized my arm, looking eagerly at me.

"Good luck! I do so envy you. Wildly. If only I could go on such a long, long voyage."

Shierbeck looked up at me and said sourly, "This I do not understand ... to go to sea like you do."

I quit that office with one last glance at the faded paintings of square riggers in dark seas rolling in neatly permed waves. The tall mates ducked under the coils of rope and blocks hanging from the rafters of the ancient building. After the stuffy atmosphere, the rich reek of the harbour felt intoxicating in my lungs.

At the quayside the ship's boat lay waiting. I heard a very English voice inquiring anxiously, "Did those cases of gin I ordered go on board yet?" The voice belonged to a passenger who would be known on board as "the airman." The question having been settled to his satisfaction, all clambered aboard the sturdy boat. I felt as if I was about to wed the sea. The one-cylinder engine chugged as the boat left the shelter of the breakwater and spray broke over her bow where I sat. Though the spray stung my face, I kept my eyes on a white, four-masted barque as we closed the five miles of distance between us. She had music in the way that she curtseyed to her cable. Her lofty spars, tapering to the skies, echoed the delicacy of a piercing violin solo. Mast and yards silvered and greyed, faded into the rose light of evening, and harmonized the barque with the sky as though she was as impatient as I to blend over the horizon bound for the southern hemisphere. A phantom I had evoked while listening to music at home had now materialized in her flesh of steel and wood. A young, tow-headed sailor who was also watching L'Avenir remarked, "Do you notice her long poop deck running for'ard of the main mast? There's less danger of being washed overboard from such a high deck."

"I'm mighty glad to see that. I've heard that a sea coming aboard can wash away a whole watch of men hauling the braces in a low-waisted ship, eh?"

"Too true."

"You speak English so well."

"I should. My father being Finnish consul in London, I was brought up in England. I attended school in Taunton."

"Now did you? My aunt lives there."

In the boat full of strangers, stung by an icy spray, here was someone who knew intimately the cosy English countryside about Taunton! I was happily unaware then that my Taunton aunt was to have an effect on my sea career more harsh than any hard-bitten wave.

"There's *Viking* on our port bow." The sailor was pointing out another great barque. At that moment spray drenched us all, even the hierarchy sitting in the stern sheets. They gulped their annoyance and also showed their disapproval of the gossip rippling between an A.B and the new girl apprentice. Soon we bobbed alongside *L'Avenir*, and one by one grabbed the jacob's ladder, scrambling up the ship's side. Swinging my feet over the rail, my oxfords clacked on the deck, and I was aboard.

I had read in the *Boy's Own Paper*, a story about an Egyptologist who discovered survivors of the ancients living on a lost plateau, a civilization he had only seen in tomb murals. His thrill must have equalled mine as I looked in wonder at the barque's deck. But now, Egyptians or no, I turned to haul up my baggage, swaying on a line from the boat. I was bumbling with it over the rail when a steward approached and took me in tow. He ushered me to a bright cabin. "Gee! This? For an apprentice?" I marvelled. A neat bunk topped newly carpentered drawers. Over the settee fresh air blew in from an open porthole. While I could not of course bunk with the crew in the fo'castle, I had expected to share some dingy hole with other women, who might be stewardesses or even passengers. I did not know that Erikson had altered the cadet's room from *L'Avenir*'s days as a Belgian training ship into a series of cabins for passengers on summertime sailing cruises in the Baltic.

"Dis yours," the steward grinned with wolfish teeth as he slit his eyes to pinpoints to leer at ... Little Red Riding Hood? This was the keeper of blankets, food, and mail? Yet when he about-faced in his white jacket and walked smartly away to attend to other more important affairs, he had an efficient air.

No one else seemed to be concerned with what I did, so with elated step, I explored my new vessel, pausing only to lean over the rail, strangely in tune with the melancholy swirls of grey water that slopped about *L'Avenir*'s steel sides. Looking aloft was a curious sensation. Was this a miniature maze gone Gargantuan, or had I shrunk to the Lilliputian size of the ship models I had built? I had the illusion that I had gone sailing in one of these miniatures. *L'Avenir*'s main yard, which in the models had been of chopstick size when carved out on a scale of one eighth of an inch per foot, had now enlarged to fifty feet long. A jackstay in the model, a thin broken "A" string from my banjo, was now the size of a high voltage cable. As for the yard's cranse irons, which I had cut from gramophone needle boxes and riveted with the tiniest of little pins, they looked here as if forged by Vulcan, and the little pin had swollen to marshmallow size. Even the royal yard, nearly two hundred feet up from the deck, might have been a telegraph pole instead of the tooth pick with braces of human hair of my models.

"Wham! Bong! Bang! Bam!" A gong sounded supper. I followed the stream of diners into an airy saloon. "Do they intend me to eat here?" I looked about for other apprentices. "Maybe they mess up forrard?" A smorgasbord at the entrance displayed appetizing food, and hunger, after a night of sea sickness decided for me. "I'll just set to." I sidled into a chair opposite one of the crew, the third mate, "Tredge," as he was called in Swedish. He appeared more like a telegraph boy, his slight form enclosed in the folds of a police-style jacket. He retreated into it like a snail into its shell when I said "Howdy do." His chin sank down on his chest and all I had before me was a hank of yellow hair nodding over his plate. After a few moments he dared to glance up quickly and smiled gently, showing some gold-filled teeth, whose elegance he then buried in a hunk of bread. Assuming a relaxed pose, he leaned back, chewing, while pressing his fork handle tip so that it kept seesawing on the white table cloth in time with his chewing.

Six passengers were gathering at another table at the end of the room, where the captain sat on a red plush settee. I was to find out later that they made up a fascinating mixture, including Percy Grainger, the world famous Australian pianist-composer, his Swedish wife, Ella, Mrs. Van Andel, an elderly lady from Amsterdam who was going to live with her son in Australia, and Miss Kronig, a yachting lady from Manchester. There was a girl about my own age, Barbara Strachey, who was the niece of historian and writer Lytton Strachey. An English airman, Mr. Barrett, and a young Finnish man, Olav Hultin, who had made the trip before in another Erikson barque, the *Ponape*, completed the passenger list.

At this first meal aboard, I listened to scraps of conversation which only gave muddled clues as to the identities of these

people. A man, fair-haired but older, entered. Oddly, he had a
kind of magical tenor about him, like those entities of Inuit
mythology who can take the form of a bird or man at will. If his
form hovering over the smorgasbord had changed to that of a
gull, and if he had picked with his sharp beak of a nose and
grabbed a chunk of food and flown to settle in his chair, I
wouldn't have been surprised. But a more earthy character, in the
form of the airman Barrett, was making an observation of the
magic seagull's plate. "You have no meat on your plate. Don't
you like it?" he queried.

"Well, I am a vegetarian," Mr. Grainger-gull replied.

"How will you survive the diet of 'salt horse' and pork after
the fresh vegetables run out on this voyage?" Miss Barbara
Strachey wanted to know, looking at him with wonder through
her spectacles.

Ella Grainger broke in with her pretty Swedish accent, "The
sea air, is *so* good! One doesn't need to worry too much about
what one eats, don't you agree?"

Tredge was scraping up with relish the last gummy threads of
his *frukt soppa*. Ugh. I thought this awful concoction, fruit boiled
in starch ... *icky*. I sped back on deck and had resumed my
fanciful investigations of the rigging aloft when I heard at my
elbow, "More people are killed in these ships by falling down
holds than from the rigging." It was the tow-headed sailor,
Dennis, of the ship's boat. He went on, "For instance, our
carpenter fell down the hold a couple of days ago and hurt
himself badly. He was taken away to hospital and our sailing's
been delayed till we sign on a new carpenter." So, this was the
cause of the delay in sailing that Mr. Calder had told me about in
London. "*L'Avenir* must wait. A telegram has come from Erikson
of the Aland Island." This was surely one of fate's ways of mixing
up one life with another, as the carpenter's bad luck became my
good fortune. "We had a Finnish girl aboard *Viking* last voyage
when I was aboard," Dennis continued, "but she was helping the
steward most of the time."

"Oh," I exclaimed, "but I am an apprentice seaman." He
smiled. "By the way, have you a nickname?"

"Well, the Manchester Line boys tagged me with 'Jacky'
when I sailed from Montreal in their cattle steamer, coming over
from Canada to England to interview Erikson's agent."

29

A tough in a cheap jersey came strolling up to join us. "Christ," he swore, making me jump, "My last ship was *Russel*. Chesus! ... Here!" and he spat from a sarcastic mouth into the scuppers. He stood at least six feet above the deck. Dennis was not to be outdone.

"I was in *Hougomont* when her masts went overboard in a blow. They bent double like curtain rods. Some of us fellows were aloft at the time. No, surprisingly, all escaped injury, You see, the masts crumbled so slowly everyone was able to scramble clear. We made port under jury rig."

The tensions of the previous frantic days had given me a rip-roaring headache, but even so, when I went below and snuggled into the cosy bunk which was now my new home, I felt very happy.

Next morning I donned my dungarees, ready for work. "But what will you wear?" was the universal question asked me by experienced sea captains as well as young ladies, as though becoming a deck hand was like going to a party. If my clothes had been my only difficulty, how easy. For my gear I had used the list for an "Ordinary Apprentice's Outfit" which the Shipping Federation considered essential for an apprentice outward bound on his first voyage.

It was the custom, I knew, to give a green hand about twenty-four hours to "sling his hammock," but I was not prepared for the two more days I had to hang about, which resulted more than ever in my finding the surroundings weird and even strangely hostile. That the *sjoman's Svensk* (sailors' Swedish) was unintelligible to me added to the bewilderment engendered by my still prejudiced British upbringing. Also, as all I had read of the nautical world had been exclusively British books, with their narrow-minded, superior attitudes, describing foreign sailors as "Squareheads," "Dagoes," and the like, I had unwittingly absorbed this bigotry. Now, fear of this unfamiliar ship and crew caused me to take refuge in that defensive attitude. I took a little comfort from a quotation in Dana's *Two Years Before the Mast*:

One Johnny Crapeau, two Portugee,
One jolly Englishman can lick 'em all three!

At last the Captain beckoned me to follow him to his stately quarters aft. He entered, but I hesitated in the doorway. How awesome his dignity when he turned to face me, backed up as he was by his bird's-eye maple furniture, crimson plush upholstery, and brassbound fittings. "Do you want to work?

My jaw dropped. Why else had I come on board? "Of course." The master's eyes widened. "Well ... you can keep watch. You understand? You can go now do some brass polish around the wheel. You will be taking trick at the wheel when we are under way." I turned eagerly to go.

"But wait! I was in *Viking* when we have girl aboard. She fell in love with one of the crew. Believe me, we have more trouble with that girl than we have with the whole ship. *You must not* be doing same. Or I will have to put you ashore in Australia. You will not like *that*!

I smiled, half in amusement, half in indignation at his vehemence. What did he think? Fall in love with that bloody lot forrard? Hell no! "One jolly Englishman ..." I thought, but I said nothing.

The master continued, "You will be staying aft with us here. Also you must be locking your door at night." I doubted if a jammed, locked cabin door in the case of a shipwreck wasn't more dangerous than any prowling Romeo. However, I meant to be a sailor, and it was not my place to refute the master. That unfortunate man had the responsibility for a girl in addition to his concerns in running, shorthanded, a ship with thirty hands all told, but which in the barque's palmy cadet days had employed a crew of eighty.

Captain Nils Erikson might have welcomed the addition of a hefty young man. But "this gurl! she is so thin and weak!" he had complained to Mr. Barrett, the airman passenger, when they were ashore in Copenhagen the day I arrived. "This is no use whatever round a capstan or for hauling lines. I cabling owners, I not taking such on a trip with us." Alas for him, the owner remained adamant. The "gurl" was to sail. Despite being the owner's nephew, Erikson had been forced to sign on this "thin broomstick" to holystone his decks and flourish his capstan bars. I was hardly a potential Barnacle Bill in his eyes, yet he proved to be a most kind master during the good and bad of sea life, and I was fortunate to have served under him.

Unaware of his innate good heart, I retreated quickly, closing the door so as not to reveal my unmanly tears of resentment. "So, they think I am a useless flibberty-gibbet, a mad American come on board for a lark," I raged as I pounded up the ladder to the platform, amidships, on which stood the wheel. Karl Ekstrom, an ordinary seaman, was there already. He appeared snakelike to me, and was green-handed with verdigris from polishing the brass. A nest of torn rags lay on the platform beside him. I snatched a strip from the pile and waved it at the young man's nose. "All right I polish with the rag?" I said, trying to be hearty and agreeable, knowing that we must work together in the months to come. He froze. Presuming that meant the rag was all right, I poured some polish on it. "Nice job, what, eh? Polishing a bit of brass like this." I thought that added a bit of Cunard deckhand cheerfulness.

"Oy, Oy, EEEEE, Aw, NO! NO!"

He muttered inanities, and, I learned later, was aghast, never having seen a woman wearing trousers in his life. We polished on for four hours without a word, till all work parties were dismissed below.

Down in my cabin, I pondered the captain's question, "Do you want to work?" Was it to be polishing brass and other minor token amusements, and never any real seaman's jobs? Childishly, I had expected too much too soon. I had a moment of doubt and thought to sweep up my gear and get ashore. Then slowly, the shapes of the articles around the cabin faded in my imagination into the hulls of the vessels I might have sailed in — a berth in a yacht, a naval "ship" ashore, a passenger liner, a fisherman, or a coaster, or in a cable-laying ship, or an Arctic missionary schooner. Then finally, a four-masted barque, a great ship of 3,650 tons, the most unlikely of all to have signed on a girl, yet the most genuine vessel on which to gain experience on one's first voyage. I recognized my great good luck.

Later, I joined my first muster in the well deck. Though the evening light was dimming, I might have been lit up with phosphorus like a putrid fish, the way everyone goggled at me from a safe distance. A big, sea-booted "Russian Finn," as the British sailors called them, closed in on me, his red-whiskered mouth bawling,

"Oh HO! *Komm her* ... Lehtonen ... *Sass'n Fliskan!*" (Come here, Lehtonen ... a devil of a girl.)

Lehtonen shuffled up stolidly on his wooden clogs, and

placing his hands on the hips of his wide-bottomed pants, stood looking over my head, as if I wasn't there. A shorter version of this seafarer, scraping his clogs nonchalantly, his chest bursting in horizontal rays out of his jumper, strolled up and leaned his arm on Lehtonen's shoulder. Redbeard tapped the leaner's beret. "Ho! *Flicken som jungman!*" (Look, Girl as apprentice). It was as if I were some creature from another planet that they must define. Ohman tossed his head back, while drawing on his cigarette as he contemplated this apparition. Then he blew out the smoke at me. Both Ohman and Lehtonen had granite-hard, but frank, countenances. Cheeky, but not vicious, I assumed. Looking away towards the sea, I observed an older sailor, who resembled a respectable, middle-aged British tar, standing by the rail. I strolled towards him, offering a matter-of-fact "Nice evening." The tar spurted out a harsh laugh and backed away. A bevy of fingers pointed at him. "Ha Ha! Oh Bergman! You lof gurl?" Where were the nice quiet men who had greeted me the first day, Dennis and the German "Chesus"? I spotted them in the fo'castle doorway, hovering discreetly in its shadow.

I was as much an outcast as Conrad's "Nigger" of the *Narcissus*, that lone black in the fo'castle of a British ship. Instead of his splendid physique and dignity to come to my defence, I had only a weak smile and ears that picked up smatterings of disapproval among this crew. "A girl ... for hell's sake, a goddam girl." This last came in clear British accents from Johnny, an apprentice from Suffolk, who looked as if he had the spiritual markings of a future clergyman.

More impressions, coloured by shock, included glimpses of a mongol-eyed monster, squatting on a capstan sputtering out bawdyisms. From behind him, half hidden, peered a stocky dwarf, whom the airman later nicknamed Jumbo. And what a quixotic irritant he was to become to me later in the voyage. At that moment I was happily unaware of this as he drew on a cigarette, gazing at me as if I were good to eat and he was hungry. Finally the mates strode to the break of the poop. For a moment the first mate surveyed us haughtily, his palms resting on the rail, his arms forming a great gothic arch. "Alri! *Poiken, VAST!*" he rapped out. The hubbub stopped as though it were turned off by a faucet. Names were called as the mates chose their watches. There were about twenty men, Belgian, Swedish,

Finnish, German, English, and even Scots. There were two new crew members, a little fifteen-year-old Danska, and last of all, one Canadian, and a "gurl" at that.

I wish I could say that all became twee, twee, and sweety-pie between this crowd and me, but it didn't. While *L'Avenir* bucked seas, I battled hooligans. Different nationalities, boys and "gurl," whatever our prejudices were, we all met at musters every few hours. In storms we greeted one another with curses, half awake and jerking into hastily drawn on jackets and sea boots, and in doldrums with hair plastered with sweat, and crossness oozing from every pore.

It was September 23, 1933, and supper time. I sat by the second mate, who, having taken his fill of lobscouse and fruit soup, unbuttoned the breast pocket of his khaki work jacket and pulled out one of his Finnish cigarettes. This economical European affair had only half its length filled with tobacco, however, he drew its fumes contentedly. Smoke drifted through the skylight overhead, and mingled with the fog outside. The fog had delayed our sailing. Mrs. Van Andel, the elderly Dutch lady, raised her lorgnette to her eyes and surveyed the Second's broad face and burly form. Apparently approving of him, she started a conversation from the captain's table, where she was sitting alone.

"Then mine goot man, you go on Baltic cruising with this ship, so I am hearing? It is goot, is it not?"

"These cruising is hart work. This ship is full, full, with ever so many passenger. They is eating all the time. Big dinner every hour of the day. Then we have to put lights up every night. Those passengers, they is dancing on deck. We must anchor, so they can be going ashore everywhere. I telling you, we have too much hard work. Those people they cuddle, kissing, sitting on coil ropes. Every time we must bracing yards, we must be getting them off coil ropes."

The Dutch lady clucked a blend of disapproval and sympathy. "You poor crew boys! Ach, so hard it must be! They are getting too much exercise in summertime, then. It is not so nice."

"Well, they have learn pretty goot how to sail. Now we are leaving for Australia these crew boys have had to make and take in sail many times, while summer cruising in Baltic. All crew except 'Lilla Danska' and this 'Yackie' here."

He looked doubtfully at me across the table. Suddenly a shrill whistle sounded three times on the deck above us. The mate glanced up at the skylight, then rose quickly and climbed up the companionway. Hearing shouts of "*Alle man pa dack*!" I followed. On "*dack*" I found coils of rope thrown off, belaying pins, and blocks squeaking as tackles were hauled. Black figures swung up into the shrouds, jiggling them. Others were already straggling out along the yards, leaning over them, while their hands scrabbled at loosening the gaskets which had been holding the sails to their yards. I gasped to see one or two figures stride along the top of the yards with the nonchalance of riveters, high up in the steel. So high, so dangerous, could I *ever* ...?

Cowering in the scuppers, sheltering under the main shrouds was "Lilla Danska," as new to the ship as I. The mate spied him, rushed up, grabbed him by the collar, cuffed his ears, and booted his behind. The boy leapt to the rail, looked aloft and then wriggled down again. With a wrathful bellow, the mate jabbed Danska, forcing him up again. Escaping him, Danska climbed higher and higher, even over the difficult futtocks, where he had to go almost upside down to get out and over the wide platform called the top. My eyes followed as I trembled in the lee of a deckhouse, wondering if it was better to be ignored or to suffer Danska's treatment. At least booting would be a cure for fear and enable me to learn my sea trade faster.

Next day, coming off watch from chipping rust in the coal hold, I found we were drifting in heavy mist past a shoreline topped by a turreted building, half hidden in drizzling rain. The young woman passenger, Barbara Strachey, sat on the main hatch wearing a drab "mac" while she knitted away her impatience making a sweater. I remarked, "Say, what a dreary looking building. Why, it looks like a castle though."

"Didn't you know? That is the Danish castle of Elsinore ... Hamlet's home."

"I've never read *Hamlet*. It was always sea books with me."

"I'll lend you my volume of *Hamlet* if you like. Come below and I'll give it to you now to read."

Barbara stuffed her knitting in a bag and obligingly got up. She had what was formerly the priest's cabin, when *L'Avenir* had been a Belgian training ship. The cabin traversed the midship section, but had no port hole, only a small thick glass in the deck which let in dim daylight. The mizzenmast grew up through the cabin like some tree allowed to grow through the living room of an eccentric house. The bed, double size, had red velvet curtains draped over it. It was altogether quite a dramatic scene with the mast. A table was spread with papers, drawings, paints, and bottles of ink. Dresses hung over chair backs. Barbara took down the slim volume of *Hamlet* from a good sized row of books on a shelf, and turned to her activities that lay on the table. I went up on deck with Hamlet's story in my hand. Standing under the sombre sky as we drifted by his phantasmic castle, I found my dreams sliding into dismal despair.

What an alien crowd of workers they were with me, who indulged in no "Cheerly Man" chantying or bantering about the decks, save for Dennis's little cheep cheep about rabbits and Aussies. There were some of them now, with fists grasping scrapers tightly, bending their plum-pudding faces over rust chipping, scratching bits of dirt from iron fittings with the solemnity of the croupiers I had seen in Monte Carlo, scraping up millions from the green baize. How ridiculous a picture they made suddenly came to my mind while chipping in the coal box on my next watch. I burst into chuckles at the thought. "What making you laughing?" the dwarfish Jumbo, who had looked at me so hungrily at the first muster, asked angrily. He even stopped scraping, in his indignation. This made me grin even more widely. At that moment Tredge arrived with an electric rust-chipping machine under his arm, carried reverently as though it were a great modern marvel. He switched it on with a flourish. It started with a great roar. All stopped work, mouths agape with wonder just to see the machine go, until the dust it raised hid everything surrounding it. There remained only the ear-splitting noise, quaking and rattling and screeching and whamming for hours and hours. But so rapturous was I, to actually be aboard and under way, that the prison-box of coal dust and noise ... well, *nun's fret not* ...

A few days later the first mate came down into the coal box and touched my shoulder. "Come wit me." He led the way into the sail room, which occupied the space under the long half-deck, where the sixty Belgian cadets had slung their hammocks, when *L'Avenir* was a training ship. When Erikson bought her, he had changed this room into dining space for the Baltic cruises in the summer, adding rows of tables and benches around the sides. They looked like those in a Canadian ice cream parlour. Sometimes I dreamt that a good old Canadian fudge sundae might appear on one of the tables as a change from the "salt horse" and sausages of the Scandinavian sea diet. (Actually, "salt horse" was only a term for salt meat. It derived from the last century, when horse meat had been substituted for pork and beef by parsimonious owners. In the same way, "Harriet Lane," a term for canned meat, came from the name of a murdered woman, whose flesh was chopped up and processed for sailors' use. Other less disagreeable sailor slang for food included "Burgoo" (porridge) and "Lobscouse" (salt meat and potatoes mixed.)

The tables still had a generous amount of space left on which to spread out sails and canvas to cut and mend. On this day, coils and coils of ratline stuff stood in a corner, stiff as soldiers. "You be winding these," the mate introduced them to me. The sailmaker took over from there, explaining that they had to be rewound in short lengths, making sort of hanks of twine for use aloft. There I remained for several work days, making figures of tight turns and trying to be extremely neat. As I worked on, I began to feel at ease with the sailmaker. The oldest man on the ship by far, he had a reputation for skill as the best sailmaker in the Erikson fleet. As familiar with every part of the world as most people are with their own doorsteps, he took even a Canadian apprentice in his stride, except that he could not resist a remark.

"Say Jack! I don't believe you are a girl. You don't look the right shape for one. So you are a Canadian, eh? Hardest skipper I ever sailed under was a Bluenose. Christ! He was a driving man! Good enough sailor, though."

This testimonial to one of my countrymen made me wish I could claim to be a "down Easter" too, instead of a mere Quebecer.

A sailmaker, especially one of such ability and experience was held in much respect on board a windjammer and held the rank of petty officer. When the captain came in to consult on the cut of a new sail, even though their discussion was in Swedish, I could tell that the master followed the advice of his petty officer in these vital matters. As a humble, first-voyager apprentice, therefore, I wound on at my ratlin balls in quiet deference, not speaking unless addressed, and not pestering with nuisance questions, just watching to accumulate lore. This attitude arose out of my mother's wise injunction, when, as a loquacious eight-year-old in South Carolina, I chattered on telling my black riding master all about my vast array of horse experience. My mother heard and counselled me, "Don't you try to tell him all you think you know. Just listen and learn from what he has to say." That horse sense easily translated into sea sense as well.

As we worked the sailmaker gradually thawed and told me something of his life at sea. Incredibly, there had been a time when the sailmaker had been a shy young boy. As a young sailor, he remembered seeing the Czar of Russia.

"You know in those days, the Aland Islands belonged to Russia. The Czar liked to take his summer outings with his family there. Aland being my home, it happened that I got orders to row him ashore from his yacht. There he sat in the stern sheets, and me, a young boy, I didn't dare speak. I felt I might do something wrong."

"Just imagine! You felt so afraid of the Czar! Why?"

"Well you know, they thought him a very high man, like a God in those days. Me, I was just a kid. I was terrified what to say if he spoke to me."

"I bet you wouldn't be like that today. Supposing the Czar could be in this sailroom now. He'd shake his sides laughing at your stories."

Of America, where he had worked on the railway in Minnesota for some years, the sailmaker said, "I wouldn't stay there, though. They treat you badly, driving you to work, all the time shouting 'get along with you, you damn squarehead.'"

The new carpenter, passing through the sailroom, stopped to listen. Then he remarked, "Lucky for you Jacky, you didn't sail in an American ship or, by God, you'd be having a rougher time of it than in this one."

"How do you know that?"

"I lived a long time in the States too."

The carpenter gave a knowing nod. His hair was a thinning thatch of wire, glistening red like newly sawn fir wood. On the voyage I was to find him a silent man, given more to expressing himself by the rasping of his saws and the banging of nails than by his voice. He was capable of cutting teakwood in a ship lap double dovetail, accurate to within a sixty-fourth of an inch, which he did while constructing a new deckhouse on the trip.

In contrast, a dour, thin individual assisted the sailmaker. Barbara had sketched his portrait, exclaiming as her pencil moved. "He is *so* handsome, and clever too." Her nickname of "Sonny" for him stuck, perhaps because it was so contrary to his nature.

He was stitching sails when the sailmaker began telling another one of his merry yarns. "Hey Jack! Did you ever hear the one about the Turkish admiral? I'll tell you that in English." Sonny stopped work to follow the sailmaker, as he too spoke some English. The story was about a nancy boy, as far as I can remember, but I cannot recall the details. I responded with chuckles from the depths of my happy chest. It was great to be accepted in the club room atmosphere, among men.

Idly gathering up wispy threads with the toe of his boot as they lay about the bench, the sailmaker must have been reminded of something because he started off on another yarn, in Swedish. Getting the gist of it, I realized it was about threads, because the point of the story came with great guffaws when the sailmaker took a handful of the threads, chopped them into tiny pieces and dropped then to the deck. I was so intrigued that I asked to have the story translated. It seems that a shipowner (it might easily have been Erikson) always took care that his sailmaker should be economical. He was instructed to use up his sewing thread to the very last inch in the needle, but the sailmaker could not be bothered to save so diligently. Every time the shipowner was sighted coming along to inspect his work, the sailmaker would gather up a mass of the threads lying about his bench and snip, snip, snip them all into tiny little pieces. "*Goot, Goot. Myket bra.*" the shipowner complimented him, delighted to have so superbly economical a sailmaker in his employ. Our Scheherazade of a sailmaker with his thousand and one stories even kept the cook, steward, and cabin boys spellbound as they halted, sometimes on their swift commutings between galley and dining saloon, shocked and convulsed at the old mariner's stories. "EH! Eh! OOOH! *Sataaan*!" they shrieked, slapping their thighs. As these stories were in Swedish, my attention wandered to Johansson, the sailmaker's assistant. He needed only the bowler hat, striped jersey, and bull terrier to make his sturdy body into an Edwardian tonic ad. His moustaches kept lengthening gently with amusement at the sailmaker's jokes, and he continued turning his serving mallet, running it smoothly, as if it were oiled, about the rope he had stretched tautly between the hold pillars. Sonny rebuked me.

"We unnerstan a gurl if she vas meking lof to de boy. Efter all, a gurl she iss for dat. But dis fun here. She talk like man. She laff at such story. Wat for gurl iss dat?"

I flung back at him, "Oh you're kind of an old prissy." A prissy? Was this some British sailor cuss word? He wasn't going to ask me, not after acting the school marm to such a baffling girl. The sailmaker sewed on, satisfied with the hearty effect of the Turkish admiral. Somehow he was secluded from the youthful crew by oceans of experience. All that, they had yet to discover. He sat, very much alone at his bench, with only his tools by his side, and even they were tucked away, with professional neatness, in a pouch. His huge, calloused paw held his palm and needle. He sewed with quick twitches, despite his massive form. The old walrus! I looked at him with envy. By the time I am a middle aged mariner, I wondered, will I have his yoke-like shoulders, tensile-steel rib cage, bull neck, and leather skin with which to resist icy winds and burning sun alike? Perhaps I will be able to bellow about the decks with the same foghorn of a voice. Yet, with all his outer toughness, he had the simplicity and dignity typical of a generation of toilers of the sea that is extinct today. They wallowed in drunkenness, dirt, and foulness for a few happy days in port, maybe, but at sea they awoke and laboured for months, with an integrity, courage, and fortitude which was incomparable. Association with so imposing a character leaves a memory I treasure that is a link with former sea days.

For several days *L'Avenir* had been trying to beat against headwinds round the north of Scotland. Finally the skipper altered her course to tack through the English Channel, exchanging the dangers of beating against a strong headwind with the dangers of a collision in the Channel. *L'Avenir* had hardly poked her jib boom past the white cliffs of Dover before she was in and out of patches of mist and rain, and surrounded by a confusion of yachts, tugs, and tramps, travelling athwart the Channel steamers as they sizzled across the Channel. Some Finnish steamers appeared, to the joy of our crew, as did a Dutch freighter from South America, duly pointed out by the Dutch lady. Coasting topsail schooners provoked arguments pro and con of the definitions of a brig, brigantine, hermaphrodite brig, snow, etc. Thames barges waddled under their Venetian red sprit sails, and I recognized the black and blood-red funnels of the Cunarders. But I did not see the one vessel I knew to be approaching England, and the one I wanted to signal to most of all — *Bendigo* of the British India Line, in which my sailor friend, Ben, was quartermaster. I had planned the message I would wave in morse, to tell him I was here, aboard a square rigger, Australia bound. No *Bendigo* as we slid on past a myriad of other vessels leaving the Channel and entering the treacherous tides of Ushant, just about the worst place a sailing vessel could be in fog and mist. Not every steamer's navigator was familiar with the manoeuvres of a sailing vessel in avoiding collisions.

"First mate's below, sick, " Dennis explained as we saw Tredge, the third mate, now in sole charge of our watch. Tredge scurried from the wind dodger at the break of the poop to look out, and then darted into the chartroom aft. "Look at Tredge there, " Dennis laughed. "His clothes! So big for him he seems like a girl in boy's clothing. And his cap! EEEnormous. If his ears weren't holding it up, it'd drop right over his head onto his shoulders." Occasionally the sailmaker bolstered Tredge by rocketing up on deck to bawl stentorian advice. Fog came down, thick, and the master came on deck. He joined Tredge and the sailmaker, listening for foghorns. They resembled three horses in a meadow, attentive, ears pricked as though sensing a rider approaching with a bridle — or would it be sugar and apples?

The trio now swivelled their heads and noticed the fog swirling in wispier shreds. They conversed and came to a decision. Tredge gave two blasts on his whistle, setting us to hauling braces, swinging yards to clear the ship down channel. We hauled in time to Tredge's unique chantey, as he moaned weirdly, "OOOOOOOOoooo, oar! Hooonde OOOver Hooooondy! Loooong Haawl."

The haulers joined in, sniggering, but his hollow tones rather scared me, amid the salty grey sea, the fog, the dripping ropes, the menace of dimly outlined ships, close as Sunday traffic on a road. Poor Tredge, I thought, he's as new to being an officer as I am to being an apprentice. We rarely see ourselves as others see us. Tredge had a completely different picture of himself from mine of the fumbling officer. At table, his shyness receded, and he told me sagas which I strained to follow.

"In other ships where I was, officer of deck he cruel man. He making me stay aloft long, long time in much snow. Cold. Cold. I freeze to yard. But I no crying to come down. I know he only do this for bad. I brave."

A real hazer, that mate, I agreed, while Tredge continued with other heroic epics of battle with cabaret crowds of seamen in South American ports. "Caramba! I knock out seex beeg man ... So!" He thrust his fists in all directions, his large jacket riding the flailing arms valiantly, while his eyes rolled with remembered frenzy. "Dey all falling to ground, tooth gone. Blood from mouth. I strrrrong ... I boss." His arms now held militantly rigid at his sides, his chest rose in pouter pigeon pride as he rose to go on deck. But he had a dreamy expression in his eyes, and his mouth just couldn't attain the severity to which he aspired; it had a give-away sweetness.

Chapter 4

Shipmates

About a week later, the Channel safely negotiated, *L'Avenir* swung about in nasty seas in the turbulent Bay of Biscay. Seasickness, with merciless octopus tentacles, reached to the depths of my belly, day after day, to the very bottom. Even so, despite all the retching over the lee rail, I was struck by the masterfulness of the driving ship, tearing through the wild water. The thrumming of her taut shrouds and straining canvas exhilarated me.

One unforgettable night, while the rain teemed down making all black as a witch's brew on deck, everyone found the right lines with admirable alacrity. Outlandish orders, snapped out in Swedish, bewildered me. Everything was cold and harsh and the wind kept knocking me about. Shivering and sick, I hung onto the spanker sheet, which we were hauling in. The mate yelled for a *nagel*, but I hung on, not knowing what that might be. Taking me for a Finn, he grasped me by the collar and shook me, till I felt like a topsail when a storm racks it to shreds. I swayed and trembled, too sick to care, till little Danska, more prompt, brought a belaying pin. Of course! *Nagel*, nail, a belaying pin to make fast the sheet. For a short moment I wished there was no such thing as the sea, but I knew how lucky I was to be sailing aboard so fine a vessel.

Fine vessel or not, she was bound to be drenched with spray on the fo'castle head, where it was my turn at lookout. The deck reeled, my innards retched, stiff with the exercise. A snake of water wriggled in my coat collar, icing my spine and wending its way to sea-booted toes. I cowered under the pelting rain. How could one *ever* see a ship's lights through all that? All I could see was round my feet where water coursed down in rivers, this way then that way as the deck rolled and pitched. I sloshed back and forth, pacing between the ventilators, and suddenly was surprised to discern beside one of them a stumpy man's form huddled in its lee. It was the German, "Jumbo," who had kindly come to endure this lookout watch and distract me from the misery with tales of "Yermany."

"I have been in Hamboorg Amerika Line ... steamer is so very better than this bad sail ship ... Mine *onkel* is of the alt Yerman army ... Ya! He wear the Prussian helmet with spike ... Hitler? *Ach*, Iss not so bad, Ya, we haf one dog at home, *ein dakker* ... Dachshund you call dis? Hamboorg steak, we make this goot in my home."

I listened with distraught, but polite attention, hardly daring to open my mouth and struggling to hold down my retching. If he had been the Angel Gabrielle blowing the last trumpet, if he had come bringing the news that I had won the Derby, I would have had no spirit left to respond. Indeed, it is to be hoped that if I had sighted another ship and we were in danger of collision, I could have given the ship's bell the required clang, one stroke for an object on the starboard bow, two on the port bow and three dead ahead. I checked with Jumbo. "At least that is the way I remember it in transatlantic Cunarders, when I climbed up in the crow's nest." I matched my Canadian-British life with his "Yerman" one. Misery loves company, so I revived somewhat, becoming more garrulous by the time eight bells rang and it was time to go below. All my wet clothing was too ponderous to take off, so I just dropped onto my bunk and fell into a sickly sleep, while trying to decide if I had the vim to bother pulling off my oilskins in the damp cold of the unheated bunk. Bay of Biscay!

A new broom sweeps clean, they say, but I didn't. Fellow workers swore at me for awkwardness in washing down paint work and decks, coiling up lines, and steering.

"Ow! That sea! Flung right outta my bunk!"

"Whose wheel is it?"

"*Helvete Flickan till roos*" (Hell girl at the wheel)

"That bloody whore at the wheel?"

"*Ach*, No getting slep dis vatch."

"Chesus, Ain't much sea on ider. Yet she's lettin the old hooker yaw about sumpin' unholy."

The fo'castle quivered with their cursing, while the barque's loose freeing ports slammed and banged echoes of those protests. Her jib boom crazily measured the altitude from horizon to Pole star. Her trucks circled dizzily downwards, as though fantastically intent on reversing their roles with the heels of the masts. In the navigation room a pair of dividers slid off a chart, piercing Tredge's knee with the sharpness of a pair of hornets. "*Caramba!*" Tredge leapt up with all the angry fervour he must have shown in knocking out all "Seex beeg sout Americans." In the saloon over the rudder head, the master, hearing the rudder knocked about as though Neptune himself was slamming it with his fists, altered the balloon of his cheeks to a face of box-like severity and clambered on deck. He ordered the mate to screech the whistle to summon a substitute steersman. A red head bobbed up the steering platform ladder. It was a fairly new hand, named Mom. His fingers talked triumph in the way they grasped the spokes of the wheel. I passed the course to him, ashamed and sad. English speaking crew members nailed up my steering coffin. "He's been in the ship only a little while longer than you and can steer a bloody sight better." The foreigners hammered it down with extra blows. "You best go home, gurl. Stay and wash the dishes there."

Below, Frasne, the ship's cat, offered solace, purring and weaving back and forth against me as I paused by the after hatch, stroking his soft back. He didn't care whether I steered badly or not, even though I had been endangering one of his nine lives with my zig-zag helmsman ship.

"Dees deck — iss *so* vet, I may be fallen."

The Dutch lady stood near Frasne and me. She clutched a cleat of the hatch, but still looked as though she belonged in a limousine, ordering "Home, James," to her chauffeur, instead of sliding on the heeling deck of a windjammer.

"Could you holding my arm and going a little promenade with me?"

"Gladly," I offered, and while we toddled around the poop, she expressed a little matriarchal concern.

"If your Mudder could be seeing you *now*! Only tree weeks away now and yet so strrrong you are becoming on dis voyage. You looking so well. So different from when we first seeing you ... pale ... tin ... weak. Now this will be so good for you, in the day when you have a familee you are becoming so strrrong you can have many children. So verrry fine is it!"

I retreated below, more shocked at her idea than at the most sailmakerish story. The prospect involved strength, no doubt, but had no "strrrong" appeal for me, amazonian Annette, lover of freedom.

Olav, the young Finnish passenger, knowledgeable from his experience in *Ponape* the previous year, predicted weather, explained customs and what might follow on this trip, especially to Barbara Strachey. After about ten more days passed and the reeling decks steadied somewhat as *L'Avenir* picked up the N.E. trade winds, he accompanied Barbara aloft, where she triumphantly managed to stand on the jigger cap. Despite the blue skies and steady seas in this trade wind area, I struggled still with my steering. One evening, coming off watch rather glumly, despair setting in, I spied Barbara swaying in a hammock that had been rigged up for her by Olav. Long, slanting rays of sunlight became stripes of gold as they filtered through the boards of the boat skids, under which Barbara lay, tinting her with orange tiger beauty. Such a life, I thought, perhaps with a twinge of envy for the luxury of having hammocks rigged up for one, and being able to recline in lovely clothes. I stopped for a chat.

"You look pretty comfortable there. I tried sleeping in one of those things. Some chap had left it empty up forrard, but I just dozed off when, WHAM! One of those devils let go the clew on me. Wow, I hit the deck a thump. Now, when I nap I stay as low as I can, on the deck planks. At least no one can open those up to make me fall through."

She responded, "You've been in a mix-up all round these days. I heard you made a pretty botch of steering too." I thrummed my fingers through her hammock clew, as though its strings were those of a harp, while I tried to change the subject away from steering.

"Yes, but I'm lucky, That fellow, Mom, you know, the

apprentice with the red hair and the bright blue shirt, he came late to relieve me at the wheel today, but my regular relief is a prompt fellow named England.

"Oh I know the one you mean," she said, "a thick heavy boy. You'd hardly think he's only 17 and although he can't speak a word of English, England is his name."

"No, especially by the way he walks — like a clockwork man. I can't help but be reminded of the Frankenstein monster in the movie ..."

Barbara stopped me. "Hush, Hush. Who might be hearing what you say? And you are on a foreign ship you know. Diplomacy and all that sort of thing." The tact exerted by her forefathers in the Indian administration was on her mind. Years later, however, Mrs. Grainger informed me that surprisingly, England had become a scholar of distinction. His "patience and perseverance made a Bishop of his reverence" as the saying goes.

Barbara continued, "If you are wise, you'll be careful not to get people's backs up more than you have to. You may have a lot to stand up to. I hear the crew were ready to accept you at first, when they thought you had just come on board as a sort of hobby, but I understand you are really serious about making a go of it. They don't like that particularly. I'd love to know what you expect to accomplish by being part of the crew of this ship."

I explained that I was putting in my four years sea time to get a certificate as second mate. The British Board of Trade had nothing to stop me receiving a certificate of competency when I had put in the necessary time and passed the exams. Their regulations considered a "person" as neither a man nor a woman. I was sure of this, because I had a letter to that effect from the Board of Trade to a commander who had written to them on my behalf. Commander F. Cooper had previously written an article in the *Nautical Magazine* saying that he did not think much of boys going to sea nowadays. "Perhaps," he suggested, It might be better if shipowners tried the experiment of placing six girls in the apprentices' half deck and training them instead." Not realizing that this was literary sarcasm, I had written to him through the magazine. "You have a splendid idea there; I volunteer to be an early candidate for the experiment." Intrigued, the old ship's captain asked me to his home for tea. Discussing the best way for me to "explore an avenue," as he put it towards going to sea, he had recommended that as a first step I try to attend a navigation school. That was how I finally managed to get to the King Edward VII School for Masters and Mates in Limehouse, London.

I continued explaining to Barbara. "Even though it's pretty tough going here, and the boys are pretty mean to me, I must say that one watchmate, Dennis, takes a motherly care of me, all of us, really. He is the senior apprentice, and he'll always tell me where to find paint brushes, rust hammers, lanterns, seizing stuff, and even the officer of the watch. When we were in the roads at Copenhagen, I was with him trying to learn to go aloft. You can't imagine the ghastly way the thin top gallant shrouds wobble. Right there and then I balked. 'I can't.' But he just prodded my behind and yelled 'YOU CAN.'"

I swung Barbara's hammock back and forth with enthusiasm for guardian angel Dennis. She replied, "He seems rather a child to me. One never knows what a child will do, either." What a mysterious knowledge this sophisticate possessed of the inner workings of the people on the ship. All my life I had been more partial to the workings of rudders and cranse irons and types of anchors than those of ids and egos. "That Jumbo, he's turned out quite kind. I like him all right," I said. She responded,

"A mixture of German brutishness and sentimentality, I know from the things he says when I talk to him. Anyway, don't you go forgetting your sailor sweetheart in England. I presume that is his photo you have in your cabin? Are you engaged by any chance?"

"Golly, I don't know. Do you realize that Ben got me this voyage? He interviewed Captain Erikson of *Parma*, and Clarkson, the agents in London. Pleaded with them to take me to sea. He's a good pal, but I want to roam the sea, free as a bird."

"Even birds have biology. Watch out yours doesn't catch up with you."

I sat down on the deck. "It won't, although, dammit, I don't know what to do about it all. But for sure I do know where I am bound."

She grinned saucily while swinging one leg loosely, like a puppet's, down from the hammock. "Just imagine," I began, "that old Dutch lady, she has an idea that I made this voyage just to gain strength to have a large family."

Barbara replied, "That means fulfilment to a woman. It is

what she is made for. Like *L'Avenir*, which was built to carry cargo. I'd like to have a big family. I was engaged before I set out on this voyage."

"Oh yes, so you were telling me. That was to the man your parents sent you on this voyage to forget?"

"Yes, but I shan't forget him; he is so *handsome*, so *wonderful*! His parents are Jewish and intend to disinherit him if he marries a Christian. Really rather a mix-up, you know. My family don't worry about such matters too much. They are more interested in discussing abstract ideas. Important topics to them are 'Why Music Pleases' or 'The Value of an International Language.'"

Barbara went on to say that she felt as much at home in Austria or Italy as she did in "the Mud House" that her mother had built with her own hands in England. Hers had been a remarkable childhood, influenced by the personalities of her uncle, Lytton Strachey, author of a famous life of Queen Victoria, and *Eminent Victorians*, a book which changed the idea of what a biography should be, and family and friends which included philosopher Bertrand Russell, the art historian Bernard Berenson and the circle of writers and artists, including Virginia Woolf, known as the Bloomsbury group. She soon returned to thoughts of her fiancé and asked a peculiar question. "Ever seen a man cry?" Shades of my British governesses prompted my response. "Oh no, a man never cries."

"Oh ho, don't they! I made a man cry. It's a frightful sight, I can tell you, to see a man cry."

I smiled as I noticed the second mate's expression, mistrusting his English at overhearing Barbara's odd statement. He had stopped on his way to check the taffrail log and passed under Barbara's hammock. As he lifted the clew, tattoos of mermaids, snakes, and an anchor shimmied with his muscular movement. I exclaimed, "Zowee! What a pair of arms! If only mine were like the second's here! By Golly there'd be lot of men crying round these decks I can tell you. I'd sure lay into some of those fresh young bums. They would quit hazing me after that, for good."

The broad features of the mate creased into a pleased smirk in response to my admiration of his manly arms. He reminded me of the brass God of Plenty that Ben had brought me from the east. As the mate strode aft along the deck, we watched him disappear behind the chart house.

Amused, Barbara continued. "You'd find the boys a lot easier to get along with, they'd accept you better if you were like a friend of mine. She rather wished to make this voyage too, as a sailor. A big, womanly Scottish girl, she's so feminine the boys could not have resented her. You're too masculine; you compete too much with them." Then, noting the flash of pain in my face as I retaliated with "Yes, but heck, I just don't *want* to be a big, fat womanly Scottish girl," Barbara rummaged in a bag beside her. "Here, have half," she said and generously offered a big bar of Fortnum and Mason chocolate. I accepted with the joyous gulp of a greedy spaniel. The first mate was passing to join the second in reading the log dial aft. "Chocolate?" I offered. He sniffed in disdain. He may never have heard of the musical comedy *The Chocolate Soldier*, but "Chocolate Sailor" he named me. "Vat's dat for a sailor? Now if only dat vas a goot glass of beer ..."

We were now being driven ahead under the trade winds, blowing steadily from the northeast over cobalt-blue water. The sun glittered on the wavelets cut by *L'Avenir's* bow like millions of diamonds. Her sails, filled out by the wind, looked like a series of magnolia petals on her masts. It was easy to maintain the course, and as I steered, I made slight sways in time to the contented roll of the deck. Maybe the crew had tossed me out of their midst like children tired of a painted toy, leaving me to weather away beyond the Pale, but now the trades revived the bright colours of my enthusiasm. Never mind if later storms might chip some of this cheer off the toy chucked in the scuppers of discouragement. But now, as the planet Venus rose in the sky, her brilliance seemed to signal that an earthbound past could be shed as a snake discards its old skin. Night fell, the sky an immense dome over *L'Avenir's* four masts. The air was lush, so filling my lungs with ozone that I felt that I was expanding to great heights. The whole environment was so enchanting that were it not for the man-made rectangles formed by the shrouds and ratlines, it would have seemed that we sailed through some fantastic dream. At the change of the watch, even the voices in the well deck sounded awed by the atmosphere, only murmuring as if in church. I was glad that no one knew my country, my family or friends. What a chance for a metamorphosis. Beside me, Johnny, the English apprentice on the port watch, leant an elbow on the rail, chin cupped in his hand and echoed my thoughts. "I'm glad to be away from home, in all this. My family didn't want me to come to sea. But they couldn't have known ... never saw this!" So, others felt this too.

Now that we had warmer winds, the crew in night watches lay on the fo'castle head rolled in blankets, getting forty winks. They trusted the one who had "police" duty to awaken them if necessary. One night when the little Danska had police duty, he curled up like a puppy and dropped asleep. When the mate's whistle shrilled to summon Danska aft, it was only answered by the ship breathing a bow wave and the buntlines whipping the foresail. A second whistle was mocked by the chuckle of the foretack scraping the bitts. The mate's trill scratched the air for a third time with such acerbity it neared sweetness. I had long been awake nursing my sides aching from the hard deck. When I lifted my head I only saw snoring humps around me, so I stumbled aft to answer the whistle in Danska's place. "You not being police now." The mate was suspicious. Not wanting to get Danska into trouble, and remembering how the mate booted him into the rigging in Copenhagen, I lied. "I don't know who is police." The mate sprang about four feet into the air and charged forward, walloping all the sleeping humps with brutal kicks from his leather sea boots.

"*SAAATAN! Perkele*! Rise hup! Rise hup, *Yevla Poike*!" (Rise up, damned boys)

Some humps only grunted in annoyance, but others yelped "yiii yiii" with pain in dog-like falsetto. As though in hopeless disgust, the mate left abruptly. The humps rubbed their eyes, muttering. Was this just a bad dream? Proud of being "pure" Finnish Finn and not a Swedish Alander, Dennis explained to me that all the Aland Islanders were like the mate. Outside of this mild comment, they took their punishment more meekly perhaps than a British crew would have done. But I wondered if, like the donkey who saved his kick for seven years, later on in the voyage their resentment would take the form of some hideous revenge. "So this is discipline," I remarked to all and sundry, watching them nurse their bruises. They knew the mate meant business. He never needed to repeat his performance during the rest of the voyage.

During the dog watches everyone was at ease, and there was some leisure. Jumbo offered me matches, blankets, and such. He was the exception to his shipmates, with his "anything you need, at your service," attitude. I accepted all with equanimity. Anxious to make himself better understood, he enrolled Miss Kronig as interpreter. They chattered together sometimes, glancing at me across the deck as though I was the subject of some plot they had concocted. Then Miss Kronig said to me "He wishes to assure you that he is pleased to do anything he can to help you. If there is anything you are short of and he can get it for you, don't hesitate to ask." I sensed that she could have added something more, but discretion checked her. She explained her fluency in German. "I am partly of German descent. During my young days, I remember gay times when I visited in fairytale castles there. Ones with spires, turrets, and dungeons, all standing on craggy mountains overlooking rivers. You know the sort of thing." I nodded, as I had seen similar castles in Austria. She continued animatedly,

"Such wonderful fun and parties we enjoyed with relatives and friends in those glorious surrounding. But you have done a lot of yachting as well, I hear."

"Oh yes, I love the sea and that is why I have taken this trip."

Jumbo's geniality did not include coming to my defence when Ekstrom, no longer the shy violet boy of the first day's brass polishing, slithered up, catching me in a wrestle, half playful, half menacing. I wriggled clear and retreated to the side of Ceysen, a Belgian crew member. Perceiving my boredom and resentment of Ekstrom's games, Ceysen excused him, "*Ces Alandais ... ils ne savent pas mieux. Quand j'étais dans leur île, j'ai vu les Finlandaises se battre couramment avec les hommes. Elles sont très fortes!*" [These Alanders, they do not know much. When I was on their island, I saw Finnish women fighting regularly with men. The women are very strong.]

Well, it was some comfort to know that the Finnish girls fought strongly. Ceysen must have found the discordant League of Nations in the fo'castle trying, because, jerking his head in Jumbo's direction, he added, "*Ces Allemands! attendez qu'ils arrivent au port. Ils se tiendront ensemble en chantant et en poussant les gens loin du bar. Ils se croient seuls au monde à avoir le droit d'exister. Quand vous serez en Australie, vous verrez bien comment un tel groupe se conduit!*" [These Germans, you wait until they arrive in port. They stand together singing and pushing people away from the bar. They believe they are the only ones in the world to have the right to exist. When you are in Australia, you will see how a group like these conduct themselves.]

Despite his three years of rubbing elbows with rude Vikings, Ceysen had retained his gracious French manner and I found him the easiest and most pleasant of my shipmates.

My easy relations with Ceysen were far from what the captain had with some of his passengers. He had to tack around their odd ideas, keeping everything on a happy, safe course. Just how much, I never knew, because although I had the occasional conversation with the passengers, as did others in the crew, most of the time I was on duty, or sleeping. The Finnish passenger, Olav, whose eccentricities had brought him fame when he had sailed in *Ponape* the previous year, hardly made his presence a joy to the master of any ship in which he might choose to sail. Olav had travelled all over the world, so he said, dropping hints that his millionaire father allowed him the cash and time to accomplish these gorgeous voyages.

While Miss Kronig and Jumbo were conversing one evening, Olav strolled up, a dead cigarette dangling from his pouting lower lip. "Oh Mees Kronig," the cigarette rode up and down as he spoke, "hev you seen Barbara anywhere? We making such a nice party tonight — you will be coming and the airman too — all wearing our evening clothes. Just as if we were in a big liner, not in sail ship, way between Africa and Spain."

"I'll be there," said Miss Kronig, livelier than one expected of her fifty-odd years. "Barbara tells me you have been all over the world in liners too, haven't you?"

"Yes, my fader, he being very rich, he has many affairs in far countries so must send me there to look after them."

That evening as I dashed up the companionway going on watch, sounds from a cabin indicated that their party was going off with a bang up start, especially for the airman, who later made a crash landing at the bottom of a ladder. Next morning I saw Miss Kronig making exploratory pinches of the wincing airman's arm. "I did a lot of nursing in the war. I am sure I can put it in a sling for you," she told him. The captain stumped up to them, so angry he could hardly wheeze out his edict. "From this time on, all passengers must be staying below deck after eleven at night." Sullenly, the airman watched the captain's stolid back going down the passageway. "Maybe from now on," he parroted, "we will be allowed to look out the porthole on Sundays, or take Frasne [the cat] to bed for a treat."

A bearded Dane who looked like the King of Iceland [King of Denmark] on that country's postage stamps, and who had been a medical student (we called him Dane Doctor) was called forth from the fo'castle to see if any bones had been broken in the airman's arm. He and Miss Kronig concluded that none were, but just the same, Miss Kronig made a very natty sling for the arm which the airman wore for some days. Indeed, the sling was incorporated in a painting Mrs. Grainger did of the airman, Miss Kronig, Barbara, and Olav. Mrs. Grainger painted on deck. On one occasion as she stood back from her easel to look at it, I remarked, "That is so original, having the airman with his arm in a sling."

"Yes, it is rather charming the way his sling is so decorative. It makes an opposing rhythm to Barbara's scoop-back bathing suit. Miss Kronig's suntan, too, gives a picturesque black, brown to work into my painting. But too bad! She suffered so when her whole skin ripped off. How silly of her to lie in the tropic sun all day. Lucky she didn't become very ill, poor soul."

Mrs. Grainger had studied painting in Paris and her ability brought life to *L'Avenir*. In addition to a sturdy portrait of the captain with his pet cat Frasne in his arms, she did some idyllic heads in pastels on the walls of the smoking cabin, which the carpenter had built on a voyage out to Australia. Her sea sprites gazed at each other across from wall to wall, with inhuman eyes. They did not look the type of people who would join in with the stout captain and the weather-beaten mates, smoking cigars while discussing what braces ought to be rove with new rope or what pigs might be ready for killing, or the cost of beer in Adelaide.

Chapter 5

Changing Sails

"A fine day like this, for sure we'll be shifting sails," Dennis told me at one six a.m. muster. "Shift sails?" Innocently I looked up at our storm canvas wearing itself against the masts. It flapped to *L'Avenir's* easy roll as she idly swung her bowsprit in the doldrums. Dennis might have been suggesting it was a fine day for a picnic, for all I knew, instead of a day of the heaviest labour I had ever known in my life.

"*Shifta segla*" ordered the mate, turning both watches to. Soon, Dennis staggered along the deck under a monster block splaying long tentacles of thick rope, proclaiming proudly as he passed me "I'm just about to go up to the truck with this." Two helpers took the tackle aloft in three stages, bringing part up to the top, then another coil up to the cross trees and finally Dennis carried it right up to the truck by shinnying up the royal backstay with that block, half as big as himself. When he had stopped at the truck it provided a sheave through which the mast rope could be rove. Led forward by the sails, this rope now became a sort of elevator by which to send sails alow and aloft.

There was no time to gape in admiration, because I was turned into one of the moles, sent down into the sail locker to burrow out twenty-five tons of canvas, sail by sail. They were made more heavy and awkward because their rigid folds hid the heavy iron clews. Smelly lanterns hardly cast enough light to reveal the identifying markings. Once we knew that the top gallant was being called for on deck, and we were not mistaking it for the royal, it was hoisted on our backs. The sail emerged from the locker as a long white caterpillar, wobbling up ladders on our staggering legs, to be dropped with care and ceremony at the foot of its proper mast, as though that were an altar receiving a sacrifice. My shirt soon became so heavy with sweat that I could have wrung it out in audible drips. Unused to toiling like a beast of burden, my knees quivered and I stared dizzily at the horizon, but faint as I was, I would not for the world have admitted it. Nevertheless, after some hours, when given a turn to go aloft, I jumped into the shrouds with alacrity. What joy and relief. Imagine that I had considered stepping ashore in Copenhagen because I supposed that "Yackie" would never be given a chance to do any real sailors' jobs. Well! Which and where were the rovings that had to be slashed with my knife? Where to place the stops of cable yarn round the sail about to be lowered? How far and how quickly those sails had to be grabbed as they sped up, swinging and swaying, on the mast rope? Then even little Danska jerked and snarled about the exact placing of the centre grommet on the jack stay, as though he was already a veteran of the seas. I was in everyone's way, and was called the whatnot frequently.

"Hell! Pass that roving the *other* way."

"Let GO that headrope, Chesus, you bitch."

Chesus ripped the headrope from me so sharply that I nearly lost balance on the footrope. Instructions in short, Anglo-Saxon English were fired at me, except from Ekstrom, who only spoke Swedish and joggled on the footrope beside me. In cat and mouse style, he pretended to claw me off the yard by grabbing my "*litten hande*," prying it loose to kiss it mockingly. "I'd like to '*litten hande*' you, by God!" I thought. Instead, I scrambled out of his way on the bunt to the yardarm where the big Finn A.Bs. worked. Lehtonen and Ohman were seated on the loop of the Flemish horse, rocking with the joy of four-year-old girls swinging in a garden. They hammered pins out of shackles and sorted out the right chains for the sheets with skillful movements like the porpoises that played about *L'Avenir's* bows. They didn't even bother to chase me back to the bunt of the yard, where tradition says a greenhorn belongs. Their serenity began to infect me. Here, aloft, after five hours standing on the cutting footropes, I began to look at the Finn's clogs, merely picturesque on deck, with respect. By contrast, my thin sneakers left my toes feeling cut away from my heels.

It took two days, with all hands turned to, to change sails. As I became familiar with the rigging aloft, my intense acrophobia slunk away like a devil before daylight. I was always afraid aloft, but super fear lessened after the session changing sails.

Chapter 6 *Work and Music Aboard*

Music at sea took various forms, such as when the Dutch lady conducted a safari of our crew, loaded with gramophone, records, blankets, and countless accessories to the main hatch. "Now you must put blanket heer," she would begin. It had to be arranged perfectly, each fold spread out tidily on just the right section of the hatch, so that no spot might spoil her Dutchly clean dress. More directions followed in "English," the Esperanto of our vessel.

"Slooow ... no bang when you put gramophone down. Ach, Zoo! Ceysen, you the most carefool. You must putting on records. Let not ozers do dis. Wind no zo hart. Break no spring. Valenstrom, you must be sitting away from records. You heer better near where Danska is. Ach! *NOW PLAY*. Goot iss it. I em zo heppee."

That was a controlled concert for docile deckhands. It was more higgledy piggledy when Olav brought his gramophone to the fo'castle head on Sundays. He was liberal in lending it and records freely to the Lido for sunbathers there. His generosity was his virtue. The airman also contributed with a stack of old English songs on record.

If anyone had bothered to notice Johnny — erstwhile public-school boy before his voyage in *Penang* — as he hunched himself up, arms drawn around his knees, inconspicuous in a corner, they would have seen him in rapt elation as he listened to *Ave Maria*.

"Stoooormy weather ... since my man and I ain't together ..." I like that. Say Jacky, what about a whirl? Did you ever hear Duke Ellington and his band?" Dennis asked.

"Who's he?"

"Do you mean to say you live in America, a debutante I hear, go to dances and don't know *Duke Ellington?*"

"Never bothered with dances. Saved the glad rag money for my sea apprenticeship fee. Now if you asked about *Haul Away Joe ...*"

"You're hopeless! Just as sleepy owl eyes, damn you."

"Pipe down, the lot of you. Let someone else enjoy his music too," snapped the airman, putting one of his Noel Coward urban nightclub recitations on the turntable and settling down to puff his cigarette in peace while listening. He had hardly squelched us into silence when the donkeyman began cackling in Alandese to Ohman, who appeared indifferent, sitting like a lump of stone on the bitts. Nor did Ohman, a former house painter, seem to be moved to wonder when a sweet song wafted down from aloft. Surely that could not be Josephine Baker high up in the rigging? Dennis looked up with wonder, but Ceysen following his glance, said disgustedly, "Argg, *Quel bête*!" It was his uncouth countryman, Albert, monkey-shining from the fore t'gallant yard while imitating Josephine singing *La Petite Tonkinoise*. Albert turned and twisted, sliding down clewlines with the grace of the hunchback of Notre Dame high among the gargoyles of the Cathedral. Jumbo scorned the "Little Indo-Chinese Girl," deaf to the song. He flicked through the stock of records. "You have nothing Yerman," he protested and retreated to squat behind a hawser drum. I was able to see his black trouser leg and foot moving in a pettyish rhythm to his own Teutonic love and hate music in his mind. These emotions were a force beyond my Celtic ken. Olav, the opportunist, however, squirmed over to Jumbo to thrum him up to a higher pitch by using him as a guitar on which to strum his own mischief. Then, when the airman found a sentimental German lullaby, Jumbo returned to the charmed circle. He approved because at last a "Yerman" piece was to be heard.

When the airman's record "Daisy, Daisy, Give Me your Answer True" whirled around several times, it became such a hit

62

aboard that even the most Finnish of our Finns picked up the chant. "We cahnt afford a carriage" came floating up from the depths of the hold to the main top for the rest of the voyage.

When polishing the brass bars over the glass of the skipper's saloon skylight, I heard chunky Swedish polkas emerging from his quarters below. These knocking, stiff Swedish tempos had little appeal for me, not even the popular "Irish Bolja." Nor were the hymns, the lullabies, or the sentimental ballads my favourites, and least of all, the singers moaning about their "Heeearts." I wanted to travel fast in music, something wild to race along with, free, like Spanish flamenco, or African drumming, or even folk music, if we had had that. The airman's "Tiger Rag" came nearest, with its "Hold that tiger ... Grrr ... he's caught!" I liked a series of early ethnic records that Mr. Grainger had and sometimes played for us. "We Weep to See the Sun Go Down" a Madagascaran tune, was a quiet, slow, sweet song that appealed to me. When the records palled, photo albums passed from hand to hand.

"*Vem ar det?*" (Who is that?)

"What ship ...?"

Chesus's mother looked so hard-bitten she could have chewed glass. She stood with power in her spine, her jaw set, proud of a life of toil, expecting the same unrelenting labour from her family. Jumbo's mother had a wide face, eyes deep with kindness. It was easy to see who looked forward to a plate piled with his favourite foods on his return from sea. Olav had a portrait of his family posed around a fine aspidistra. The ladies, weighed down by enormous hats in Edwardian style, sat in velvet chairs, while saucily showing some buttoned boots. The men in their black frock coats stood erect behind their chairs, wearing monster watch fobs. "Oh no, this is not my grandparents," Olav insisted. He claimed to belong to one of the aristocratic families of the country. Either Finnish blue blood was conservative in the extreme, clinging to pre-war styles, or so fashionable that it didn't matter what they wore or did.

As I had left my past behind in my desire to metamorphose into a Barnacle Billie, I had no family album with me. No photos of paintings of King Charles's mistresses, or English country hunting squires, or Huguenot Irish forebears to refute my paint-spattered dungarees and begrimed features under a short, mannish haircut with a forelock hanging down towards my eyes. Hair sprouting in that peculiar fashion, D.H. Lawrence had written, is only seen on the heads of British workmen, the result of their descent from a crude tribe of ancient Britons. "Jacky," Dennis remarked, "you and the donkeyman might be brother and sister; you look so alike, your hair growing in the same way." Laughing, Dennis pointed me out to the Finnish donkeyman, "*Dinna syster.*" `

"*Minna syster?*" exclaimed the donkeyman in a "You crazy Dennis" tone of voice as he surveyed my work-worn form with his eyes crinkling. I looked for some resemblance in "*min bror*" too. He stood with one hand over his heart and the other limply at his side, the shoulders drooping as if cramped from constantly bending over his machines. His greasy shirt revealed a fragile frame, and his face looked as though he washed it in the greasy water around the winches. Sometimes, off watch, his thin legs seemed to give way and drop him to the fore bitts with relief. Then, his grainy chin waggling, he emitted poultry cackles of Alandese, making his audience roar with laughter. He was hardly the person one might have thought, to keep the precise mysteries of the dynamos and the antique winches and windlass running with gleaming perfection. But he did just that.

Ceysen might have found himself at home in *L'Avenir* because of her Belgian origin, an atmosphere that hovered about her, traces of a scent that had once pervaded her. Her white hull and spars and lavish brass brightwork had a Latin gaiety, but there was Flemish burgher richness in the red plush seats in the dining saloon as well as in the upholstery of the master's quarters, which I had glimpsed with such awe in my interview when coming aboard. *L'Avenir* had sailed from Antwerp on her maiden voyage in 1908 with a full compliment of officers and crew as well as twenty-four of the flower of Belgian youth, training aboard as cadets to be the future officers of Belgium. In a flight of fancy I like to picture the barque as she was then, as though she were part of a medieval painting by Memling: *L'Avenir* setting her canvas in argent hillocks, standing emblazoned against an azure sky, their white as new as untrodden snow, as unhandled as the uncleft seas that had yet to be cut by her forefoot. The royals would have been brilliant with their fresh-painted coats of arms far above our heads, with their smattering of that same heraldry that must have been so much admired by those watching her sail away from Antwerp down the Scheldt in 1908.

The practical Finns, who now had possession of those painted harridans of sails, when getting them from the locker would toss them aside angrily saying, "the oil in the paint is eating troo that canvas. Now is so rotten it's breaking. Anyting will happen when that sail is up on mast."

Her hull had also suffered in the long time she had been laid up in Antwerp while awaiting a purchaser. By the time Erikson bought her in 1932, her skin of steel plates had flaked with a rusty canker, which sidled into cracks around her rivets and gnawed away at her angle bar joints. Cavities had bitten into some of the teeth of the winch gears, and decay into the strands of the standing rigging, *L'Avenir's* muscles. Even the steel plates of her yards were pitted and flaking, all except the royal yard, which was made of wood. Like children trying to empty a beach of sand with little pails, *L'Avenir's* meagre crew were set to task tacking away with their rust chipping hammers all day long, in hopes of surgically cleaning her of rust. The cleaned plates in the hold were covered with two sticky thick coats of grey paint.

The monotony of tending to *L'Avenir's* ailments had not been expected by one member of the port watch when he signed up for a life of adventure. Bill MacDowall, the Scot-Swede, and the reputed relative of a baron, had expected seamanship of a higher order, and to have it handed to him on a silver platter. Squatting beside me, he ceased plying his hammer, and lifted his gob-style cap to air his sweaty locks. Running his fingers through his hair, he relieved his pent up feelings. "This Goddamn Finnish ship! Chipping rust *all* day. I regret coming here. In Sweden," he complained in his musical, girlish voice, so incongruous, yet common in these great Nordic hulks, "there we have our own good school ship, *Abraham Rydberg*. She is easier to work on aboard, carrying many more cadets. They learn everything well there too. No one bothers to teach anything in this hooker here. During one year in that Swedish school ship I could be learning as much seamanship as during the two years or more, in this crazy Erikson-run ship. Chipping! Scraping at muck."

He was right about muck scraping, because at the bottom of the holds, old boards and empty wheat bags had been placed to prevent the cargo from touching the damp sides and deck. This protection, known as dunnage, was now the filthy home of thousands of rats who lived and died in it. We spent many days clearing this dusty rubbish out of the holds. If any of the crew hoped it might break a girl's heart to have to pick up dead rats plus their excrement in sodden sacks, they had another think coming. Animals of any sort I had always loved, and I could clean out a horse's stall or a pigsty without unwarranted disgust. Indeed, as an adolescent, I learned how to move about a stable from a great friend, Jose de Mott Robinson, once a famous bareback dancer in the Barnum and Bailey Circus. Many many happy hours I spent helping her, cleaning the livery stable she ran, and grooming and riding her horses. She never boasted of it, but I heard that this tiny woman was the first to perform somersaults on one horse, instead of somersaulting from one horse to another. Undoubtedly, there was a difference between rats and horses, however, clearing out the rats' bedrooms came more easily to me than if I had been a stewardess having to clean up after seasick passengers. For that reason I had never felt a call to be a nurse or doctor, even when a kindly doctor I met aboard a transatlantic liner advised me to graduate in medicine with a view to obtaining a position at sea as a ship's doctor. That was one way I could sail the seven seas; a very rational solution to my dilemma, but it did not attract me. It might be, of course, in a doctorless ship that I might be called upon to treat sickness or injury as a senior officer, if and when I became one. Perhaps I would even emulate one of those masters on a sailing ship who operated roughly, but successfully, on an acute case of appendicitis, when it appeared that the victim might die in any case. But by that distant time, I expected to be hardened to everything on land and sea. I had no wish to become a professional medical person, but I realized that, living on such intimate terms with crews, I must acquire a nurse's poker-face toward naked men sunbathing or pissing in the scuppers. This attempt at *sang froid* was taken amiss by Sonny, who rebuked me, saying that a "real lady" would have had hysterics and run right away from such chance encounters. "I'd be more taken aback if the men couldn't act so naturally," I tried to explain, using the analogy of the London bus conductor who said to the Victorian lady "refainedly" fussing with her skirts before going up the steps to the top deck, "Lidy, legs is no treat to me." Rat piss, scupper piss, it was all one to me.

66

But what a relief, one scorcher of a day, when a hail from mate leaning over the hatch coaming resounded to the depths of the hold. He called MacDowall, Ceysen, and me away from dunnage clearing and rust chipping to come on deck. MacDowall clattered briskly up the long ladder from the hold, hoping that a real job awaited him on deck. He looked suspiciously at the bevy of barrels the mate pointed out to us as needing our attentions to move them aft.

"What's this stinking stuff?" I demanded to know, after sniffing inside the open butt, and reeling back from the greasy effluvia from the whitish corpse inside.

"That? Never you mind. All you have to do is be taking it all the way along the main deck, down to the well deck and under the fo'castle head. Mind, you must not be spilling one drop." The mate shook his fist at me.

"God!" I see it now, this is salt pork," I said to MacDowall, while we swayed and staggered with a heavy barrel of the stuff towards the break of the poop. "You'd think it would grow rottener, if possible, in this blazing sun after being slopped about on deck here."

The Swede surmised gloomily, "It's probably made several voyages before this one."

I gagged, "And we're going to eat it?"

MacDowall grumbled, "It's that bloody steward and this crazy Finnish ship."

I decided to stick to the flat black rye bread. "It's good, really," I enthused, "and did you know it is what their Olympic runner, Nurmi, trains on?"

"Aaach, aaagh" Ceysen gargled his French disgust. "*Ce pain plat et noir? J'en mange avec dégoût. Assez de ces galettes.*" Ceysen dismissed the square riggers he had slaved in for the past three years.

After the barrel-moving day, I was set to work on tearing up old sails for the sailmaker to use for patching. Nearby, Otto, a German A.B. made new footropes to replace the one which Dennis described as "rotten as politics." Otto was serving the new lengths of footropes and bending stirrups on them with fancy rose knots. Before sending the completed rope aloft, he tested it by stretching it and whacking it with one of the great capstan bars. He did this with all the strength he had, but he had to pause often and lean on the bar. His thin chest heaved like an overdriven cab horse, dripping and shining with sweat. He kept clearing his throat with a sawing noise and spitting into the scuppers. I thought to encourage him while he rested.

"Good to see such a hearty job is being made of those new footropes. Rose knots too, I see! Aren't they about the most difficult of the fancy knots to make?"

"I know all the fancy stuff, rose knots, star, Turkish sennit, I can do anything." He spoke excellent English, but he was panting. "I've been four years in sail. I'm going up for my ticket as soon as I'm home in Germany."

He spoke pleasantly, but intuitively I felt a black undercurrent of hate running through the courteous answers. "Jumbo and Chesus, " I asked, "they'll be getting their tickets too, won't they?"

"*Ach*, them? Those bastards, they can *klydia m'arse* (kiss my arse) for all I care, as they say in our native Hamburg."

He swore in Hamburgese when the other Germans were mentioned because, as I soon learned, they all repulsed each other like magnets of the same polarity.

As *L'Avenir* approached the equator, "health and joy" as the fortune-tellers say, increased, delighting greatly. Sunsets exploded, and the albacore playing about the prow arched into rainbows as they leapt out of the turquoise water, spilling a cornucopia of exotic colours. What a change from the north, where the cold lays a harsh hand on hues, forcing most to be greyed, browned and well-bred. In this tropic zone, lapis lazuli blue brought reveries of minarets, turbans, rickshaws, Bengali Babus, yoga, dhows, and scimitars. Might I not partake of these on future voyages, a Sinbad the Sailor? Many times at the wheel I yielded to the temptation of looking away from the compass and down at the tremendous spread of shining, rising, and falling ocean. If that water had been a blue wine from heaven, what a draught from the divine Lethe, the river in Hades. To drink its waters produced oblivion.

"*Up n' da vinde! for HELLVITER!*"

The master's roar sent me jumping back to the compass. *L'Avenir* swayed drunkenly, a couple of points off her course. I found that the wheel and I became close companions in these doldrums. "Only three out of each watch need take wheel, lookout and police," Dennis had informed me at a muster. "The rest are to be day men — work all day, sleep all night — lucky bastards. You are to remain on watch." On watch we three watch keepers were sometimes forced to keep hauling braces all night long, because the fickle airs of the doldrums jittered about from every point on the compass. Pools of sweat streamed off us, dripping onto the deck in a series of punctuation marks where we had been bracing.

I did not envy the day men their fill of sleep, however, for they endured mouths and eyes full of rust chip dust collected in the roasting oven of the holds. They emerged from the holds in the evening to go off watch as soon as the decks were hosed down. Eager to get that job done, their haste turned the rotted canvas hose, with its projecting wires, into a zig-zagging dragon, ripping the bare feet of any hoser who didn't jump clear. This dragon received yells of pain and beautifully hissed oaths in homage. "Horry up." Bergman whisked a deft slash of the hose over my bare toes. "Hah! Ha! Yackee, dat make you wash. Queek, Queek!" He stretched his unshaven chin in a grin of pleasure as I jumped in pain at the scratches on my feet.

After all the sweat and grime, it was sweet and pleasant to gather together, seated on the fore hatch during the dog watches. Then the seamen would yarn, play cards, read, and sometimes dispute. Their arguments raged endlessly on odd subjects about which they may or may not have had a great deal of knowledge.

"You think the royal ratlines here are bad! *Penang's*, God! They were a damn sight worse'n that here. Practically all gone on the main shrouds when I was in her," Johnny pronounced, with quite the air of an old-timer in sail.

Dennis asserted "You can eat Chinese eggs boiled."

"The hell you can!" Johnny disagreed.

"I have eaten them boiled, they come all that way to England and they're still good."

"Phew, they're hardly fit for frying!"

This controversy raged on for weeks. Chesus prided himself on his American background. He found some of the continentals and Britishers affecting superiority to him in this respect. "Well, at least the traffic laws in England are better than in America!" Chesus found the airman challenging him. "For instance, in England, the cars have to stop to allow the people to get on and off the trams."

"Christ, they doing the same in America too."

"The hell they do!" refuted Dennis.

Chesus drawled, "Wot you knowing about such things. Yuh ain't never bin to Amurica," and turned his back on the whole untravelled lot.

"All American women is very lazy," announced Danska, never before out of Denmark in his fifteen years, "getting machines to do washing and cooking. Going out all the time. Having fun themselves and leaving their babies alone at home with the machines."

I laid down the law. "Just as it should be, cooking and washing is machine work for sure." Danska turned fiery red at my adamant declaration of independence. Fairly hopping with rage, he was the Rumpelstiltskin of the Danish fairy story. His stamping and screams entertained the lollards on the hatch. Tredge strolled by to see what was going on, but he ignored Danska's raging because he was absorbed in his usual dream of days of yore and past glory. He began telling me about *Herzogin Cecilie*. "When I was in her, sail very fast. Sven Erikson much goot skeppers. Youngest in Erikson *flotts*. I knowing. I seeing how fast he sailing." Kind words of praise, though, are rare among the hatch company.

Forehatchers began grumbling about a newcomer on board. "Mom? He'll make one lousy sailor. No nerve. Pisses his pants, he's so damn scared aloft. His hair stands so stiff with fright it could sandpaper the mast." That cap of frightened hair fitted my own head too well, and I felt like retreating before any one else had a chance to describe my symptoms aloft. But the talk drifted off to the pubs in sailor town, in London. When "Charlie Brown's" was mentioned nostalgically, Sonny broke his Trappist-like silence, and challenged me with "Charlie Brown's! Dat vere voman goes. Voman in pub drinking beer and giving some also to little baby she is holding. You dere," and he shook his finger at me, "you tinking dat orlright?"

I stuttered, "I ... I dunno exactly. I never held a baby, let along fed one beer!" This had all the effect of Marie Antoinette's "Let them eat cake." Sonny, on hearing of a woman who had lived to the age of 24 without ever having handled babies, went rigid and remained silent in shock.

Olav, ever present, cocked his head on one side like a robin listening for a worm. No doubt he reckoned this last statement of mine as an echo of the confidences I had exchanged with Barbara about my biological quandaries. He had become very chummy with Barbara of late. Olav sought to relieve the tedium of the doldrums by concocting a cure to make "Jacky" grow up. He would use Jumbo as a nostrum. What fun, to set fires alight and watch them burn. The pyromaniac!

Just then a ball of flame dropped dramatically on the horizon, but it was not the one plotted by Olav. It was the sun, as it does in low latitudes. A procession of clouds dignified it, majestic forms of djinn, dhows, all a fabulous pageant. I drifted into a reverie, wondering "where, after death?" perhaps to an existence among hues only, forever floating like *L'Avenir* among the seas and surrounded by those radiant golds, heated reds, electrical greens, and lush purples, where none of our concepts of time and space in the universe hold true. The sea whispered to me of mysteries I dreamt it would fathom for me.

Olav only saw my body on the hatch, while I floated free of the petty plots aboard. But my scatter brains, how they tangled me in the orderly shipboard routine. I tried very hard to live up to the mate's meticulous standards. No "holidays" in paintwork, no spots left on brasswork, no untidy coils, no paint splatters on deck. These were the essence of good discipline, but were impossible for a sea gypsy.

On lookout in a chilly night, shivering in thin tropical whites, I snatched a blanket that had been left tumbled on deck, to ward off the heavy dew, and swathed it about me like an Indian. When my relief arrived, I strolled aft, smiling as I reported *Clare lanterne* to the mate, unaware that I still had on the picturesque but incorrect attire. The mate froze, stony. He was either too taken aback to reprimand me or else he thought "This Canadian Indian is too wild even to bother reproaching." The boys soon found tongue, on hearing of the enormity of my immigrant outfit. Casual style, I learned, was a *faux pas*, simply *not done*. "Reporting the lights while wrapped in a blanket, by Christ." Even Dennis despised me. "I have no more use for you, doing a thing like that."

Chapter 7

Crossing the Line

Why is it that a ship's bow has such fascination? Perhaps it is because the bow is the end of the ship which is the beginning, unlike the stern with its wake of past mistakes and hopes tumbling about and finally disappearing in the sea.

One night, asleep on deck near the bowsprit, I awoke in an atmosphere of mysterious repose. The moon shone in easy glimmers, forming "in" lines of Japanese art on the water. They were lines of super perfection because they lost perfection in breaking as the ocean swelled and fell. Only in oriental paintings of celestial dreams was such a divine night revealed. *L'Avenir's* concave bow moved through the water with a gentle sough. The wonder of so much beauty moved me beyond words and I cried out. Olav, creeping behind a capstan heard my voice, and nipped into the fo'castle to tell.

"I hear Yackie! She moaning so loud at moon on deck. She's in love with steward. She must be this because she being so cold, cold to the poor, poor Jumbo and I see her making eyes at steward. How about we arresting her and making charges to her for treating the poor Jumbo so badly?"

He roped in some A.Bs. "Hey Dennis. There is a nice, nice pipe, a really new one. This is salary for you if you be judge. I can be juror. Sonny here, he never talk much. He good one to be quiet like the peoples of the public."

His enthusiasm for a mock court caught on, and the next dog watch found Jumbo and me dragged, kicking and protesting under the fo'castle head. "This court is accusing you of disdaining Jumbo the German," the "judge" admonished me. He waved his pipe at Olav. "There is a witness to that fact. Also, you have been seen making eyes at the steward. Having truck with a low-down steward! Breaking our sailors' tradition." Held fast in the callous grip of Redbeard.

I stamped my foot. "What an utter lie!"

The "juror" now cross-examined the "claimant," Jumbo. "You loved her once is not that so? But she has killed every feeling you had for her, by her coldness."

Jumbo, wriggling against those pinioning his arms, hissed "I haf nozzing to say."

The "juror" swung his thin arm and pointed his sharp finger at me. "*There now!* You see the error of your ways. Don't you know what it is to be a gurl?" The court whistled and guffawed their applause. "Why do you continue in the same stupid way?" Olav lectured.

I laughed scornfully. "I don't know what you are babbling about. Anyway you know nothing about girls. I may *be* one, but more importantly, I am a human being."

This plea confused the onlookers, so the "judge" waved it aside. He summed up. "You know, you really ought to be kinder to Jumbo, because the communists may shoot him any day when he goes ashore, to revenge themselves for splitting on some of the crew who were sympathizers to communism, when Jumbo was working as Purser's Assistant in the German East Africa Line."

"What the hell has that to do with me!" I retorted. "If ever there was a bunch of baloney," I announced in their grinning faces. "Anyway," I plunked down my ace card, "I promised the captain not to fall in love on this voyage. So *that's that!*"

The "judge" banged his marlin-spike gavel, shouting "Olav's right. I pity Jumbo with an iceberg like Jacky. I condemn her to ... C'mon fellows, give her a fitting punishment. One she won't forget, by God." The court wrangled in such a welter of confusing exhortations that I managed to slip my cable and drifted to a remote corner, escaping further indignities ... for the moment.

I might have been forgotten entirely, only we were nearing the equator, and "Crossing the Line" ceremonies intruded. Scandinavians have combined that raucous frolic with extra fertility rites (they would!). These were designed to prove that the initiate was ripe enough to join his shipmates when sowing wild oats ashore. Already, a secret enclave plotted horseplay for the arrival of Neptune. Olav lifted his head from the huddle, on seeing me scuttling way. "We are fixing *you* all right! You being so sorry on *doppa ligna* day." He left me shuddering with fear of a ducking from high on the mainyard, let down in a bosun's chair into the sea while the ship drove on, choking and half drowned until returned to the deck, half alive. I had heard stories of having the genitals smeared with hot tar in full view of the roaring ship's company. Ignoring Olav, I stuck my hands in my dungaree pockets, drew my chin down into my collar, and tried to remain as inconspicuous as possible until the awful day arrived and was over.

When *L'Avenir* neared the equator, Redbeard in the guise of the Ancient Mariner, holding a mock quadrant made of slats, took a sighting of the sun and pronounced her right on the line. Jumbo honked the foghorn with zest, summoning King Neptune and Aphrodite, his queen. They crawled up over the bowsprit accompanied by an alarming army of followers, named from ancient times the Doctor, the Priest, and the Bears. These last soon rounded up the trembling "greenhorns." I starched my face into a calm smile like a wallflower at a dance, appearing not to care. If only I *were* a wallflower in this festivity! To have a girl crew member at their mercy was a one in a thousand novelty for the crewmen. Inside I shivered as apprehensively as an Aztec princess about to be cast alive down a bottomless well. Any show of fear, and I knew they'd pepper up their fun with antics not even contemplated. Clerical in a long black oilskin coat, the ecclesiastical tabs of white under his grizzled chin wagged as the Priest, our tough donkeyman, interrogated his victims with his ribald wit. His fair skin blenched with fear, Mom was the first greenhorn thrust forward. His green eyes widened as he listened to Neptune droning, "Carl Mom, you are now about to receive holy baptism into my kingdom. Do you swear to be loyal forever, to the sacred band of seafarers?" Mom could hardly nod. He was forced to sit on a barrel. The Doctor seized him roughly, making his face smart with a rap. Then as his mouth dropped open, aghast with apprehension, the Doctor popped in a billiard ball of a pill. The Bears held his jaws shut on the concoction of tar, coal oil and sawdust. Knowing those rogues, I dreaded to imagine what else. Gulping this, he had not time to breathe as he found himself upended into a barrel of water, heels in the air. He was dunked and held under three times before he was let go, sputtering and choking, face streaming, red hair splintered down his forehead, relieved at having suffered no worse.

The canny Danish Doctor turned the tables on his tormentors by jumping up suddenly during the shaving and bestowing a great smacking kiss on the barber. This was an uproarious hit with the onlookers and put them into an easy mood. That, and the presence of passengers watching the hijinks restrained this rowdy company from indulging in too rough exuberance when "Yackie's" turn came. I too was ceremoniously upended into the water barrel and given the tar and sawdust pill, which of course, one then spat out as soon as released. Treated the same as the others, I relaxed. All the neophytes were formally presented with a certificate in Swedish, sealed with tar and ropeyarn, confirming that they had been admitted to King Neptune's realm.

It wasn't such a bad day after all.

Chapter 8

Jumbo Proposes

Olav's insidious prodding set Jumbo to questioning me. "Yackie, how alt your fader be?" Sometimes he asked, "How many room in your home?" To Jumbo I was an American, another word for wealthy to Europeans, who did not differentiate between Canadian and American.

Alone with me upon the fo'castle head, one pink, romantic evening as we leant towards each other over the capstan, Jumbo seized the opportunity to declare "*Ich liebe dich.*" Finding that I did not pick up one of the capstan bars and beat him over the head with it, he gathered up his courage and burst out earnestly, "Vould you been my vife? I do all dat you been happee."

Marooned on the lone isle of *L'Avenir's* deck by the shunning of her company, I felt tempted to accept the hand of this Man Friday without protest, even if it were proffered in marriage instead of comradeship. But I turned as though trying to sight someone beyond the golden horizon. "I've got another sailor waiting for me in England," I murmured.

"*Ach*, I knowing this. You all times talking so of de other sailor. Perhaps he not be waiting for you. We sailing so long away."

He smacked this awful sea across my bows to loosen my

rivets and sat back to observe the effect. I wobbled, "well, you are rather cute...."

"Only *cute!* Me?" He stiffened indignantly. "Cute? What is this you are saying. I have you knowing I would been officer, high up in Yerman army, if only not so short being." His stature was the result of the starvation suffered as a child during World War I. He drew himself up, at the same time, trying to smile. "Then you can be coming to mine home in Hamboorg. My mother see you there. At last you can be telling this damn, bloody Erikson shipowner to go to hell. You not for him work more!"

"But Erikson is the only man in the world who ever gave me a chance," I maintained. "And I tried all the good shipowners in England, but not one would sign me on. Only Erikson."

Jumbo did not acknowledge my point, and continued with his plan. "We go round the vorld, together in small boat. Then we coming back to Yermany. Having big schloss there, I go ridin round the land. See after all is well ..."

I broke into his dream. "But who is going to buy that sea boat and that fine castle?"

Jumbo gasped at this arrow sprung by his intended. "*Ach,* that I not knowing just exactly."

Although he was an experienced sailor, and a schoolmate of the nephew of Count von Luckner of *Sea Devil* fame, Jumbo's interests were entirely military. He kept up a correspondence with Prince Oscar, who was a great Nazi. Jumbo believed that the old monarchy might one day return. Unfounded rumours that he might be an illegitimate son of the Kaiser rippled through the ship as a consequence. Jumbo would show me these letters and tell me about German generals. For the life of me, I cannot now recall their names or which Prussian general opposed what new Nazi general, as Jumbo's anecdotes went in one ear and out the other. These stories might have been advantageous to a Mata Hari, but to a Canadian merchant seaman, the solemn array of the old guard with their spiked helmets was too much.

Then mischief provoked me. Because I had tanned to a deep brown, my skin charcoaled by the sun, the boys kept saying "*du ar neger,* Yackie." This worried poor Jumbo to the point where he inquired anxiously "Den dis might be zo, Jackie? Dat you the nigger *blut* haf?"

"Oh no," I said seriously, "we are a proud family. My father is descended from a long line of Indian chiefs. Very fine. Not nigger at all."

Poor Jumbo was distraught. "*Ach*, but dis alzo still very bat. Ver bat is it. Hitler not allowing dat any Yerman should be marry an Indian."

While *L'Avenir* sailed down the South Atlantic off the coast of Brazil, I had been ripping sail cloths clear of old stitches and the stiff leather sewn onto the clews for the sailmaker. Now, I flopped on the pile of canvas, exhausted by the Brazilian equatorial heat.

"This is like living in a furnace. From the chart, I see we are pretty close to Pernambuco. What do you think our chances are of meeting a pamparo, hereabouts," I asked the sailmaker. A pamparo is a cold wind that blows across the Argentinian pampas, and when it hits the unstable tropic air at sea, causes severe storms that strike with little warning.

"Christ," he swore at the very mention of a pamparo. "Don't talk bout those winds. I seen one rip the mast completely out of a vessel in just a few minutes. You can see one when it's coming; a queer shaped cloud it is, like an arch. It sweeps down so quick you ain't got much chance. Ah no, not likely we'll meet one of those, Jacky. We may be close to South America, but we are too far North for one of those goddam pamparos." Our position on the wind chart didn't seem to warrant the sailmaker's calming statement in that unstable atmosphere, so saturated with heavy intensity, and I was not so sanguine.

A hint of the exotic land of macaws, pumas, and coffee buzzed aboard and landed on Miss Kronig's bare shoulder.

"Ugh!" she shrieked, "whatever is that?"

I pounced on the insect as it flew from her with rattling wings. "A locust, I think, but look at its colour!" The oil-on-water hues of its wings and body set me dreaming of the luxury of palm trees and Pernambuco, where brilliant butterflies floated against the dark of the jungle.

"How *can* you pick up such a thing, so ugly? It's disgusting!" Miss Kronig said.

"Oh no," I defended the insect. "One reason I went to sea was to be able to see such creatures of nature in all parts of the world. I used to collect butterflies when I was seven years old. I bored our dear old cook too, telling her all the butterflies' Latin names. How patient she was. But mostly I regret having killed all those butterflies with gasoline. I still dream that I am one, too; caught and stifled with gasoline. I'll let this lovely locust go." It whirred off, landing as a speck high on the main sheerpole. It was gorgeous, yet with its cloak-like wings, it was a miniature witch foretelling the turbulence forming in the suffocating air that hung about *L'Avenir*.

That evening breezes fluffed from every point of the compass, chasing ruffles of rain hither and thither in *chasses* about the greying sea. Squalls roared past; a deluge flooding the air so thickly we might have been able to swim in it. Fiercer and fiercer the wind and rain blended, thumping the sails. Finally, in the night a sound like a pistol shot announced something carried away. Almost by instinct the mate announced that the mizzen sail had parted. Being close by the clew of the staysail, I snatched a block and tackle and wrestled, trying to hook it. It was like trying to put a bridle on a dray horse gone bronco. By some fluke, or perhaps from my experience with horses, I had the hook in the clew by the time the rest of the watch arrived. They tailed on and made the sheet fast.

"You idiot," Dennis scolded, "that bloody clew could have cracked your skull open." Feeling like a greenhorn again, I apologized. "I didn't think ..." Yet in the stances of the rain-dimmed forms of my shipmates, I sensed a grudging acknowledgement that my spurs, or more likely, my marlin spike, had been won.

Horizon and sea were one; thick driving rain made our hair stream in arrows down our foreheads. The mainsail snapped sharply, breaking loose from its buntlines. "*Uppa riggin! Tag in storsegal,*" the mates ordered, their shouts coming faintly from the deck below. We streamed out along the mainyard, with the mainsail shuddering and then flapping feebly, like the last twitching of a netted fish. That capricious wind from Argentina must have had some of the Iberian temperament and love of quick change. The winds of the world are as varied as the row of men of different nationalities wobbling on the footrope of *L'Avenir*'s mainyard, as they bound the mainsail with cablegarn.

Because our fresh water was low, after weeks of searing sun, both watches turned to, slopping about in a continuous bucket parade to fill the water tanks. We lifted several tons of fresh water by this method. They were poured into a tank under the galley and into barrels forward of the navigation room. Rivers of water ran off the sails over our sodden bodies. After four hours of this, in the light of early dawn I saw that my fingers had crinkled into hideous ridges, like those of sea sand, from their long soaking. Dane Doctor predicted gloomily, "we shall all get malaria. It is hidden in such tropic rain."

I tried to tease away his melancholy. "Why? I bet the bucket brigade is too much for you."

After all that, it had not been a real pamparo. Darn near, though.

Chapter 9

The Westerlies

S oon the warm delights of the tropics receded like a fadeout in a movie. From South America the navigators planned on *L'Avenir* picking up the forceful westerly winds sooner than if she had attempted to sail straight along the West African coast to round the Cape of Good Hope. In the westerlies, *L'Avenir* was driven one quarter of the way around the world on a monster sleigh ride. Travelling half way between the Cape of Good Hope and Antarctica we reached the longitudes of Australia. To do this, we had to repeat the task of changing sails, doffing the lighter tropic ones for the heavy canvas *L'Avenir* needed to brave the westerlies. The sailmaker and his assistant had cut, sewn, and roped a goodly number of these board-like creations already. No Parisian couturier ever surveyed the curves of his dresses with more intense satisfaction and sharper criticism than the master and the sailmaker as they oversaw the fitting out of the ship for the high season of storms in the South Atlantic. The elegant curves of the leaches on the topgallants, the smoothness of the topsails, the slight flutter on the head of a royal, all came in for notice.

In her storm canvas, *L'Avenir* appeared crisp as a trained nurse in her starched uniform, and ready for the business-like breeze which struck her from the west. An albatross hovered over the yards when we braced around to accommodate the new direction of the westerly wind. Our heads gyrated, following the swooping of the bird with its rock-brown wings — our herald of the westerlies. He was a thousand times more graceful than the dainty gulls, who are at home only in the blue waters further north. The albatross ranges over the great rollers of the South Atlantic that can spread a thousand feet in length, because they are uninterrupted by land, except for Cape Horn. They travel right around the world in the latitude of the "roaring Forties."

In these seas, *L'Avenir* did just as she pleased with me at the wheel, and I was soon banished again. "You needn't think you can get out of any work that way. You are to take extra lookouts in place of the wheel," the senior apprentice ordered, "and coil up all the braces by yourself too, after the watch has gone below. Mind you coil them down in perfect fakes, all clear for running."

"Okay, Dennis"

"The lower brace so ... in this figure-of-eight coil. You see? One fake exactly inside the other."

Dennis demonstrated with quick, able turns, which I too was able to make after faking down miles and miles of lines for weeks. Compensating for my failures at steering in this way kept me at work an extra half hour, after my watchmates had clattered to their bunks below, glad of a rest after a sixteen-hour work day.

Despite my steering, I had slowly begun to gain some respect from the master and mates when they realized that I knew how to work a sight. In those Finnish ships, no navigation instruction was promised to the apprentices, in spite of the fifty pounds premium they had paid. At the end of their four years of service the Finns attended a state-subsidized school for navigational theory. When I told the mates that I had taken a correspondence course in navigation, they laughed, just as in the magazine ads for piano courses by mail — "I sat down to play and they all laughed."

"You do dat? We taut you was crazy gurl, and now we know."

But they became more curious when they heard that I had also attended the real sailor's school in Limehouse in London. I could even work a Marc St. Hilaire (a newer method of fixing a position used in steamers to accommodate the longer day's run).

Aboard sailing ships they used the Sumner method. One day about noon time, the master approached me as I clambered out of a hold, laying down my rust chipping tools. "From now on," he said, you can leave your job a half hour early so you can be working out the noon sight with us." Exultant, I marched up to the senior apprentice and announced, rather tactlessly, "you can bloody well coil up the braces yourself at noon, if need be, 'cause I'll be taking and working out the noon sight then."

"You blasted gurl! Taking the noon sight indeed! You've got no business doing that, you ought to be washing baby's pants instead."

"And you ought to be wearing them," I retorted, thumbing my nose. "Yammering like a baby. Hasn't got a rattle to play with. Can't use a sextant. YAH!" He shot into the fo'castle to proclaim indignantly the news of "that bitch's" latest effrontery. Sour eyes could be seen sometimes, looking aft when I joined the goodly company of master and mates as they held sextants in their hands, standing steadily on the pitching deck and then reading the spray-coated verniers with neat accuracy.

L'Avenir drove along handsomely, in about latitude thirty-seven degrees south, when the three islands of Tristan da Cunha hove into sight. In the centre of the South Atlantic, these islands are considered to be the most isolated on earth. Their black cliffs were grey in the drizzling rain, and the six thousand foot mountain top of Tristan had a cloud weighing down on it.

I said to Ceysen, "Tristan ... *triste?*

"Arrgh," he shuddered, then remarked in English, "What is that, like mud on the water all round the island?"

Mr. Grainger, standing nearby looking though his glasses at the island, said "That must be what I saw on the chart as 'Kelp.' A sort of seaweed, isn't it, Jacky?" He handed me the glasses.

Mrs. Grainger shivered. "Oh so cold, so lonely, it must be for those people on that island."

But her husband refuted her: "Oh I don't think so. Perhaps they only stay there because they like it. Not everybody wants to be in a crowd."

The inhabitants, who had begun settling there in the early 1800s, are reputed to have the best teeth in all the world. This happy byproduct of life on Tristan da Cunha was their good fortune, but some of them also had the lachrymose lot of being the last humans to glimpse the barque *Kobenhaven* driving by in the rain just before she went missing in 1928.

"Did you ever hear of the barque *Kobenhaven*, Jacky?" It was the sailmaker, come on deck to see the islands, even though he was familiar with the sights of the South Atlantic.

"Yes, wasn't she the largest sailing vessel ever built?"

"Yes," he affirmed, "she was, and a Danish training ship too." I asked him, "How do you think she came to disappear. I read that she went down in the Atlantic near this island, even though she was very well manned. No one could understand why she was lost.

"It's my belief that when a square rigger is built beyond a certain size, the sail becomes too much for her crew to take in, and something's bound to happen. Steel masts don't break like wooden ones would, and so the wind can keep on blowing her over till she capsizes."

Thinking of Dennis's description of his escape from the *Hougomont* disaster, because the masts had bent and broke under the strain, and the barque remained afloat, I said "Better to be dismasted than overturned."

Tristan da Cunha was to figure in *L'Avenir's* history again, about six years after she slid past the island with us on board. *L'Avenir* was destined to leave her own last evidence there, as had *Kobenhaven*. But *L'Avenir* was not sighted by the natives. Instead they found her figurehead of a young girl holding an arum lily washed up on their shore. This was published in a sea magazine, *The Trident*, about 1957, in a piece which described the figurehead as "a maiden with an arum lily." But I remember her figurehead as the Belgian coat of arms, which was removed when she was sold to Germany in 1938. The maiden with the lily was on her tailboard. Could that have been washed ashore at Tristan da Cunha? The Germans restored her as a cadet training ship and, breaking one of the great superstitions of the sea, renamed her, but her new figurehead of *Admiral Karfanger* was not ready before she sailed with her big crew of Hitlerite cadets.

Gustave Erikson had the grace never to change the names of the ships he bought, and *L'Avenir* retained her Belgian name when I sailed in her. Perhaps because Erikson had not defied the superstition against changing a ship's name, I was spared from washing ashore to Tristan da Cunha with lilies on my breast.

During my lookout watches in the westerlies, with the sky so clear that the stars seemed to hang within reach, I wished I could reach up to take Orion's Belt and wear it to hold up my rust-laden dungarees. On stormy nights on watch under sodden skies, I remembered hearing as a child, Walter Damrosch's rather guttural accents on the Children's Radio Hour, telling the story of the *Fliegende Hollander*, the Flying Dutchman doomed to sail forever in his haunted galleon in these very same waters near the Cape of Good Hope. Then too, from all my avid reading, I recalled how Vasco da Gama called the Cape of Good Hope "Cape Despair" as he beat against a dreadful headwind in rounding it. His victory over "Cape Despair" comforted me four centuries later, for it showed that a seemingly fruitless quest can turn out to have great meaning, Other nights, the horizon cut hard against the sky as we tore along. No trees or houses obstructed the view, leaving me to realize how stingy our planet is, with its thin layer of air, and a pittance of land to live on, compared with its vast seas. Even the small comfort that this speck of a ship harnessed the wind to carry those aboard to where they wanted to go could not reduce the awesome awareness of the vast size and emptiness of the sea.

To allay the immense loneliness, I gulped in the air that blew over my face from across thousands of unpolluted miles. It seemed to fill my chest with hope and swelled it to the sailmaker's barrel size. One night, I stood in the lee of the ventilator, moved to sing and not caring that I tortured others with sounds out of tune. The swing of the waves and ship brought cheer to a gay "Habanera," while the sound of the wind in the rigging recalled "Lowlands." The line "she came to me, all dressed in white," was no dead girl, but *L'Avenir* herself, with her moonlit canvas towering above me. Ashore, worship of a ship becomes ridiculous, but aboard for months, there is something bewitching about a ship to those dependent on her.

Alas, being on board also meant never-ending contact with the others aboard. No eccentricities could be hidden, singing sessions on lonely watch included. Next day, the sailmaker grasped me and held me up before the crew. "Oh Ho! Singing away last night, weren't you? We knew! Everybody gathered at the bottom of the ventilator shaft to hear you. We all had a good laugh." Then he added softly, in a curiously gruff voice, "but you made us all feel so sad, we were just about dropping tears." He imitated wiping his eyes on a piece of sailcloth. "Why did you sing so mournful like and sweet?"

I blushed crimson. "I sure wasn't feeling that way," and wished I could crawl away and hide. But we floated on the ocean and there was no place to hide. I recoiled from having my feelings bared before that crew of harsh rovers, but I had to stick it out, like a barnacle on the ship's bottom. I had endured the sneers of Redbeard, who stood arms folded, sea boots ready on deck for a hard kick, and the mockery of that wretch of a cabin boy, who tried to wrestle with me all the time. Would they ever let me live my singing down?

Another night there was music at sea again, and this time the free watch gathered, squatting on the piled up canvas of the sailroom like a flock of penguins on an Antarctic rock. They were huddled in a nearly hypnotic trance, listening to Mr. Grainger's music from the broken down old piano. This tattered audience, who usually went about cursing their rotten meatball dinners, slapping each other, or clattering buckets of wash water on the iron plating, did not move so much as a sea boot, so as not to rasp a sound across their canvas "dress circle." Even their breathing was restrained as they listened while Grainger played Brahms, Tchaikovsky, Grieg, gay Irish tunes, Chopin, and sea chanties. Percy Grainger obliged everyone's fancy, ending up in waves of rustic laughter with his own compositions, *Country Gardens* and *Molly on the Shore*. The crew swayed their heads like cobras fascinated by an Indian fakir. They cannot all be meatballs, I thought. They respond to this music. Were they dreaming sentimentally of home, of girls, or Charlie Brown's pub in London?

For my part, staring at the bulkhead as the music drummed and cried, I seemed to see Neptune and spiral shells, mermaids calling from sea caverns; the music, the sea rising and falling became existence itself. So far away had I travelled that I was jolted awake when the ever-correct Dennis proclaimed, "Such a treat for us, sir. The boys forward say they never heard anything to equal your playing, Mr. Grainger."[2]

A smile, archaic and faint, flitted across Mr. Grainger's face, indicating the pleasure this compliment had given him. Coming as it did straight as it did from the hearts of the young sailors, it was even more to be treasured than the most elaborate praise from a newspaper critic. Grainger liked simple folk — farmers, sailors, lumberjacks, and bailiffs. He wore dungarees and lumberman jackets, and climbed the rigging at dawn.

Once, standing on the fo'castle head by the anchor crane, he pointed to its top and said to me, "One could injure oneself just as badly if one fell the few feet from this anchor crane, perhaps as from a royal yard, depending on how one fell." Mrs. Grainger backed his comment, describing how he once leapt safely from a third-storey window! The captain joined in, agreeing and kindly letting me hear his testimony too. "I was in a ship once, and dis boy, he falling right down from royal yard. Yet he not hurting himself. Yes. He bounced all the way down from one sail to de other. He only hurting himself very little." Still, while I kept my counsel, I felt that such luck didn't happen very often.

Mr. Grainger's pre-breakfast exercise included an appetite-whetting game of tennis. Although he was an Australian by birth, one might easily have taken him for a native of Norway or Sweden. Grieg had found in Grainger the soul of Norway. Other times, Mr. Grainger held the passengers entranced with the sagas of ancient Nordic monarchs, whose deeds and names he told with the same familiarity as an ordinary Britisher might recall the lives of the Kings and Queens of England. Thus, at meals I heard Mr. Grainger and the other passengers talking of many strange affairs in one part of the globe or another. The mate, however, ignored the tales and bent over rolling and lighting his cigarettes, as indifferent to the talkers as the Sphinx is to the camel-riding tourists who pass it. Munching away at his elbow, I imagined that he must have super knowledge of the ports being discussed, too vast to reveal, except perhaps to another sailor. Once at early coffee, when the passengers were not yet there, and alone with the mate, I warmed my hands by circling them around the coffee pot, gazing at the reflections on the nickel surface, as though they were the varieties of experiences to be seen voyaging the world. "You must know a lot about those places the Graingers and Barbara were talking about," I probed.

"Huh, dose passenger!" he said scornfully, "Dey yust talk, talk, talk, gabble noding." How disenchanting! To the mate, foreign parts were just varied beer parlours. Yet maybe it was the fiendish wakefulness that a sailing ship demanded of a mate that rendered him too careworn and hollow eyed to do more than just be a link in the chain of the "Erikson *flotta*."

One day, as Jumbo and I were painting the winches, the mate came to scrutinize the work. As his stooped figure and lined face went on to check others at work in the well deck, I remarked to Jumbo, "Gee, the mate looks old, but he's only three years older than I am."

"Ach, dose Finn, They alt many year before they must be."

"Is that a racial tendency, or is it like what happens to Canadians sapped from hot dryhouses and crackling cold," I suggested, but down-to-earth Jumbo refused to bother theorizing about it. I might have gone to Mr. Grainger for one of his original pronouncements, but he was so Nordic-minded that I felt he would say Finns were no different from Australians in that matter. The sailmaker, the most well-read man in the crew, would discuss it, perhaps, but then, being a Finn himself, he might not admit any shortcoming.

The sailmaker had loaned me a book which I showed the mates at supper one evening. "Look at this book by Basil Lubbock. Surprising ... he says those old colonial clippers sailed as far south as Latitude 56° when rounding the Cape, as we are doing now.

"There's lots lies in books," said the second mate, disdainful. "That's lies telling that any sailing ship went that far South."

"But look at these," I insisted. "The extracts of the logs of those old vessels. The sailmaker believes they sailed that far South. At home in Canada too, I have an original edition of the geographer Maury, who believed that better winds could be picked up in the lower fifties south."

The first mate corroborated the second's statement. "They couldn't go that far south; too much ice, for one thing. Look at cold and snow this barque is having, and she is only forty-three degrees south, now."

Going off watch the second mate thundered his fist on my door. "Rise hup dere. Show a leg!" Like a cow in a stall, I shuffled to my feet. "Midnight already and time to turn to?" I yawned, fuddled. From my bunk I could see the scuffling of white suds burying the port hole. Thuds shook the shell plating. Storm!

With a fireman's haste I threw on oilskins and sea boots and tumbled through the black alleyway, fumbling for the companionway. It slanted straight up and flattened down like the funhouse floor in Dominion Park in Montreal. Cautiously I squinted through a crack in the deck door. No gushing water, so I leapt out. The door slamming shut with dynamite force behind me could hardly be heard over all the noise on deck. I joined the group of line haulers. The mates barked orders, and like steers in a herd we scuttled about, sorting lines hastily thrown free of the pins in wind and water. Finally we had the royals clewed up. "Get aloft and furl them." Up I went in my first storm, as squalls of rain mercifully dimmed the distance to the deck.

Get that canvas in on the royal yard. Go to the weather side first. Reach forward, it's dangerous, and grab the ponderous leach by the rope and strain, haul, lift it atop the yard. Grip stiff canvas in folds. Now bring the wiry leach up to the jackstay. Got it! Now bring up the foot of the sail. I have to lean so far forward to do this. So heavy! Both hands. The worst is next. Squat low on the footrope, reach forward under the yard and snatch at the gaskets, one by one, to wrap around the sail as I sway, slide, and teeter. Work and pound at the canvas till it is rolled into a skin to prevent the wind from tearing it loose again. Hardly is this completed before we find the t'gallants are already clewed up awaiting furling too.

Finally, when everything was taken in except the topsails, we descended to the deck. My eyes, now used to the dark, could make out dishevelled cordage awash on *L'Avenir's* deck as though it was her hair, and the deck her greyed face, the heaving seas a labour bed, bathing her in a sweat of agony as she tossed and groaned at the birth of a fast day's run. Her deck had been so golden in the tropic sunshine.

The gale took on "Barney Bull" size, as sailors say. We heard a screeching as though a thousand pigs were having their throats cut. It was the master shrieking, "The TOPS'LS, get them in!" A panic shot through me like quicksilver. Three whistles from the mate brought the starboard watch up on deck, stumping and resentful.

Dennis, standing by the topsail halliards with me, bawled in my ear. "I hope all his bloody sails would blow to ribbons if he starts a halliard." Sure enough, the topsails had hardly crunched down while we lowered the halliards, when the cat of a wind stroked its claws across the canvas. Shreds streamed out like banners in the wind. The starboard watch, half awake, hissed "*SSSatan FOORbannade,*" (oh the Devil, for hell's sake!) as they stared at the great rents in the sails. With the shrouds slackening and tautening, threatening to snap us off them, we clumped aloft and were soon crumpling the torn canvas under our bellies and making the remnants fast with robbands. As dawn broke on the horizon, the port watch was dismissed below, leaving the starboard watch on deck to secure and tidy up the remaining mess.

As I went below through the alleyway, the Dutch lady greeted me, distraught. "Oh dose poor boy! Dose poor boy! Up in rigging in dis tereeble storm. Sleep I must not till I am knowing they not fall down and die." As I shook out my dripping oilskins I chirped unfeelingly, "Oh they're all right, they're loving it up there. Anyway, everything's nearly all made fast. The starboard watch is just working on finishing up." Mrs. Van Andal looked incredulous, and remained standing outside her cabin, wringing her hands and shuddering as every pounding sea hammered *L'Avenir's* side. While the ship hung steady for a moment, as though shocked by these blows, I added, "They're young. Those boys came to sea for this." I tried to soothe her and convince her to go back to her bunk. But, like the ghost of Katherine Howard, forever pacing the hall of Hampton Court Palace airing her misery, Mrs. Van Andel haunted the alley in her trailing night robes, moaning about the agony she imagined the dear boys must be suffering.

Next morning, *L'Avenir* rode light as a cork over the heavy swells left from the storm. She rolled with a wrenching weaving of her masts in the sky. Dangling up in the rigging, the snapping motion made it a struggle to keep from sliding sideways on the footropes. We were replacing the torn canvas — seven sails lost in the night. The spiralling sensation only equalled in terror the climb over the topmast crosstrees. There I felt like a fly on a gigantic pendulum. Indeed it was worse than any fly as I did not have the wonderful suction cups on its feet that a fly has. I had only my dead tired hands to grip with. They had hauled a thousand lines, dragged sails up on deck to be bent and hammered onto the yard, all in the previous few hours. I had a bizarre longing to drop off into the sea, to quit this harsh struggle. I nearly reached the nadir, and gave in, but then, as the ship rose to the zenith of her swing, the roll boosted me upwards, and I ran up the futtocks with comparative ease. Gravity held me to the rigging where I had been clinging, and instead of weighing me down, the roll sent me upwards. This taught me to look for ways to make use of opposing forces in turning my female muscles to good account. Acrophobia did not altogether account for my unease, however, for our work could be very dangerous. From the t'gallant yard I glanced out at the sun, shining palely over a steely sea. Far, far below, a sea broke over *L'Avenir's* stern like a dirty lace curtain. When Redbeard and Lehtonen pounded out onto the footrope beside me, they made it sag so much that I sank right down till my chin was level with the yard. I was just getting used to this when they leaned forward to catch the sail coming aloft to replace the one sent down. That shot the footrope backwards, and short me was left stretched out full, from jackstay to rope, fingertips to toes almost. "Oh, Jesus help me, I'm slipping!" That wasn't swearing either, as I struggled to lean forward, catch the sail and master the fear that I could not reach that far, and would surely skid off the footrope. *L'Avenir* levelled with a lurch before the masts and yards whipped with the shock as the next sea struck her. Even my watch mates froze under the impact. "Look aloft, look aloft" I recited in my mind the mariner's adage passed on by my father. "Look alow!" is the temptation of the devil, for to glimpse that splinter of a deck is to see oneself falling, whirling down, down, bouncing on the braces and stays to crash onto the deck far below. Would one be conscious in such a fall, to clutch at every line on the way down before cracking on the deck, with spine driven through the skull perhaps. I wished I were a thickheaded Swede, but my head pounded with visions of limbs thrown out at monstrous angles, or the agony if not killed outright, and screaming "kill me, kill me." If I fell into the sea, my sea boots would fill and drag me down. But if I stayed afloat, there was the lifetime to live before the cold took over, seeing the ship sail on as she must. There would be no chance to launch a rescue boat in seas like those below.

Blast the custom of greenhorns stopping at the middle of the yard! I wriggled out to the Flemish horse at the yardarm. Looking at the foremast, I identified Chesus, calmly moving his long frame about. How I envied his height and long reach, or that Belgian,

Albert, and his bravado, always sliding down a thin clewline from one yardarm to the lower one. It made me retch just to look, and I turned back to the swift passing of the cablegarn through the cringles on the new sail head. Concentrating on the yard gave the illusion that I might be on deck doing the work, and gave at least an impression of safety, shortening the time in the rigging.

On the upper mizzen t'gallant yard, the sail being sent down caught on the main t'gallant braces, resisting all attempts to jerk it loose or haul it off. The mate ordered us aloft. Dennis grumbled to me "What the blazes does he think we are? Monkeys, to go out on the brace and clear that sail?" I couldn't help but think that I would have given anything to be a monkey at that moment.

While I struggled to master both mind and body and learn my trade aloft, the other young woman on board was making decisions about her future. One Friday, as Dennis and I chipped rust in the after hold, he shot out, "Do you know what is going to happen today?"

"Let's see, it's not lobscouse, salthorse, or stockfish. Sure, I know, pea soup and pancakes lunch!"

"Pea soup and pancakes be blowed! No, no, you dumbhead. Barbara and Olav are engaged to be married and will make the announcement tonight."

Apparently everyone else in the ship had known for many weeks that something of the sort was in the wind. That evening, every one on board had in their hands the means to "splice the main brace." Glasses clinked and wishes for good luck chimed high over growls that they must be giddy to have become engaged at such a speed. The couple had sought the opinion of an elder, and Miss Kronig had advised as best she could. But the mate remarked to me, "What Miss Kronig know about dis? She old maid." As a marriage consultant, they probably thought that a twenty-three year old tomboy hadn't much idea either. The Graingers agreed that both Barbara and Olav had artistic ability in common. They had painted souvenirs for the passenger on parts of the topsails that had been blown to pieces in the storm. The caricatures in this book are Barbara's too, so clever and amusing.

Up forrard, Dennis seemed silent and worried by this turn of affairs, and Dane Doctor was critical of the follies of the young and rich. I upheld Barbara's courage, maintaining that if she really felt so strongly for Olav, then she should demonstrate this by taking the bull by the horns and standing firm in her decision. Olav and Barbara asked the captain to marry them right away, but he answered "This I cannot do. Even so should I be vanting to, I am not allowed to by the law. It is not true that a ship's captain can be marrying people at sea."

I noted down in my journal at the time,

Olav does not hold too much popularity with the crowd forrard, nor with the afterguard, having a reputation for tale bearing from one end of a ship to another. But he has good points too, although he has never earned a cent in his life. But he enchants Barbara with fabulous tales of his wealth. Barbara, really worthy of a better fellow, cannot be argued with though. Such would be folly. Her broadminded sophistication spreads about her as a protection. So, should this ship of marriage sail onto the rocks, she could get spliced again without worrying about a wrecked life and all. One might as well predict the outcome from a box of dice, as how a marriage will turn out.

At Christmas, everyone was given a small tot of schnapps. Thinking to get rid of mine, I swallowed it in one manly gulp. It was like swallowing a swarm of bees. As I hugged my belly and grabbed my throat, my mouth in an "O" of astonishment, the mates guffawed. They only sipped their tots. This, the slaughter of a pig for dinner, and the Christmas festivities, delightful though they were, did not prevent the ship from demanding service on Christmas Day. It came on to blow, so some of us spent most of the afternoon taking in the royals and t'gallants. The buntlines on the mizzen upper t'gallant broke, and it took a swift duck to avoid the danger as it slatted backwards over the yard. This holiday workout had not appealed to those too full of Christmas spirit on deck to volunteer for it. Maybe the schnapps had bolstered my courage, but willy-nilly I managed my side of furling the royal to the satisfaction of some of the old-timers gazing up critically from the well deck. Even Redbeard joined in, giving me some of the hearty slaps on my sweaty back as I was welcomed back on deck from the yards. It was the best Christmas present ever.

That evening, everyone dressed up. Even the sail room was transmuted. The Dutch lady stood in the centre, Santa Claus style, giving out presents from Holland to all. Once couldn't but admire her kindly forethought in laying in presents for the whole crew before we sailed so many months ago. It did help to make it seem like Christmas, while she hugely enjoyed running the show. A brass plaque tumbled out of the wrapping when I tore my present open. Jumbo sidled up to look at it. "Very goot. Lufly! For our home, dis," he whispered, delighted. MacDowell and his chum Segerstedt united in a duet at that moment, which made my gurgling reply inaudible to Jumbo. "Hi Diddle Um Pum" (Swedish version of the Village Band), they chorused, then rollicked into a sea chantey.

"Johnny Boker, Oh do, my Johnny Boker
Come rock and roll me over."

This became the companion piece to "Daisy, Daisy, Give Me Your Answer Do" for the rest of the voyage. Dennis, choked up with whisky from God knows where, lisped a recitation of sorts. Then after rounds of excessively sweet, but potent Swedish punch, the crew faded from the festivities in the sailroom.

At supper, Mrs. Grainger looked angelic with her braided golden hair, wearing a heavenly blue gown, and smiling charmingly. The first mate, gold braid on his sleeves, uniform aglitter, sat smart as an admiral. What a chameleon change from his usual utilitarian overall. Barbara indulged in an after dinner cigar, inciting hot controversy among her table mates, and even among those who only heard about it. Some thought it scandalous for a woman to smoke in public, while a few brave souls leapt to her defence. In the midst of the fray, the captain, officers, and passengers disappeared for a further feast and drinking party in the cabin saloon aft. As a deckhand, I never entered these quarters. Up on deck, I tapped poor little Tredge's shoulder, indicating that he should go below and have what fun remained aft in the saloon. As mate, he had been standing watch during all the gaiety. He would even have taken my lookout as a favour to me too.

L'Avenir running before a gale in the southern ocean.

Captain Nils Erikson, holding Frasne, with first mate Hugo Karlson.

Some members of the crew, (left to right): Herbert "Jumbo" Zublke, William "Bill" MacDowall, Sven Bergman, Annette Brock, Evert Segerstedt, and Karl Mac.

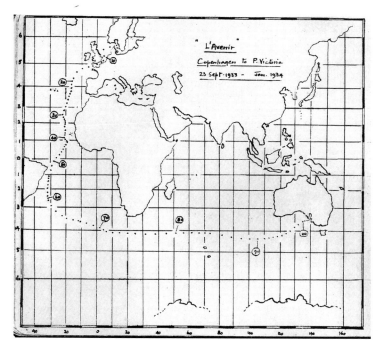

Chart of outward voyage from Copenhagen to Port Victoria, Australia.

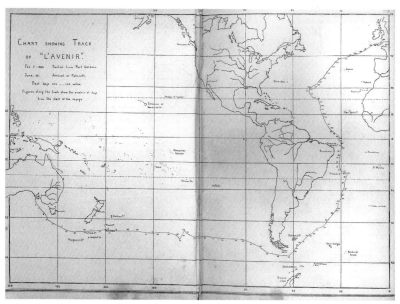

Chart of return voyage from Port Germein, Australia, to Falmouth, England.

Two men at the wheel of
L'Avenir, in a gale in the
southern ocean.

Sailmaking on deck; John Sommarstrom with his helper, Lansen,
as passenger Miss Kronig looks on.

Changing sails on the foremast, showing the spreader
for the upper back-stays.

Crew in the rigging, furling a sail.

The watch working on a yard. Annette "Jacky" Brock is second from the right.

L'Avenir arriving in Port Germein, Australia.

Main Street, Port Germein, Australia.

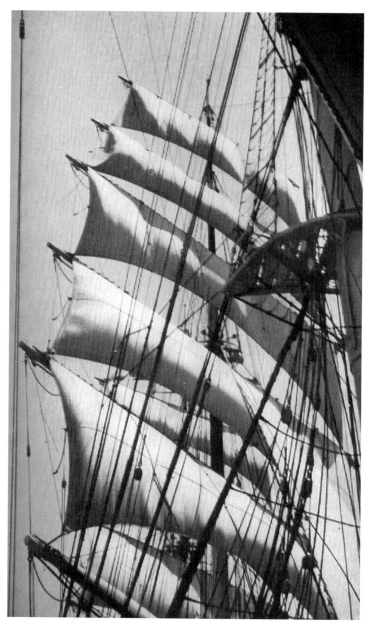

Sails and the tracery of the rigging. Looking aft from the forecastle.

Tredge lived an exacting life, no better than in the days of Dana's *Two Years Before the Mast*. He had to pitch into every task alongside the hands, and at the same time, keep to the fore front as a sort of banner, waving them on to greater effort. In the night watches, the boys slept, guarded and awakened if need be, by the vigilant "Poleez." Even little Danska was vigilant now. But Tredge must keep himself awake, pacing the poop, praying for matchsticks to prop his eyelids open. There was always danger at sea, no matter how safe it seemed. There was danger of collision, and in these high latitudes, of icebergs. During half his mealtimes, he had to stay on deck, working out sights and entering the log. Only in that he was not required to rush aloft for every trivial chore did Tredge fare better than in the days of wooden ships and iron men.

On lookout, I danced with the vigour of a moujik, trying to keep warm. My woolen work trousers had been hastily shoved on under a Russian style silk tunic, my only festive dress, worn for the sailroom entertainment. A rowdy laugh stopped my Polovtsian footwork. "For goodness sake, Yackie, what the hell are you doing? What you got on there?" I clumped solemnly around, turning to Danska with mock curtseys, swishing my clownish outfit. His laughter went on, until halted by his homesickness. "This day not at all good. Not like Christmas at home," he mourned.

"Why," I asked, "didn't you like your dinner? I thought we did pretty well stowing away pork chops."

Danska dismissed pork chops. "Bah, those chops! You should see the Christmas dinner we eat in Denmark. Sometimes chicken and prunes, or liver pate and cucumbers. Wonderful!" he recalled nostalgically. "Then lots of side dishes, crayfish and egg and chopped herring. Then my mother, she takes hours and hours making us the most tasty fruit puddings. Mmmm, we have lots and lots of sweet pastries," and he smacked his lips at the thought.

"And marzipan too?" I asked, adding a Germanic candy I craved to this mental feast.

"Oh yes," he said, "I like too, best of all."

I added, "I'd almost trade in my sea career for a bit of that now," but the best of the ship's culinary efforts could not bring forth those thousand and one Danish delicacies, so dear to

Danska's stomach. Nor did *L'Avenir* carry all Danska's family, and "the marvellous surprises my mother would have ready for us all after dinner. Lots of good times and games." A boy facing a long life of toil at sea must leave behind these homely joys with his childhood.

To distract him and cheer him up, I related the tale of my Christmas in Rome when I was 13.

"When I was in Rome I had an audience with the Pope," I told him.

He retorted "Go on with you, Yackie! Now you are making up stories. You never did such a thing as go and meet the Pope, Yackie."

I insisted, "Sure I did, all dressed in white too, with a long veil over my head and every fitting that goes with it. Wouldn't you have laughed to me then — Yackie, all in white. To show what a pure girl I must be. All young girls got to be dressed like that, you know, to go to see the Pope." Danska listened with intelligent wonder as I described being brought to the entrance of the Vatican, where we were conducted by the Swiss guards, dressed in helmets and breastplates over sixteenth-century costumes of orange and black. They even carried halberds, and the rooms through which they led us were so magnificent. "You could hardly believe they were real, Danska. The treasures! Sparkling crowns, model churches of solid gold, and robes of silk embroidery. You don't believe this? Well, I bowed low and kissed the ring of St. Peter too. Yes, the stone St. Peter is supposed to have worn. "

"But you are not a Roman Catholic, Yackie?"

"No, only they like to have Protestants view these marvels in case they might change their minds. I went up in the golden ball of St. Peter's Church in Rome too. See our main truck there? Well, that dome is another hundred feet higher. But of course, no rocking and rolling while climbing there. Stairs and ladders all the way. It's hot as hell in that metal ball at the top of the church. Catches all the sun."

I yarned on and on, and so Danska, the little Danish apprentice, forgot his homesickness, losing himself in the glories of Rome, while under our feet *L'Avenir* rushed through the dark Indian Ocean that Christmas night in 1933, now so long left in our wake.

Water had surrounded us for so long that land, like childhood, had only a remote reality. Noah's dove appeared, but not on wings. Our harbinger of land was the ponderous accommodation ladder we carried. We gasped and staggered with it around winches and over hatches, to the side, getting it set for use. Except for the "ughs." "Aws," and "phews" under its weight, the starboard watch became mute as elephants bearing teak wood. Next we became snake charmers to the wire mooring lines, persuading them to coil up near their various bitts ready for mooring. Bergman got in some more of his spiky "fun," shrieking "Queek, queek, Yackee!" as he jerked the lines through my palms. These had hardened somewhat, so that he didn't get such exciting reactions has he had with the spiky hose earlier in the voyage.

Ninety-one days out, the promised land was sighted. It was South Neptune Island, with cliffs white and chalky as those of Dover that we had left behind in the English Channel. The Dutch lady took it in with one glance. "Oh, we are coming in to land, right away! Packing I must now, all things." The captain cautioned her. "It is sometimes taking two weeks or more, before we have no head wind and can be going inside Spencer Golf, far up to Port Victoria."

"*Ach!* so long it can be, then?"

An object seen from the other side of the deck held everyone's attention, so she went to join the mates there. They took turns watching the *Archibald Russel* through a pair of field glasses. Each mate passed the glasses to his fellow, flicking his head over to mutter in his ear about the set of the ship's yards, the number of days she'd been at sea and perhaps the condition of her plating. The rust red of this showed plainly as she approached, with her hull high out of the water because she was in ballast. Her masts described arcs through the sky as she swished near to *L'Avenir*, like a majestic queen, her great wake a frothy train in the sea. She too was a four-master like *L'Avenir*, but was three hundred tons bigger. The mates scanned all this raptly, but no idea of hailing the vessel seemed to have entered their isolated minds. If these vessels had been English, what a signalling spree would have been on! I ventured to ask if flag signals were to be used. "Bodder wit all dat? What would we haf to say?" Was that non-committal Scandinavian attitude the result of being silent like the sea itself under its blue skin? Even when *Russel* passed megaphone-close the following day, they acted as if she were not there. It made me begin to feel as if in this finding yet losing contact with a real object, I was slipping off into the world of illusion. Annette, rather than Alice, had stepped through the "Looking Glass" mirror of the sea, magically into one of those watercolours of sailing ships by Spurling, such as *Russel* now seemed to be. Chesus expressed no such childish fancies on sighting his last ship, but just the same, he was practically convulsed by the thrill, as he clutched my arm.

"See? Get a look at her wheelhouse, aft." He turned to Johnny. "Chesus! Ain't that sumpin'? All sheltered there, housed over. You never roast in the sun, Yackie, steering in *Russel*." He pointed excitedly over Dennis's shoulder. "Watch, now. As she heels over. Now! Didja get a load of them bilge keels? She'd roll God awful, if it weren't for them keels. Jest the same I seen her roll bad. Chesus! Dipped her main yard in the sea, she went over so far."

"Bullshit! You're a lying bugger. No ship's ever rolled that far over and lived to tell the tale. That's as far fetched a roll as your story."

"Christ Chesus, I'm jest a telling yuh," Chesus witnessed, "I was aboard *Russel* when it happened. I seen it wit me own eyes!"

Seventeenth-century "shippes" with their bluff bows had to await a "faire" wind. So too did a sharp-bowed, steel barque when entering narrow straits such as those into Spencer Gulf. *L'Avenir* darned the water off Cape Catastrophe, the entrance to the gulf, tacking day and night. At intervals of about three and a half hours it was "ready bout ship." Even the carpenter and sailmaker were called out. As for Yackie, with extra braces to coil after the others had gone below ... this lasted ten days. Every change of watch the mate chucked fore braces to the deck, off their pins. The steersman put the helm down. We shuffled aft to haul in the spanker sheets. Lee and mizzen braces came off their pins. The barque shivered and shook, all sails head to wind. Jib tenders jerked sheets to release blocks caught high in the fore stays. The main braces gossiped, "clack, clack." Flying hands brought in the snaking braces, fore, main, mizzen. Now *L'Avenir* was again *bi di vinde* (by the wind) on the other tack, we trimmed the spanker sheet. "*Friska tag*" (haul taut all), and we jerked the staysails over stays. "*Vacten go nere*" (watch go below). I remained on deck making Flemish coils, preparing the lines to run out freely for the next *vande* (tack).

Eventually, this wormed us into Spencer Gulf and Port Victoria. Spencer Gulf lies on the south shore of Australian, just west of Adelaide, separated from it by the narrow boot of Cape Yorke. Port Victoria is a small harbour on the cape, about ten miles south of Maitland. A frigid wind whistled through our stays. It was cold, cold, cold, and it was summertime down under too! With our sails furled, there was a "done with engines" feel in the silence. Lying at anchor with us were *Pamir*, *Parma*, and *Archibald Russel*, to be joined later by *Killoran*, *Pommern*, *Passat*, *Viking*, *Ponape*, and *Priwall*. Never again could it be possible to view such an assemblage of the great sailing ships anywhere in the world. Birds of the past. Each arrived like a gull fluttering to rest, settling her billowing topsails, folding their wings and then bobbing about in comfort on the wavelets. Green water reflection from the sandy bottom wavered on the underside of our yards.

The unique scene induced Mr. Grainger to paint many pictures of the vessels then at anchor. People looked on as he sketched, commenting, "My, I didn't know you could paint too!" He responded "I like painting. I don't like playing the piano at all. I only play music because I was forced to learn the piano when I was young I much prefer to sketch"

Reports of casualties buzzed among the seamen of the anchored fleet. *Parma* over there, she had a young fellow fall down her hold. Yes, they put into Gravesend ... sent him ashore. Spine injured badly. That was just the beginning of their troubles." Chesus added, "You heard about Ekstrom? He was washed overboard in a s'easter blowing off Jersey Island. They say he was clinging to a rail when he and the whole blasted contraption, overside they went."

Johnny interposed, "Really? The way I heard it, he was unshackling one of the lifeboat blocks and it struck him on the head, knocking him overside that way ..."

"Well, whatever," Chesus answered. "Didja hear they was aheavin' a lifebuoy after him, but o'course he never ketched that. Chesus, such a sea runnin'. Hell! They coulda never picked him up anyways. Body has been washed ashore on the French coast.

The authorities thought the whole ship had foundered when they found Ekstrom and the buoy."

Ceysen added his eulogy. "Aaargh, Veree tragique, this boy Ekstrom." I piped up almost with a wrench of momentary feeling for the cat-like boy of the wheel polishing, who had continued to tease me, "Would he be a relative of the Ekstrom aboard here?" The sailmaker answered, "Some relation I think. Knew his father. He died at sea, exactly the same way. Queer. Happens, sometimes."

Dennis broke in, reminded of a tragic tale of his own. "What about that poor lubber last voyage? Filling a bucket the wrong way made him kick the bucket too. Idiot. Didn't know enough to heave it ahead of the ship and haul it up as she passed alongside of it. He flung the bucket aft and the weight of the sudden tug jerked him right overside. Never do that, Jackie," Dennis added, turning to me. "He drowned before he could be picked up. But there was a worse fool we had aboard. Remember lads? The chap who pranced about on the royal yard? Showing off to his mother who had come aboard in Mariehamn. 'Look Mother, see, I'm not even holding on. No hands!' So he came down to the deck, a hell of a mess, I can tell you. Fool."

Chapter 10

Port Germein

Leaving behind the fleet of sailing vessels anchored in Port Victoria, *L'Avenir* set sail for Port Germein on Yorke Peninsula at the top of Spencer Gulf. When the wind failed, the anchor was let go and the sails furled. Leaning over the bunched-up topsail while we were passing the gaskets, I was surprised to see that this part of Australia was not all desert. In the light of sunrise, a braid of hills appeared behind the desert. Rose-tinted, with purple shadows, I compared their elegance with the hills I had seen under differing lights — the majesty of the seven hills of Rome, the Dents du Midi, the coast at Sorrento, the cliffs of Dover, Gibraltar, the green slopes of Madeira, and the Bavarian Alps.

A dot on the smooth water of the gulf became a smudge of smoke emerging from a little funnel. Finally plump-fendered bows showed that it was a tug to tow us. We all swarmed down from aloft, joggling the rigging in our haste to return to deck and attend to the hawsers for the tug. She swung around, stern to, revealing her name, *Yacka*. "Oh yes Yackie, *Yacka*," grinned Lehtonen good naturedly, as we held the bight of the hawser, preparing to throw it over the bitts of the tug. But once *Yacka* had the tow rope fast, no one twitted me because we were so busy coiling up about deck. *Yacka* soon frothed alongside a jetty, and everyone gathered at the rail to have a look at the "Austrylians."

We made out small figures grouped around freight cars at the end of the jetty. When *L'Avenir* swung alongside, these figures slouched over, their clothes slung on, everything from slippers to stetson hats. They reminded me of the easy individuality of Canadian lumberjacks as they swarmed over the side. They were friendly, shouting cheerfully to each other as they set to work. "Here y'are Clem" and "whatho Jo!" echoed from the furthest corners of the holds as they carried the two hundred pound sacks of wheat all day in the 110° heat. What a contrast to my Nordic shipmates, stolid, contained fir trees. Pleased, in the Depression, to be earning a pound a day, or eighteen shilling on the quay, they seemed wealthy in the eyes of our able seamen who worked two weeks or more for that amount.

"Christ, that sun brings on a scorching thirst," swore a burnt group of stevedores. "C'mon Ab, let's get aholt of that cook aboard this hooker. See if he'll oblige us with a good drink of water."

Knowing "*Koken*" I watched the stevedores shamble up under the fo'castle head with a wry smile. Sure enough, indignant outcries soon rang around the deck, this time without the good humour.

"Stinkin' lousy devil, that cook. Wouldn't tell a poor sweatin' fellow where he can find a drop of water!" I sympathized, but had no time for condolences as we were sent up to unbend all the sails preparing to wash and paint the yards.

"Ahoy Yackie," I heard the mate's bellow from far below the royal yard. "Come down here, hurry up." I slid all the way down the backstay.

Beside the mate stood a lad from shore, neatly dressed in collar, tie, suit and all the trimmings. He was a very orderly looking boy, younger than I and appearing very conventional after more than three months at sea with that picturesque crowd of seamates.

"Here is a nice boy for you. John Wood. He is keeping cargo tally for the shore people. You must be keeping cargo tally for the ship. You mark on this paper a cross for every sling of wheat that's coming on board. Every car load is holding sixty-five bags of wheat, so for every car you are having six and a half crosses on your paper."

Despite the soporific effect of counting noughts and crosses in the heat, the tally clerk and I didn't miss a sling as it swayed over the rail. We had time, too, between train loads to relax. Then I plied John Wood with questions about Australia.

"Yes, this being summertime here, it can be roasting like this, but in winter, sometimes, puddles in the road freeze"

"You break ice here? I'd feel, almost, as if I was in Canada in winter then. We, at least if the frost nips us in Canada, we don't have sharks to bite us. Do you have to keep on the alert for them in Germein Bay if you go for a swim?"

"We never had anyone bitten in Germein Bay. Why, some people swim in the dark, after work here."

"Ooh, that seems like tickling the sharks' teeth. Have you always lived here?"

"Yes, I used to sew the wheat bags up there in the storage shed on Main Street. That's where the farmers bring the wheat from out back in trucks, to wait until it's shipped. We've had bad times till now. Port Germein's been a dead place."

The quaint little locomotive, built in 1905, huffed out the jetty towards us, bringing the cars loaded with wheat bags. We moved back out into the burning sun ready to tally the sling loads of bags swinging aboard ship. Later that day I heard cries of "Goodbye Jackie dear," from a truck that was pulling away from the ship. I looked down to see Mr. and Mrs. Grainger, swaying and bumping atop a load of crates in the truck. They planned to found a museum of historical musical instruments in Australia, Percy Grainger's native land. The crates contained these instruments that had made the voyage on *L'Avenir*.

I felt such a twang of loneliness at seeing the Graingers go. They had been so good to me on the voyage. All the other passengers also left the ship for various parts of Australia. The only ones who returned for the trip home were Miss Kronig and the airman. He stayed with the ship for part of the three-week stay in Port Germein. I stayed by the ship, but working in port counted for only one-third of the time needed to qualify for the Board of Trade exam for second mate's certificate. I saw the port mainly with my shipmates: unlike my "la de da Cockney" friend, Ben, I did not go off sightseeing by myself. Australia seemed fantastic to me, rather as America must have seemed to the early discoverers after their sail across the fearsome and unknown ocean.

Danska was painting the ship's side from the homemade punt *Greta*, named after the steward's Aland Island girl. A brisk breeze came across the bay, and, *Greta* not having been made well fast during the sweltering calm, broke away from the ship's side. It drifted for some distance with Danska aboard, trying to paddle back. It was too much for him, and he gave up and started doing his Rumpelstiltskin act, jumping up and down and screaming. It was so comical that I burst out into a roar of laughter which carried across the water. The ship's boat was quickly launched and Danska and *Greta* were rescued before they became engulfed in the surf on the other side of the bay. Danska clambered aboard, red-faced. "This is nothing funny," he pouted at me, all his feathers ruffled at my laughter.

L'Avenir, as a foreign vessel, was legally able to work long hours in Australia. None of your forty-hour week here. Five thirty a.m. and everyone was up and working the twelve-hour day, except for meal breaks. The Finns didn't even take the "smoko" at ten a.m. that the stevedores revelled in. "Englishmen is all lazy, they doing no work" our skipper used to tease the airman, when he lay dozing in a hammock. When we knocked off at five thirty in the afternoon, a plummet into the shallow sea alongside the ship felt sweet at the close of a sweaty day. Who could resist water so gentle, so exotic, while all the time visualizing stringrays, with their long tails which, John Wood had warned, inflicted wounds which never healed. "They wouldn't attack you though," he said, "unless stepped on." Then they might hardly be blamed for kicking up a fuss, I thought, but still, I trod the sand warily, knowing that the stingrays lay camouflaged beneath the lovely swirls of yellow-green water. Floating about, one was free of stingray slashes, but then I thought of the sharks, which can dart into the shallowest water. The master and the mates did not indulge in the delight of swimming, but the master warned me, "We have seen very large sharks on the way to Port Pirie in the boat." He had gone across Germein Bay to the larger town on ship's business, taking Mac, the German A.B to the Port Pirie hospital. I realized that where nature is most tempting she can also be most dangerous.

Wharf-side fishermen brought up crabs in their nets. They were colourful as Australian opals, shining sapphire blue and waving long, elegant nippers, quite different from the dull crabs of temperate zones. Too beautiful to eat, yet too delicious not to, they made a break in our hot weather diet which plodded along just as if we were still in the iciest part of the ocean. Instead of greasy salt beef, pea soup and pancakes, pulpy canned sausages, fried preserved fish balls, or hard, salted stockfish, I thought how delightful to have a fresh crisp salad. I mentioned this to the mates. They squelched this namby pamby girlish desire for delicacies as if it was abnormal. Stick to the good ship food and avoid shore food was their maxim. But was it necessary in clean Australia? Eat a salad in Algiers and then you might have the dysentery that turns you inside out.

I decided to go ashore in search of a chocolate bar. *L'Avenir* was moored at the end of the longest jetty in Australia. It was a narrow, wooden affair with a lighthouse at the end, and a railway line to bring out the wheat. The jetty was a mile and a quarter long, so that going ashore meant a walk of two and a half miles. When I left the ship to go to the village of Port Germein, there were a few flat cars standing beside *L'Avenir*. With other crew members who were going ashore, we gave them a shove, climbed aboard and rolled shoreward, standing with our jackets held open like sails in the wind, which blew us and the cars along the whole way to shore. There I did find some consolation from the ship food in buying a chocolate bar, but the heat had melted it so that inside the silver paper it was like squishy mud. As I fumbled with how to eat this, I felt a thumb on my shoulder. "Chocolate Sailor" jolted me. It was the mate.

"Chocolate bar, vat's dat? Come to the real bar and haf a good glass of beer wit me."

Rendered dumb by this honour accorded me by a superior officer, I plunged in with him, Tredge following, through the gay nineties swing door of the saloon. Through the fog of smoke and fumes came shouts of greeting from my shipmates. "Yahoo, Yackie! *For Sataan!* Drink with me!" Ekstrom waved a glass at me with his lean arm. "*Nay, komma hit,*" Bergman waved his tattooed, callused hand at a captain's chair for me to sit on. Even Redbeard in a corner, sharp knees crossed, lifted his bottle, calling "*Med mit,* Oh oh Yawkie, dis vay" Twinkles appeared through the creases of his eyes at my startled surprise at the greetings. As confused as a kitten running about a room with everyone trying to catch it, I deserted the mate's proffered glass of beer at the bar and took the Australian "plonk" held out by the sailmaker. Not that I liked the sailmaker better than the mate, it was a case of bitter beer versus sweet wine. After swallowing the plonk, which struck me as the sweepings of the winemaker's floor, I reeled towards the door, barely able to thank the sailmaker in all the hubbub drumming around me.

Outside, a few gulps of air revived me enough to join Dennis and Sonny, togged out in their Scandinavianly scrubbed shirts, their slicked-down hair quite refreshing to look upon in my wine-and-desert, sun-dishevelled state. Other *L'Avenir* crew members wobbled up the dusty street to join us in the shade of the porch of the only store. I was to write to my mother,

> The village has two hundred inhabitants, tin corrugated roofs and fences, a Post Office, a bank open once a week, a barber who comes every two weeks, and a bar. It looks like a wild west show, especially with all the Australians in their bright kerchief and huge stetson hats.

We gazed at the false-front houses of grey weathered boards, and some of the wagons with their large wooden wheels, which were loaded with wheat and dragged from the farms to the wheat sheds by dray horses. A frontier scene, perhaps, certainly not quite the night life the crews may have hoped for. We walked towards a group near the beach. These were hands from *Mozart* and *Winterhude* lolling amid the sea grass which partly screened them, as they gazed towards their ships far down at the end of the jetty. Our crew, who at sea baptized me sometimes as "that splitass meechaneek" now conducted me towards the other crews. With pride, mind you, *L'Avenir's* crew shoved me forward, introducing me as "our own girl apprentice." Mozartians and Winterhudians sprang up from their sand hummocks, clicked heels and bowed. Some kissed my hand with courtly grace. *Winterhude* or *Mozart* might sail to windward better, perhaps, than *L'Avenir*, or possibly their crews displayed super talents in their seamanship, but one distinction they did not have was such a curious crew member as the boys of *L'Avenir* had in this girl. Even if those vessels had had a pet monkey aboard, they could not rival this.

After some questioning in German, Finnish, and English on the novelty of a girl apprentice, they sought to alleviate boredom by straggling towards a big bleak shack painted in peeling white. It was round, with large letters encircling it, announcing with all the comic dignity of a kookaburra bird, that it was the *Palais de Danse*. As we approached, a pianola could be heard through the ramshackle boards, reeling out *Ten More Months and Eleven More Days*. How absurd, I thought in this vast panorama of sea and desert. Inside we found a few couples shuffling desultorily around the floor, as the pianola began its other tune, *Looo wheees aiana*, while others sucked soft drinks at tables. Danska touched me on the shoulder. "You come dancing with me Yackie. Come on."

I warned him, "I'll try just to please you, but you remember Dennis calls me sleepy owl eyes because I can't dance, and don't even know who Duke Ellington is." Danska didn't believe this until he had a round of the floor with me.

"Ow! You can't dancing! No good for a girl."

I retorted, "You couldn't paddle *Greta*! No good for boy!"

Danska yelled "Go!" and gave me such a shove, I whizzed across the floor, startling some of the dancing couples as I banged into them. I found refuge in the company of Ceysen at his table.

Suddenly shouts broke out at the door, and a crowd of men pushed in, ousting dancers, and everyone in their way. "*Ces Allemands*," declared Ceysen, "there, you see it as I told you. When those Germans are together it is as if the place belongs to no one but themselves." Ceyson shook his head at the sight of beer glasses waving to *Hogh die Tassen*. The room shook with the Teutonic power of their shouts and songs. Onlookers cowered in the corners away from the onslaught.

Jumbo caught my eye, "This is Yerman. All zo goot. Ach, this being the right way to ect."

"Aaargh," growled Ceysen, "this is too much noise. I go back to ship, to sleep. We have much work tomorrow," and he set out to walk the mile or so of pier to our gangplank.

His place at the table was immediately taken by the bearded Dane Doctor, with Johansson, the sailmaker's assistant, in tow. The latter was so swathed in bandages that he looked like a dummy set up to demonstrate first aid. His head had been broken open by a bottle wielded by the donkeyman in one of his black rages, brought on by liquor. Johansson had been taken to Port Pirie to have his wounds stitched. They healed slowly because ashore, he kept falling about and reopening them. However, he was a happy-go-lucky soul, and kept nodding and smiling approval of the tale the Dane began telling me. "I am a very old man." As though I didn't know! He had always disdained the frivolities of youth and jazz on the fo'castle head, emitting mutters of disapproval behind his beard. "Yes, look at me now," he continued, but I had turned away to watch an outburst from the Germans. They were applauding one of their number who was playing the piano and caterwauling his version of *Dein ist mein ganzes Herz* (yours is my heart alone). His eyes sparkled like the sea on a day of squalls, tickling my sense of humour as though it were a lively dinghy. The Dane tapped my forearm, to bring me back to his melancholy story. "Yes, look at me now," he repeated with a sob in his voice. "I took girl from the streets and married her. Later I found her in bed with my brother." ... *du bist mein* ... the singer continued in his screeching voice. Startled, the Dane stopped, and then brought out painfully, "Yes, my own brother, can you believe it?" I squirmed with naive embarrassment. "I must pay him back," he went on, "so, I took his wife. He didn't like that when it happened to him." The Dane pounded the table, making little waves in his lemonade. "But my people, they did not understand. No. I must go away and leave it all, for a long, long time. Oh God! In a sail ship. The time is *so* long." Johansson confirmed the emphatic parts of the Dane's story by jolly wags of his head. Sobbing, the Dane took comfort in sucking the straws in his lemonade. "Would you believe this is whisky? See the policeman over there. He does not know I am drinking whisky. Ha ha. But I have a bottle in my pocket and can fill this glass with it when he is not looking."

At that time liquor could only be bought in licensed places in Australia, accompanied by a mountain of regulations about where it could be drunk and so on. I looked at the policeman, and decided he probably knew more than the Dane reckoned about Jack Tar ashore. An Englishman, he had gone to sea himself, but had deserted his sailing ship in Australia, and many years ago had settled in Port Germein, where his family became bigwigs in the village. "Take care, you," the Dane suddenly jerked me back from the policeman's past with a warning. He shook a prophet's finger in my face. "That Jumbo, money mad." His beard wagged with the force of his words as he continued.

"We shared a room in Copenhagen before the ship sailed. I found out while we together in Copenhagen. He is thinking of nothing else. Money mad. Hee hee." The Dane got up and trailed off, screeching "money mad," his accusing voice growing thinner and thinner as he flopped through the door in search of more whisky at the hotel. Perhaps he could drown his sorrows over his brother's perfidy and the works of such knaves and fools as Jumbo and I, and even Johansson, who was the victim of his own good nature.

By this time only a few people were left in the dance hall. Johansson floundered to his feet, and began to stumble his way back to the ship. He'll finish by breaking his neck if he falls off that pier on the way, I thought. I should go back with him and see that he doesn't fall off. To encourage him along the straight and narrow, I sang songs with him. We chanted loud and clear to the starry sky, his interspersed with shout of "Hip hurrah! You goot gurl. You come marree me," all with the full power of his lungs. After a monster belch he added, "Live in Aland. I making you goot home dere." He might not have made such a genial offer when sober, but it sobered me into remembering that I was "the gurl," which I had forgotten in the good humour of shipmates ashore. "Oh Yohnny, come down to Hilo," we sang as we stumbled along, our bellows fading from the ears of the shore folk, but soon picked up by those aboard *L'Avenir*. Johansson, tipsily but safely reeled up the gangplank, wobbled off to the retreat of his "round house" up forrard. Alone on deck I gazed at the white tracery of masts and yards pointing crosses at the stars. What a life I had chosen to lead! It was both ethereal, as in this barque and sea and sky, and yet grotesque, as in those goings-on on shore.

Suddenly Jumbo popped out on deck. His mouth foamed as he spat out "Very bat. Dis very bat!" Now what's wrong, I wondered, as I bumped back to earth. He complained often about the food, especially in hot weather. This time, the Dane's whisky-laden warnings, the jolly pier proposal, every move I had made ashore had so outraged Jumbo's German passion for propriety that he could only scold, sputtering, at my back. I didn't stay to listen, but drifted off below to sleep soundly before turning out at five-thirty a.m.

Next day, when everyone knocked off for dinner, the

stevedores munched hearty sandwiches and swigged at bottles, while sprawling like seals in the shade of the deckhouses. Even the little locomotive ceased puffing, and its driver, who had his three-year-old son along, made a dining room of the cab. I hopped over the bodies as I threaded my way below to wash up in my cabin. I was swilling my face in tepid water when Barbara burst in. She almost wrung her hands as she plumped down on the settee.

"I don't know if I am making an awful mistake. I have been in Port Pirie, making arrangements for our wedding to take place in Port Germein church ... and yet ... I don't know. Am I right in marrying Olav? What do you think?"

Taken aback, I hid my face in my towel, wiping slowly. How could such a clever woman, with all her sophistication and talents imagine that I would know more about the happy married state than she? At best, in my simple way, I had thought of it as existing, while practically a prisoner in some place like Notre Dame de Grace, a Montreal suburb peppered with newly weds, perhaps in a dull duplex in a dull row of duplexes. Perhaps one might seek respite for a moment relaxing on a tapestry sofa in a frowsty parlour, while contemplating the inevitable picture of "The Bridge of Sighs" in Venice. A wife's days would be employed, when not bearing babies in agony, in bouts of dish washing, laundry, and other dreary household rounds. Marriage, it seemed to me, was a condition to be avoided at all costs, and hardly was one to encourage Barbara to attain. But then, she felt differently, as her cable to her mother revealed.

Delicious trip. Have fallen unmistakably in love. Intend marrying here immediately. No conceivable misgiving. Everything perfect.

Mrs. Strachey's reply struck me as the essence of common sense and reasonableness.

Tons love but please dont be precipitate. How can we approve without knowing nationality age profession income plans and a thousand items besides charm. Would fly out if possible. Marriage rather serious affair.

"My mother," said Barbara, "what can she do? She can't make the decision for me. This is my own to make up my mind about." Then, as though this declaration had given her the answer, she rose from the settee and stood tall.

"I *know* I'm right. I am perfectly sure now. One knows deep down."

I lifted my hands in a gesture of despair towards my oilskins which swung on the back of the white door as Barbara closed it behind her. I felt so incompetent at being unable to pilot her through the awful, deep mysteries of giving and taking in marriage. Later, while I tallied wheat sacks on the jetty one morning, Barbara and Olav approached. They hailed me jauntily, proclaiming that their marriage was to take place that very afternoon and they wanted me as bridesmaid. "Didn't you have Miss Kronig in mind for that?" I asked.

"Oh, poor Miss Kronig, it is too bad, but she is still in hospital in Port Pirie. The blood clot that formed in her leg when she injured it going ashore in Port Victoria in the boat is not better yet. So you must come in her place." The couple begged special permission from the captain for Dennis, Sonny, and me to be granted leave so that we could attend the wedding. Barbara rushed below to help me scrape up my most dress-like possessions to make the change from stevedore to bridesmaid, complete with flowers.

A Fox Film man took pictures of the happy couple, posed in various parts of the ship. Barbara might have gone through a wedding every day, so calm and casual did she appear. She dressed in the hotel, where the woman reporter fingered her dress, speculating on whether it could be described as crepe or *peau d'ange*. It struck me as so odd, attending Barbara getting herself spliced in this outlandish village, where none of her own people could be with her to help her. I had grown fond of her, and vainly wished I had the power to help her more than I knew how to do.

Outside the church a great crowd had gathered. The country folk were very curious, and eager to catch a glimpse of the "couple from Pirie" and their attendants. Dennis and Sonny were in shirt sleeves and I wore my beret and red, Russian-style tunic — the only dress and hat I possessed to fit the occasion. We must all have seem extremely exotic to the locals. Even Olav in his spic and span white suit did not quite come up to their expectations of the frock coats and silk toppers they regarded as normal wear for rich European families on such occasions.

Inside, the church was bright and richly decorated with flowers, but Barbara and Olav looked rather out of place as they knelt before the altar. Still, this, the first wedding I had ever attended in my life, did please me with its casual freedom. Perhaps it was infectious, as the next wedding I attended was my own. Indeed, so casual was this occasion that the archdeacon upbraided the Australian onlookers for coming merely to gape. He gave the newly wedded couple a jobation as well, exhorting them not to be frivolous and not to take the holy state of matrimony lightly. This so touched the bridegroom that he broke into audible sobs, and sniffled and wiped all through the rest of the ceremony.

After, we all drove off to Port Pirie for the wedding breakfast. Lots of champagne flowed, to the accompaniment of speech-making all around, except from Sonny, who was reported in the newspaper as "suntanned and silent." That evening, the bridegroom's best man and I went to the movies. But how boring the picture! Perhaps real life, so virile, alive, and exciting since I had followed the sea, outrivalled artificial adventure so that it no longer brought a thrill.

Returning to the ship, I found Chesus at the head of the gangway, taking his turn as night watchman. Beside him on the bench was the steward with a parcel on his lap. It was a present of silken lingerie for his girl, Greta, home in Finland. He proudly unwrapped it to show me, asking whether he had got a bargain. I agreed that the garments were very elegant at the price, but actually I was as much at a loss to advise the steward on silken underwear as I was to have helped Barbara about her wedding. I was a wearer of heavy "woolies" at sea, the stiffer and more board-like the better, because they served as a windbreak. The steward seemed happy with my appraisal, smiled wearily, and after stretching and yawning, disappeared below.

I took his place beside Chesus on the bench for a chat. Chesus spat after the departing steward. "That stooard! He's getting big money, nearly as much as the skipper." From Cunard ship gossip on many Atlantic crossings I knew that the deck department always suspects stewards, so I said, "He has a lot to look after, pleasing the shipowner, the Board of Trade and You!" That provoked an even stronger outburst from Chesus.

"Look after! I guess! Godammit, all he looks after is himself. Doesn't give us anywheres near our due. Stooards make money out of us. You'll see, that stinkin' bastard'll not be ashore much here. He knows he'd be in for it. We could beat him up ashore. The ship couldn't do nuthin' about it. Got no say in what we do ashore. He knows it too, that lousy stooard."

Well, if times were tough for me at sea, at least I was petted ashore, unlike the "stooard." Some consolation!

Suddenly from far back on the pier, we heard a disturbance, a raucous, topsail voice announcing in hoary Scottish accents, "the auld songs is best. Those new ones is only nigger music." It turned out to be the sailmaker, who when tiddly on "plunk" reverted to the accents he had picked up from his early days spent about Scottish barques. He buttonholed every passer-by, holding each up against the railings and not letting go until each had agreed with his opinion that "the auld songs is best." Then along came the mate, tense on tiptoes, triggered to fire his fist at anyone, after many a *goot gles* of beer. Another young hand lay in the well deck until dawn, his flaming red hair a halo in the beer he had retched up. The carpenter arrived back aboard next, transformed into a sort of Flying Dutchman about the decks, burrowing under ropes, opening doors, peering in ports, then becoming bothersome and amorously trying to chase me. Jumbo's already outraged sense of propriety endured yet another shock; his hair nearly standing on end.

"Terrible it is, that carpenter, he chase you."

"Oh hell," I boasted, "one shove and I can knock that monster right over, the state he's in now."

Lehtonen and Oman returned, exuding joviality, up to a point — the point of their knives. Danska's tongue wagged like a puppy dog's tail. "Those pure Finns, they throw knives when drunk, they are dangerous." Lehtonen had gone after that traditional butt of sailors, the cook, pushing his knife hard against poor *Koken's* adam's apple. *Koken's* eyes had nearly popped right out of his head with fright. According to Danska, at this crucial moment the donkeyman came to the rescue of *Koken*, who remained completely shaken up for several days after.

One evening, as I stood in the main street, uncertain whether to bother with the joys of the *Palais de Danse* again, the airman hailed me. "I have a lift to Port Pirie," he offered, "with the mate and second mate. Want to come along?" I got in the car, which was driven by the local garage man. The man from Fox Films who had photographed Barbara's wedding got in also, but had to ask several times for the car to be stopped so that he could throw up. After each bout of retching, he would beg my pardon for being drunk. On one of these interludes, the garage man suggested "Let's all have a go at the little girl, right here." I stiffened, but the mate cut in before another word could be said, murmuring "No, she ain't that sort." Still, I was relieved when we reached Port Pirie, even though that only meant another bar where more rounds were served to my already wobbly escorts. They filled the car with bottles of beer. The airman, who had made the long voyage partly to get away from liquor, said that he really did not want to get "paralyzed drunk" and begged me to see that he got back to the ship if he did.

It was a miracle that the car survived the streets of Port Pirie as we whizzed around corners on two wheels, and through the traffic like a Keystone Cop car chase from the movies. That crazy garage man headed deliberately for other cars, and showed off his "skill" by turning aside at the last moment. Although used to the speed of planes, the airman was scared stiff, and when we stopped at another bar, consulted with me on how we might get back to the ship in a different car. Since neither of us had enough money with us, I could not see any way out, except that I might try to take the wheel, having had driving lessons a long time before (and no practice since).

The trip back to the ship was tougher than any sea I had ever been in. The mate lay fast asleep in the back, while the driver kept yelling at me, "I'll frighten you. I'll frighten you. You're mad with me, aren't you?" He kept swinging the car onto two wheels as we went at top speed along the bumpy road. Finally I got the wheel, but that was almost worse, because I hardly remembered how to shift gears and had to relinquish it. But the second mate, thinking that I still held the wheel, became quite bellicose. At each swerve and heave, he roared "Don't do DAT! You bloody bitch, I'll trow you out of the car. *Look out now!*" Now more or less recovered from his retching fits, the Fox Film man clutched the remaining beer bottles, trying valiantly to keep them from smashing on each swerve. Finally back in Port Germein, which I never expected to see again, the airman and I left the snoring humps in the car. All the way from the pier to the ship, he kept asking me "Am I drunk?"

This experience enlightened me sufficiently about Saturday night with my workmates that I took refuge in the company of the friendly postmistress. As I was a stamp collector, she was pleased to tell me about the new kangaroo series. I asked her where I might find an alarm clock and blankets. She introduced me to a store owner, Mr. Goode, of Port Pirie, and soon I was bumping along in his Ford to Port Pirie again. The road was still rough, but it was a very different journey from my previous ride. Mr. Goode looked like Henry Ford himself, and was just as ambitious a money maker. As we drove along, he told me many things about the country. Back of the hills, there was a small kind of kangaroo called a wallaby, and ostriches too, of a smaller sort. But beyond Port Augusta, at the very top of Spencer Gulf, there was nothing but desert. Port Pirie had been built on a swamp, and his family had been early settlers in the area. "If it wasn't for pioneers like the Goodes and the Woods, it wouldn't have been built," he said with pride.

Leaving the desert behind, empty except for strange clumps of plants with swollen branches which stored water, we drove onto a paved road, past wooden houses each with its large verandah. It was very crude, but Port Pirie actually held pride of place as the metropolis of this countryside. Mr. Goode ushered me into his general store and showed me all his wares, from coils of ropes and blocks to ladies dresses, jams and other delicacies. I was amazed to find such a place, where one could buy blankets, food, and an alarm clock (made in Canada), and I was delighted to meet the Graingers again. They were staying in Port Pirie, and were about to go off on a tour of the smelting plant. They asked me to join them and I went along.

Approaching the plant, we choked in the hot, sulphur-laden air. In the first building, the ore was smelted, fired by the plant's own sulphur as fuel. The ore, from Broken Hill mines, not far up country, produced sulphuric acid in this first process. After the initial smelting, the ore was sent to a plant in Tasmania that separated copper from zinc using an electrical process, and then the ore was returned to Port Pirie. The next step involved smelting the ore further in a furiously hot furnace. A mammoth steel bar revolved inside, further removing impurities. We were allowed to see this from the open furnace door, and the heat, added to the one hundred degree heat of the day, sent us reeling back, for the temperature was about six hundred degrees. An old man tended this furnace. He had worked there nearly thirty years, and his arms appeared to be distorted. I learned later this was due to lead poisoning. Melted ore flowed to form huge cakes, which then travelled, red hot, on a line through another furnace which separated metals using their various melting points. Poured out into ladles, the metals were lifted by an aerial truck and turned out into huge vats to cool. I learned that the dull grey, roughened surface that forms on silvery molten lead as it cools did not because of impurities, but rather as the result of oxidization. I was fascinated with this because of having used lead for the anchors of the ship models I had built at home. That dull formation had troubled me when making the castings for the anchors. Here the smelters cleaned the lead of the "rust" and remelted it. Only strong Italian immigrants could do these jobs, and even they became "leaded" eventually, but the pay was good, and in the Depression, the work attracted labour.

Next we saw the precious metals, gold, silver, and antimony in their molten state. Some glowed with colours as radiant as the blue crabs. The guide put a block of silver into our hands, so heavy that it took strength to hold it. Also we had the thrill of holding a nugget of gold said to be worth £100 sterling, which I remembered as the cost of my apprenticeship. The Pirie inhabitants had been breathing in gold from the refinery smoke in the old days, as thousands of pounds worth of gold were lost in the soot pouring out of the smelter chimney, but now it was recovered using a new process from Germany. Altogether, the smelter was a fascinating and awful place to visit.

On another day in Port Germein, I saw a girl on horseback riding down the main street. I wished I could ride there, but felt too shy to have stopped her to inquire whether there was a livery stable. However, as I polished the brass one work day, a girl came aboard and chatted with me. She turned out to be the sister of the girl on horseback. They were part of a family of twelve and seven of them were known as the "Riding Smith Girls of Warnertown," when on holiday in Port Germein. They did not have their horses with them, but invited me to go swimming in a nearby creek on our last Sunday in port. This family ran a "station" by themselves, and told me tales of their battles with blowflies, which eat the sheep alive. The heavy chores carried out in the blazing heat made life at sea seem easy by comparison.

As *L'Avenir* was loaded her rail eventually dropped below the wharf, and the bags of wheat could be slid into the hold from the rail cars using skids. The mate tallied these bags. In port the second mate had charge of any deck work. Under his regime I was set to removing the verdigris that combined with the sea salt to make a shell, plating the copper tops of the light towers, the brass plaques on all seven capstans, the rims on all four wheels, many feet of solid brass rails on wheel and compass bridges, dozens of brass portholes, brass door panels, and ladder treads, and worst of all, an army of brass bars over the scuttles. All this golden display of the grandeur of Belgium in the old days was designed to keep the hundred or so cadets out of mischief polishing brass. There I was, "alone on a wide sea of verdigris" until the boss stevedore, having dinner with the mates, was sitting across from him and commented in his breezy Aussie voice, pointing his knife at me, "Jacky, she's just like one of us. Not laike them there stuck up Europeans. One of us colonials orlraht! Say, why don't you give this little gal a break? Brass polishing' all dai, every dai. She don't deserve that. Why not a real sailor's job just for a change?" I beamed in gratitude, but more to my plate than to the stevedore. He was boss of his crowd, but the second mate was boss of me, more or less.

"I'll have you know I'm in charge here in port," the second mate pounded on the table. "What I say, that goes. If it is brass polish, then we have brass polish. I don't need to be told how I must run the ship."

"Orlraht! Orlraht!" The stevedore waved his fork merrily. "Course I ain't got no right to interfere! I'm only just atelling you what I and the boys on the quay ben sayin' among ourselves."

I had my own plan to be rid of the brass. The first hard layer of verdigris I had managed to remove, my fingers becoming so webbed with it in the process that they looked like the hind feet of a frog. The blazing sun dried the verdigris and polish till they became a sort of glaze baked onto the brass. I broke off that layer, humming, "I polished that handle so carefullee, that now I am the Ruler of the Queen's Navee," I was able to finish the whole caboodleum one hour before knock-off time. The second mate inspected this sovereign shine with an air of grim defeat at finding no speck, and all golden. He had the last word though, by flinging back a door which had a brass handle I had missed. To put a smile on its face took the rest of the work day, as it had not been polished for years.

Next day I was set to wash paintwork with MacDowall. We were some distance from a work party setting up shrouds by the starboard rail, under the supervision of the sailmaker. "See that?" MacDowall nodded in the direction I must look. "A nice job of seamanship, and who else has it but the Finns. None of us foreigners are given those jobs. Why can't I ..."

"Jack!" bellowed the sailmaker over his shoulder, his arms, back and knees busy hauling a shroud. "We need you here." As I started off on the run to answer the sailmaker's summons, Mac tried to trip me with his toe. "Need *you*!" he mocked.

The sailmaker pointed to a pile of rigging screws. "See those old rigging screws? Clean out all the tallow and rust from every one of them so they shine like your nose. SHINE, d'ye hear, Jack? Then take lots of fresh tallow from that pot. Smear it on thick. We want these to run smooth when we set them up again. And watch, too. You may learn a thing of two about setting up rigging, here with us."

The twenty-year-old shrouds had been removed. The silvery new cordage had a superior sheen, but it also resisted taking on its new duties. Redbeard was forcing it round the masthead. Then the ends, cut to the right length, were rove through turnbuckles of massive size. The wire seizings holding this had been turned in by the strong, expert hands of Johansson. He was still bobbing his turban of bandages as he bent over this work. The new wire rope screeched as it was stretched on the rack of a "handy billy." Even the deltoids and biceps of Lehtonen and Ohman swelled hard in their struggles when giving the rope its final, taut turns with a "Spanish windlass." At last, tortured to tautness, the wire became a guitar string for the wild west winds to play upon when we rounded the Horn. A forceful drama, this combination of muscle, wire, and wind, and I was happy to play even a small part in it.

Scraping away, I felt an angry presence beside me. Looming

over me, his eyes dark and bitter, stood German Otto. I was unaware of the shock he had just received in hospital at Port Pirie. A hopeless case of tuberculosis and his whole sea career in ruins. "Ha! You would go showing your stinking ass on the dockside of the ship. So all the people over there can be looking. Ooooh look, they can say, at the gurl doing sailors' work ... oohh ahhh," he went on derisively.

"You have a cheap mind," I retorted. "Can I help what side of the ship they rig?" How unjust those fellows seemed. And that Jumbo, how unjust too with his stupid "yealousies."

That evening, quite unintentionally, I was to give Jumbo more overtime spy work. This time it was an Aussie in the *Palais de Danse*, who pulled back a chair for me. He sported a small black moustache (the same style as that worn by Jumbo's own Hitler, for whom Jumbo now intended to become a spy in Norway).

"Have a lemonade, Jackie," the moustached one offered, with friendly gusto.

"Sure, thanks," I said.

"I been in Austrylian coastin' steamers," he announced, as he scraped up his own chair alongside mine, "whenever I had a chance to work aboard. Now I aim to work my wai over to Europe in a real honest-to-God sighling ship. You knoaw, for us chaps here in Aussie, it's well nigh impossible to get in a deep sea vessel as a seaman. We haven't got the ships."

"But you are not in coasting steamers now?"

"No, I'm an electrician from Balleroo. I'm come down here for a short holiday." So we continued becoming acquainted, comparing who knew the most knots, and I felt glad to find in "Balleroo," as I named my new friend, someone who talked to me as a human being. No harping on the cliché "not for a gurl." Hard as I had tried to adjust to the attitudes of others, I found this English-speaking person a relief. One could joke with freedom, without fear of offending. Balleroo treated me royally to chocolate and ice cream, while showing me some miniature carvings in stone of anchors and mermaids he had cut with his penknife. He revealed himself as kind, slow in some ways, yet clever at match and card tricks.

Johnny, intrigued by these entertainments at our table, strolled over. "What's all this conjury going on here?" He sat down to investigate. I told Johnny that Balleroo wanted to make a voyage in a sailing ship. Johnny was English, but he had to stick with the foreign crew, not the "gurl's" side. "What do you think of that?"

Johnny looked sharply at Balleroo. "Don't you dare think of stowing away, it would not get you anywhere." I glanced up, startled, as this rough side of gentle Johnny. His admonition raised a suspicion in me. My wits had sharpened after such close acquaintance with so many men and their underlying motives. It crept over me that Balleroo's friendly overtures might stem from a plan to have me help him stow away. I told him so, bluntly. Balleroo swore that he had no such intention. *Winterhude* needs a hand, I told him.

"Yes, that's just what I'm hoping. I reckon someone might be signed on her to taike the plaice of the feller who came tumblin' daown from aloft while was ahaulin' on a gasket. It broke. Just as they was acomin' to anchor, wasn't it. Hurt himself? Too raht he did! Smashed a coupla ribs on the wai daown. Now he's to Pirie in hospital there. He ain't injured too bad, but he won't be sailing in *Winterhude*."

Balleroo walked back to *L'Avenir* with me. He asked to climb the rigging, however the mate was absent. My companion was to be a seaman; did that qualify him, at least somewhat? He went straight up to the royal yard. There we compared the miseries of being tied to the shore, watching a ship sail and leaving one ashore. Dreamer and vagabond that he was, Balleroo still didn't press me for help in stowing away.

Next day, to the glee of the stevedores, Balleroo appeared, arranging nets on the pier, and announcing in his carefree Aussie manner that he had deserted his job as an electrician, and henceforth, he was taking up as a crab fisherman from this wharf. The mate prodded me in the ribs, pointing to Balleroo. "Dat little black moostache. OOO! it must tickle luvvly."

"Oh shut up," I dared to banter to my officer, "I don't care about moustaches." After the dinner hour, as we were turning to, whoopees, catcalls and uproarious cheers greeted Balleroo. He had shaved his moustache.. "Look Yackie," prodded the mate, "now isn't that nice of him? He has shaved it off, yust to please you. LOOK. Won't you even look? He's fishing here, yust to be near you."

"Yahoo, Whoopee," hallelujahed the stevedores at the mate's

remarks. This banter made my mouth twitch at the corners, and broke step in the loading routine. The stevedores straightened their backs to laugh, unburdening their spines for a moment from the two hundred pound sacks of wheat they carried to the depth of the hold.

After three weeks in Port Germein, it was time for *L'Avenir* to give her farewell dance. In the mellow glow from the open scuttles, the brass rails that I had polished sparkled and winked to the tune of gay Finnish waltzes. Such a combination had a *Valse Triste* effect on my emotions as I sat alone on deck in the dark. Going below, I saw that the source of the music, energetically swinging and sawing at his violin, was the first mate of *Winterhude*. His accompanist was the blue eyed sailor, also from *Winterhude*, who had played at the *Palais de Danse*. Occasionally he would burst out with *Du bist mei … ei … ein Madchen* again. Another *Winterhudian*, breathing "plunk" fumes thickly, grabbed me. "You do Finnish waltz." For the rest of the evening, merry mariners whirled and clumped me round and round in my British tweed suit. Finally, I plumped down on a bench, more exhausted than if I'd been fisting in a topsail in a half gale.

Tredge, all decked out in his "whites," stood before me with a tall, fine-looking Finn. "You meeting old school frent of mine, *Winterhude* sailmaker." Tredge announced. Between their two forms I saw Jumbo glaring sourly across the room.

"You like sailmaking?" I asked the Finn.

"Ah yes, I don't mind the cutting of the sails, it intrigues me. The sewing, that is another thing, that is really monotonous," he replied in passable English.

"You are a 'pure Finn' like Tredge?" I wondered.

"A 'pure' Finn? Yes." He seemed amused.

We talked of voyages. His name was Eino Koivistoinen and he had sailed to Russia under the Bolshevik regime. "If I hadn't signed on in this ship," I told him, "my best bet might have been in Russian vessels, where many women work as sailors." Eino pretended to faint at the very idea.

"Have you ever been in a Russian port? This it is impossible to believe unless to see. I have seen the stevedores there. Skeletons, wearing rags for shoes in freezing cold. Frightened to speak. Afraid any moment to be shot for the least sign of mutiny. The conditions are so terrible there, it is a wonder any human lives through them."

Turning to a more cheerful subject, he slapped Tredge's shoulder and bantered, "This man, they are all afraid of him in your ship." I was surprised. Afraid of mild Tredge? "He is writing a book about them," said Eino, "and no one knows what he might say." Unbeknownst to me, this sailmaker had novel-plotting designs on me. They emerged years later in Eino Koivistoinen's Finnish book, *Meren Tytar* (Daughter of the Sea) and in *Billowing Sails*.

Chapter 11

L'Avenir Departs

The next morning all turned to, hauling aboard the huge fenders, casting off the mooring lines and then heaving in the 120 fathoms of cable on the anchor, which had been streamed ahead. Practically the entire population of Port Germein was on the wharf to watch the departure of *L'Avenir*. Standing by the warps and then coiling up the obstinate wire mooring lines, I saw the long wooden jetty loaded with friendly folk diminish, until their hearty cheers faded to chirps in the distance, and their forms specks of dust on a match stick. Only a couple of vigorous enthusiasts were screaming and jumping enough to be heard more than the others. These greatly amused Mac and Dane Doctor, and vaguely, I wondered why. Regrets at leaving behind their kindness and even the parched Australian countryside for the months of cold wet sea ahead tugged at me as *L'Avenir* was drawn away by the stout little tug *Yacka*.

How many ages ago it seemed since Copenhagen, when Dennis had sung out to us, tailing onto halliards, "Oh hogy! Australia. Rabbits boys! Oh yes, and kangaroos." Now that was all past, except for the left hind leg of a rabbit in my pocket, given to me by the stevedore Clem, as a good luck token. I pinched it, praying, "Rabbit, I'll need all the luck you can bring."

Rough weather awaited us. Our hatches, heavily battened, ready for the savage South Pacific rollers, filled me with awe. On our departure I had written to my sister in Canada,

> Well, I wonder if I shall see you? ... shall cable home on my arrival. Our lives are very near death, so close to the sea as in a sailing ship. But it is intensely vital and so beautiful that it does not seem it would be as hard to die, as in a bed with some painful disease as most people do. The fellows get used to it. Just look on a near slip as a joke, and no matter how one feels inside, it is never well to give the least sign of fear in one's face. I guess there will be times on the homeward voyage when I shall tighten my lips; but then again, there are more when one feels absolutely happy. After all it is really living.

We anchored outside of a long sand bank about five miles off Port Germein. Spencer Gulf is so shallow that there was not enough water even at the end of that mile-and-a-quarter long pier to finish loading. The rest of our cargo of wheat came out in lighters. We lay there, far out on Sunday, a holiday, but with no one allowed ashore for fear that they might drink or desert. Free time aboard was grumbled away. We all wove about, restless. I finally came fluttering down among a group of malcontents who squatted on the sails in the cadet room. They formed a sort of web surrounding Chesus, who sat with his long black-suited limbs folded like a spider.

I imagined that his grating voice sounded like a spider's would, as he rumbled "This gawdawful ship. With her fucking crew, they don't get on at all. Too much peoples here of all countries. That's why. And the pig-faced old man on top of it all. Scared of letting anyone ashore." I couldn't believe that.

"Surely he isn't scared," I said. Chesus swivelled his head around to glance at the intruder, saw it was only "Yacky" and continued on his favourite theme.

"Why in *Russel* the master, now there was a man!" Everyone began to disperse, bored by his stale recollections.

I thrust my hands into my dungaree pockets and wandered out onto the fo'castle head. Little Danska, sitting on the breakwater, called to me. "Never in my life," he declared as I squatted down beside him, "did I ever have such a good time as at Port Germein with Phyllis. Charming!"

Crouched on his other side, gloomy Jumbo muttered, "I wish I was running away in that country. I wish I was dead. It would have been much better zo. *Ach.* Now I only hopen to be spy for Hitler and get shooten down."

That was too much for me. "But if you had run away in Port Germein, what could you do? You have no money I suppose, and how hard to get food and hide from the police in that desert. Odd jobs are so scarce too. Look at poor Balleroo. A native of the country, yet he hardly got enough to keep himself, fishing from the pier."

"Oh yes," Jumbo mocked, "he do this for you I tink. So you take him and hide him in this ship. Dis been very bat if you do dis. But for me, dere in Australia it would have been all right. I finding yob. I wish I do dis. There is nodding left for me. I het dis damn bloody ship. Ve mussen vork all times for noddings and ve haf only fish balls and pea soup."

God Almighty! Balleroo! "But I like pea soup," I countered, "don't you? Balleroo, he's for *Winterhude.* He's nothing to do with me. But what's the use of trying to convince you. The whole idea's stupid."

Jumbo refused to be convinced. "Dis you telling me. But steward, he see you take dis Balleroo in cabin vit you ..."

I laughed outright. "Snooper steward. That rat living in a world of keyholes. YOU listen to him?" I laughed until I wheezed, remembering how Barbara had drawn his picture thumbing his nose, and then hung it over the keyhole on the inside of her cabin door, so that when he snooped, he'd thumb his own nose at himself.

Jumbo angrily squeaked the worn-out soles of his sneakers against the breakwater, but Danska, so lost in youth's young dreams, paid no attention. I was glad to turn to him once more. "Oh Yacky" he sighed, "you should have met her, Phyllis. What a lovely girl. I went to her home every Sunday. I hope, oh how I hope we will be back there the next voyage. That I come again to Germein. I am never, never forgetting ..." The lighter came alongside, ending the complaints, no matter how sharply sandpapers of discontent had grated.

Fine old hulls of sailing ships often ended their days as

lighters. I gleaned the original name of ours from her second mate. It was a Scottish name which I had never heard. The lighterman had sailed all over the world. "I've voyaged with Finnish crews too. I reckon they're the dirtiest, meanest crowd one can be shipmates with," this Scotsman told me.

"Do you mean the 'pure' Finns or the Swedes?"

My mixed feelings prompted me to shake hands with him and agree "You're goldarned right, you are," and yet, I also resented him disparaging my shipmates. They were the only ones I had known. They had joked and chaffed with me, and then, who knows? We might become souls foundering and drowning, all of us together in the voyage ahead. Instead, I said noncommittally, "Oh, they're much of a muchness."

He replied, "Will you make another voyage?" I told him that I hoped to do so, but that I could not pay any more premiums for apprenticeship, and recounted how *L'Avenir's* owner had deleted the section of my contract which stated that after serving a year as apprentice, I would be signed on as an ordinary seaman at thirty shillings a month. "Then," he prophesied, "you will be kicked out, if I know anything about the owner, bloody Erikson."

This caused me some uneasiness. Finns are so reserved that no one had mentioned my future chances of being signed on again. It had remained an unspoken anxiety for me, festering in my heart for the whole voyage. Somehow, it was startling when this outspoken lighterman exposed it so bluntly. One thing was for sure though, as we watched the last hold filling to the very brim of the hatch with golden wheat, I was aboard for the voyage home at least.

Preparing for the heavy seas ahead, we thudded down the stout hatch covers and shrouded them in not one but three of the thickest tarpaulins. The last one was brand new and was sewn on to fit snugly, and then coated with tar. Bars sprung down taut with large butterfly bolts came next, and lastly, we sledgehammered wedges into the cleats. The whole affair was carried out under the close supervision of the carpenter.

A long spell of heaving at the capstan bars followed, as the anchor was raised by hand. For some reason the steam windlass was not in use. Despite the interminable rounds about the capstan, the fellows had taken on a merry mood. We were homeward bound! Spinning around with gusto, as though the capstan was merely winding a ball of wool, they even attempted a chantey. "Good bye my boyees, we're hoooomewaaard bound." On the outmost end of one of the bars I travelled fast, leaping over the taut line at every merry-go-round turn. Horseplaying shipmates on the inner ends, with only short turns to negotiate, were rowdily hopeful of pitching me down in a hilarious Charlie Chaplin tumble. It came in a shin-splitting crack across the taut wire. No bones broken, I leapt up to join the round again. The skipper ordered me out. "Lev go Yackie, you vill *keel* yourself dat vay. Give us a chantey here. On top of the capstan, Yackie. Come on, up vith you." Dennis cheered. I would dearly have loved to do this, but shyness and pain restrained my exuberance. Although the unusual camaraderie had a healing effect, I just toiled on, quietly, at the inner end of a capstan bar.

Then, anchor aweigh, and all sails to set; pully hauly and coiling literally miles of lines. The mate admonished me, "A ship's mate is always known by the correct skvaring of her yards and the croo by the neatness of her coils." I worked at coiling up even fakes. Not even in the ultra weariness of the last coiling would any sloppiness be tolerated aboard.

"Well, that's the last of the Australian shelahs," growled some of the fellows up forrard, as the barque began to slide gently away from the shoreline, "and you, you bloody bitch, you're all we've got to look at for the next months." Chesus added "Christ" and the Finns added the inevitable "*Saaartan flickan.*" But neither the barque nor I fretted over the loss of the shelahs. We shared our impatience to show our round sterns to South Australia. A light but fair wind favoured us all the way out of Spencer Gulf.

Darkness fell over the green water near Wallaroo, but we could still see the dainty blackness of *Killoran* overtaking *L'Avenir*. Her sidelights flashed red and green. Awed by the atmosphere, the crew murmured in low tones that *Killoran* could sail faster than *L'Avenir* in light air. As she came abeam to port, news in Swedish rang out, giving dates of departures of other sailers from Wallaroo and Victoria. Her rigging exquisite against the mauve sky, *Killoran* soon slid away into blackness, even her emerald sidelight shut out, evoking memories of my pirate dreams in my rowboat-buccaneer days in Canada.

Those were the ships of my youth.

Chapter 12

We were running down to Tasmania in pleasant weather and I was at the wheel, feeling fully in control. Guffaws rose from the well deck, and I smiled to hear such happy laughter on a sunny day. Suddenly the mate appeared, rising up from the well deck ladder stiffly, as though he had been levitated up it. He strode past the wheel platform, his face rigid with anger, his mouth and the lines around it making an H of severity. Then, shocked, I noticed a figure lagging behind him. It was a stranger, a man weighed down by the sack he had on his back; the rags he wore fluttering in the breeze. He looked horrible, like some ghoul risen from the sea bottom. My spine seemed almost to ripple, so shaken was I by this apparition. Bursts of laughter from the crew indicated just how horrified my expression must have been. "Jackie brought Balleroo on board," they whooped, convulsed by my expression.

In the glimpse I had of the beastly little procession, I had seen a man of the same stature as Balleroo, black hair, and unshaven. The moustache? I couldn't see. Now I was going to be bullied for breaking all the taboos and helping a stowaway get on board. Otto had said as we sailed from Port Pirie, "You are no girl Why did you not help that poor Balleroo to stow away?

He was so good to you." Had Otto been wanting to nudge me into trouble with the skipper, who would be ready to drop me over the side if he believed I had helped a stowaway. Time dragged, as I wondered what the stowaway was saying while undergoing questioning by the master in his saloon aft. A figure or two buzzed up on deck like scout wasps, then, sea boots creaking, the master appeared and marched forward of the steering platform. He stopped and glared at me in silence for some moments. The mate came up and shouted at me "Ya, Yackie, your sveethart is on bort. Aren't you glad?" The crew went hysterical, cradling their bellies, wheezing and rolling, laughing till they gasped for breath.

The stowaway was immediately put to work cleaning the pigsty. He was far enough from me that I still wondered if it really was Balleroo. Starving and roasting in some crevice below decks during the five days since we had sailed, could that change a man's appearance so much? At supper that evening I asked the master and mate who the man might be. The mate swore, "By Christ Jackie, you're the one who brought him abort. You knowing more about dis dan we do. You fed him too. He couldn't have lived in the holt dat long widout food and vater. What de blooty hell you trying to give us, anyway? *You* know what you done all right and you got plenty trouble coming ... *plentee*!" My stomach rumbled with nerves all my watch below. But the next day, a Sunday, the stowaway lolled in the sun by the foremast. I sat beside him. It was not Balleroo.

What relief! He was a stranger named George, from the Broken Hill mining district. He appeared shrunken from starvation, although bunches of muscle remained, verifying his story of having laboured on farms "out back" and his wanderings as a hobo. Through all these desert hardships he had kept his eyes fixed on a mirage — life at sea. "Most boys out back have no wish to rove," he said, "and it's bloody hard to find a job at sea in Australia." While visiting friends in Port Pirie, he conceived the idea of stowing away. They helped him to conceal himself on board the lighter ferrying the last bags of wheat to the ship. In the confusion of loading the wheat, he managed to slip on board unnoticed. He wore his best suit, had a little food and water and a lot of pluck. He never revealed who it was that helped him to find a corner among the wheat bags and passed him more food and water. How some sharp eye on board didn't spot this mere token of sustenance lying around was a miracle.

"Hotter'n hell daown there with all them bloody rats," said George, describing his five days in the hold. He had lain there in his tiny slice of space, feeling rather like the captured slaves transported on the old slave ships. Even the sweet aroma of the wheat turned to a suffocating gas smell as he lay there in the blackness of the hold, his throat cracked with thirst, wondering if he would survive. In that hole he knew neither night nor day, but he hung on until the sounds on deck told him that *L'Avenir* must be well enough on her way to keep at sea, too far from land for him to be set ashore. Then, to the wonder of all beholders, he stumbled out through a door in the tween decks in search of water.

The captain, foreseeing wrangles with British immigration authorities because of this ruffian, but noting also his hardy appearance, ordered "You'll *verk* and you'll verk *dem hart!*" He did not ask if his stowaway wanted to work. George trembled, but not from fear of work. His sunny Australian gaiety amused even the circumspect Scandinavians as he tried out his newly acquired Swedish swear words on the cook. "*Fee Fawn. Yevla Kocken!*" he shouted, thrusting his curly black head inside the galley porthole. "*Yeefa mig knuylland glass vatten, a Sataan*" (give me a fucking glass of water). Startled by the rugged face and cheeky grin, the stove-bound toilers pouted, silent. They carried a queer resentment at his poking fun at them from the sunlit outside. George then turned his robust effrontery to the chores assigned him, dancing his way through cleaning out the pigsty.

George's British cheeriness earned admiration from our new passengers. They conceded that he was worth his salt. Well they might, for one of them, Commander Butlin, had been training boys for the Australian navy. He had command of the largest warship. The second was also a naval commander, returning to Britain after years spent based in Hong Kong. He had observed the upheavals when the Japanese moved out from Korea and seized Manchuria from China in 1931, and had lived among skirmishes and the rattle of bullets. A Dutch tea planter from Surinam was the third new passenger. He was a quiet, capable fellow with a reserved manner. Indeed, these experienced people knew how to get along on board a ship. If our previous passengers' capacity for highly entertaining, abandoned and colourful high jinks had tried the captain on our outward journey, his face showed agreeable relief at having professional officers as passengers.

The commanders clambered alow and aloft, vigorous in their quest for unusual angles for their photography, while zestfully absorbing every detail of life on board. Ship model building occupied much of their time when in the cold Westerlies. Commander Fisher, perplexed by how to complete the standing rigging of his nice little scale model of *L'Avenir*, puzzled, "The donkeyman has routed out these strands of electric wire for me. Nice and fine, but how am I ever going to lay them up to look like neat standing rigging in different sizes?"

Pleased to be able to contribute a dodge I had learned when making ship models, I advised him to take an ordinary drill and put the number of wires he wanted to lay up in its chuck. "You can get right laid or left laid, whichever you need, and your miniature rope will be just like the real thing."

Commander Butlin had his pretty, young new wife along. The stowaway confided to me that he had fallen completely in love with her, but could only admire her from a distance.

As we approached the Westerlies, Ceysen, Segerstedt, Chesus, Dane Doctor, Stowaway George, MacDowall, and I were ordered to spend days rust-chipping in the deep dampness of the forepeak. One watch period we tried out our guess that if we made no noise the mate might forget us, and we passed the time without doing a stroke of hammering. Instead we became a miniature conference on international politics. Australian, Swedes, Scot, Belgian, German, Dane, and Canadian discussed "what the next war might be like." Even in 1934, the prospect of another war loomed, blighting our youthful ambitions. Then the talk turned to the Finns, and why they are like they are, and from them back to our time in Port Germein.

"You remember that ship stores dealer in Germein?" Dane Doctor was smiling, instead of his usual frown at frivolous chatter. "Eh Mac, you remember him?" he asked.

MacDowall slapped his thigh, "Don't I just, *Christ!*"

Dane Doctor explained, "That dealer came aboard whispering to us, 'could you snitch some paint and sell it to me cheap?'" The Dane imitated the whisperings of the stores

Stowaway

dealer, making the hairs about his mouth fly about like dandelion fluff. "'Oh yes, oh yes sir,' we told him, and he gave us ten shillings each for a couple of gallon cans. Not bad. We were pleased, eh Mac?"

MacDowall was giggling so hard he couldn't reply.

"That fool came back for more of those wonderful bargains. We gave him more all right," Dane Doctor added, "filled with sand and water. He never lifted the lids. Paid us well and went home. We sailed the next day." he broke off in a wheeze of laughing. Suddenly I remembered the two figures, leaping up and down on the end of the pier as we left.

"Oh, I *saw* them, those two shrieking on the pier as we sailed ..." Mac piped up, "and everyone thought he was just waving us a nice goodbye."

Untrammelled by any land mass, stupendously long rollers grow in the South Pacific. We had nothing around us for thousands of miles but windswept ocean. No one would know if *L'Avenir* struck a berg, as she had no radio to crackle into the void to bring rescue, even if anyone had been about. One night, on lookout as the eyes of the ship, I watched through hissing rain as her bows plunged over the night water. Suddenly I was afraid. Was that long stretch of greenish white a lather of foam, or was it a berg? That night stands out for sheer terror. If a berg had loomed out of the confusion of murk and black water, towering over *L'Avenir*, my impulse to rush aft and cry "I can't stand another minute up there on lookout!" to the mate would have been within reason. But on that night, had I done so, how could I have explained that I was absolutely possessed by a sense of disaster, so urgent that I clung to the rail and screamed my fright to the winds, so as not to give way to unreason. Perhaps there was some kind of kinship between *L'Avenir* and myself, a young woman, or perhaps I had some kind of premonition that *L'Avenir* would be lost in this area of ocean, four years later, when she disappeared with all sixty-eight souls aboard. Jumbo, possibly, was among them.

At last we approached Cape Horn, most dreaded and notorious of all passages for fierce storms and ferocious seas. Yet in this of all places, we had flat calm for ten days. It was incredible. Even the barometer falling to "tempest" did not bring on a storm. Where we should have been swishing by, or even

135

taking in sail in a storm, we had to tack against light whispers of air, hauling the heavy yards around from tack to tack. The crew blamed me for this calm and threatened to throw me overboard as a Jonah to appease the winds. I retorted that if a Finn had been on a British ship, he would have been shut up in the forepeak until he had conjured up a fair wind! Ceysen kindly quelled the argument, "*Ah, mais cela n'est pas si extraordinaire. L'an dernier, je me rappelle, une mer d'huile, près du Cap Horn. Vous n'étiez pas à bord, ce n'est donc pas à cause de vous que nous avons une mer semblable.*" [Ah, but this is not so extraordinary. Last year, I recall an oily sea near Cape Horn. You were not on board, therefore, it is not because of you that we have a similar sea.]

Standing by, waiting to tack, I would look over the weighty tomes on the shelf in the navigation room. They were a remnant from *L'Avenir's* formal days as a Belgian cadet training ship. The *Southern Pacific Guide*, of 1870 was a ponderous volume, but to one with imagination, it was full of exciting facts. I pored over details about the natives of Tierra del Fuego, their fierceness and their cannibalism. Some of the missionaries had been boiled in Fuegan cooking pots. Though the climate at Cape Horn was extremely harsh, the Fuegans wore little or no clothing. Unfortunately, inducing them to wear clothes proved fatal for the poor natives, because the batch of clothing sent them came from a Chilean orphanage which had been swept by measles. With no resistance to this disease, which was unknown to them, nearly the entire race was wiped out. The guide also offered advice on how mariners should deal with the "savages" of Tierra del Fuego should they be shipwrecked there, but suggested that it was better not to be wrecked there in the first place. Ways of avoiding collisions with icebergs were described, along with speculation about detecting their presence by a fall in temperature, their characteristic smell, and by bouncing echoes from them. I read about the long, narrow Beagle Channel on the south end of Tierra del Fuego, separating it from the great mass of tiny islands and rocks leading to the southernmost island, Cape Horn itself. His Majesty's frigates had passed through Beagle Channel on their voyages of exploration in the eighteenth century. After experiencing the rigours of tacking in Spencer Gulf, and now here at Tierra del Fuego, and the dangers of collision in the English Channel, and knowing the difficulty in manoeuvring a square rigger in those comparatively wide waters, I could only conclude that they must have had to tow the big sailers by means of small boats rowed through the tortuous channels. Think of the blisters, the frostbite and the slowness of all that. In extravagant Victorian flourishes, the *Guide* recounted winters spent at Tierra del Fuego. The details gave an inkling of the courage of those mariners over the past four hundred years who had sometimes been forced to winter in these hostile parts. How could they have survived, I wondered. The inhuman seas hurling bitter spray to the grey sky that I could see through the navigation room porthole made me shiver with awe at what those earlier adventurers had endured. Aboard *L'Avenir* we had only a sniff of wind while sailing past Diego Ramirez. We wallowed past that grim rock without even sighting it. I read through the *Guide* to find out more about the source of its elegant Spanish name and the life of its discoverer, and went on to the story of Magellan as well. He was a wealthy young nobleman, who set out to explore merely as an occupation, and discovered the passage which separated Tierra del Fuego from the mainland of South America — Magellan Strait.

Tredge appeared and shoved a chart of the region of Cape Horn under my nose. He had drawn it accurately to scale. Was this the same hand that did long calculations in wavy, scrambled figures, from the same head that carried the big hat that Dennis had ridiculed?

"Why" I exclaimed, "I've never seem so precise a chart done by any student in an English navigational school."

Tredge applauded his own countrymen, "Dis, it is done so in all Finnish navigation schools. All man there can be drawing such a chart."

I said, "We have to learn all the *Regulations for Preventing Collision at Sea*, more than chart drawing, in England. You know, word for word. 'On or in front of the foremast or if a vessel without a foremast, then in the fore part of the vessel, at a height above the hull of no less than twenty feet and if the breadth of the vessel exceeds twenty feet, then at a height above the hull not less than such breadth ...'" and I repeated all the thirty-one articles as easily as a churchman reciting the thirty-nine articles of Anglican faith. The mate stared in astonishment.

"Where must you have all that?" he asked.

"In England," I answered, "you must know it like that or the examiners boot you out of the exam board room. But it's international. Don't you have to be able to repeat it word for word in Finnish?"

"Well, we have to tell which lights is there, yes, but all those words."

"By golly then what's the use," I said, "when it's international, if you fellows don't know it word for word, like they have to in British navigation school?" The mate didn't reply to that, except to grunt that we had not had any collisions on the voyage, and, after all, that was the best answer.

I undertook to translate the whole log book from Swedish to English. Though the mate had expressed disapproval of my sea career, he did provide approximate English equivalents for the sea terms that could not be found in the Swedish-English dictionary that Miss Kronig had obtained for me in Adelaide. With the mate's aid, I became familiar with Swedish sea terms, and with the terse, unromantic language used in a log book. Thus armed, I hoped to be able to enter the facts about wind, weather, sails set and taken in, distance run, anchoring, hours worked, who lay sick, and so on — those thousand and one details which an officer had to observe and record accurately, even under the most dire stress. An entry could turn out to be a vital factor in a dispute arising in a court case over overtime wages, or perhaps in an inquiry into a wreck or a collision or any mishap to a ship.

"Here's an entry I haven't seen before, 'Tagit upp ett hya.' What's a hya?" I asked the mate one day.

"That mean shark. Damn fool tird mate! putting that in log," he answered disdainfully.

"Why," I asked, "doesn't one usually enter about catching sharks in the log?"

The mate snorted, "Gawd, what do you think?"

I didn't say so, but I thought how very different from each other the two watch mates, Firstan and Tredge, were; the one so practical and the other so romantic.

To amuse them I brought out the old log I had kept in my St. Lawrence catboat on Lake Massawippi. As behoved a professional teenage shipmaster I had made such entries as,

Voyage No. 2. Seamates Company Sloop *Ruth*. From

Seamates' Company dock, Lake Massawippi to Point No
Point. Cargo: One bedspring (a mother had wanted this
moved, to our pride and joy — a real cargo!)
Captain: A. Brock
Officers: 1st Mate: Mait Edey
Boatswain: Joseph Leduc
Crew: AB Mcgill Gawthrop
AB B. Tillman

Ship's Log.

Time Wind Force Sea Weather Clouds Ship's Run
4:30 SW by S 4   3   b   cumulous 5 mi

Remarks: hasty departure due to misunderstanding of an
order to cast off by a seaman. Nearly had a collision with
Flatsides, Seamates Company vessel, moored to
Headquarters's wharf.

And in the "Official" log:

Case of insubordination by a member of the crew. The
latter, name Tillman, attacked the mate, who was flogging
him for giving too much jaw, when ordered by Captain to
wash down decks. After having been captured and
imprisoned in the forepeak for a short time, he has
become very submissive and courteous.

I did not say that Captain A. Brock had found herself in some
difficulties with the authorities after marooning a recalcitrant
crew member on one of Lake Massawippi's islands. Nor could I
then have told the mates a rather remarkable by-product of all
this childhood pirating about. Of all the millions of children on
the thousands of lakes in North America, two of us in this log
book were destined to sail in real "Olde tyme shippes." Captain
A. Brock sailed in the four-masted barque *L'Avenir* and first mate
"Mait Edey," as the correspondent for *Life* in the Atlantic
crossing of the replica of the *Mayflower* about 1957.
    Pandering to another of my enthusiasms, the good mate of
L'Avenir searched out some old charts used in the ship's cadet

training days, on whose generous back I copied, to exact scale, *L'Avenir's* lines and sail plan from the Bremerhaven naval architects' drawings. I had the building of a future ship model in mind, when I managed to squeeze out spare hours for this drafting. The mate was intrigued at the progress of these drawings, but watched eagle-eyed for a slip in accuracy.

"Dere!" he exulted, "You saying, Yackee, you want to be old maid like that Miss Kronig. The old maids, they all making crazy mistakes like you chust made. You horry up, get married. I telling you. Why the other day Miss Kronig comes up on deck when the yards dey was squared. She says 'Have we still got head wind?' *My Gott!* You will be same if you keep on."

I retorted, "Miss Kronig doesn't have to worry whether the yards are squared, braced, or cockbilled. But you do. There's the difference."

Later, I caught the mate out in his reckoning in navigation — by twenty miles. "*AH HA!*" I said in triumph, "that comes of being a bachelor, by your theory." He was crestfallen. But sometimes rivalries and technicalities gave way, and the mate, steward and I whooped it up in a little horseplay.

"Why don't you marry the steward? He's got lots of money. Best paid man in the ship," the mate teased, and grabbing our necks in a clench, he banged our skulls together. Clack! The steward's mop of hair waved as though blown by a hurricane, while he struggled and I wriggled, dodging his jagged teeth. Our roars of laughter rolled over Tredge, who took no part in these shenanigans. He just ambled on, giving us a monologue about how he was going to construct an old-fashioned chip log to measure the speed of *L'Avenir*. Sometimes he muttered over a box with a ball in it which he had made, and which he claimed was the equivalent of an astrolabe. Such was the motley mob thrown together to work on *L'Avenir*. Smooth sailing depended on mutual tolerance and understanding. I was learning.

"Oh Yackie, I knowing you better than you knowing yourself," said the mate one day, boasting of his perception. I was too much of a Mother Carey's chicken [3] even to begin to rise and grasp the aspirations of this sea eagle, ranging aloof from *L'Avenir's* crew.

The mate never took advantage of my hearing the gossip around the whole ship, both before the mast and in the cabins aft. He never asked me to repeat any. "Without fear or favour" was his way of treating all aboard. But one day my idol revealed at least a toe of clay. Leaning together over the chart table, he suddenly asked me, "What do they think of me up forrard, eh?"

Forgetting the "All Aland Islanders are like that" episode, I replied, "Never heard a word against you. They say you are a fine officer." I noticed a warm colour light up his face. Was that a flicker of pleasure or vanity? As a rather naive young woman, I was surprised. So, senior officers were human too, and could be just as uneasy about their popularity as debutantes could. I wondered about our exalted captain. Could such anxieties fret even him? But no, surely that was impossible in one so stout and sure.

Night watches continued to demand extra vigilance even after we rounded Cape Horn. The weary mate and Tredge, though, began going below together, instead of singly, for their five a.m. coffee. They had enough confidence in my seamanlike abilities to leave me in charge of the watch for those fifteen minutes. Quakes of indignation rumbled through the crew forrard at this procedure. One morning it happened that we were in sound and sight of the steersman as the mate presented me with his whistle, commanding "If anything carries away, *BLOW LIKE HELL*"

How closely I watched the straining rigging, looking aloft with pride. Then I swaggered over to the binnacle, checking the course. Looking aloft again, I noticed that the steersman, Dane Doctor, had allowed her to fall off slightly, so angry and excited was he at witnessing my investiture as officer of the watch. "*Up i' de vinde, Sataan!*" I ordered the steersman sharply. Dane Doctor's beard twitched with anger as he found that he had to carry out my order because he had indeed let her fall off course.

At the change of watch, Jumbo glowered at me, muttering "The boys mat. Dey very very mat. It not official dat you take charge of de vatch." Later they had still more to be "mat" about when one night Tredge was busy with one of his long star-sight problems. At eight bells, he said, "Yackie, I have to be finishing dis. Firstan is dayman, so will you be going to break of poop and telling watch to be going below." I hopped along willingly. Leaning over the rail above the well deck, I called out merrily, "*Vacten, go nere*" (Watch, go below).

"Vas dis?"

"*Aaarrr, Roruru.*" The fo'castle crowd sounded like a group of stage players saying "rhubarb rhubarb rhubarb" behind the scenes, to give an effect of a threatening mob.

"You cannot do dis!" I heard Jumbo yell.

"Tredge must come himself," demanded Dennis.

"*Icke bra, flickan*" (not right, girl) burbled Redbeard.

"I'm only a messenger from Tredge. He told me to tell you the watch is dismissed. So go on below. Go *nere* ... but if you want to spend your free watch out here in the cold arguing about me, that's your bundle. Tredge's message is delivered to you. So ... goodnight. Sleep tight!"

I left the rail as Dennis translated all that into Swedish. What children, so easy to ruffle this way and thus pay back some of those kicks in the pants they had dealt me. "Dose are all child," the mate had described his crew to me, but added, "and *YOU* is one too."

Chapter 13

Heavy Weather

Working in the sunshine on deck, I took blocks apart and regreased them, painted hatch coamings and made sennit, all jobs so pleasant that when I noticed the cheery sailmaker's assistant beckoning to me, I supposed he had been sent to fetch me for some sail ripping or other chore too long and monotonous to waste the sailmaker's expert time. Johansson led me, with a sort of happy-go-lucky swing to his walk and a smile, under the fo'castle head. We passed the lantern room where I had passed one smelly day up to the ankles in kerosene cleaning up a spilled barrel. We passed the rope storage, sniffing its musky smell, and went on to the petty officers' mess room. Strange, how in a confined space for months discipline leaves whole cabins that one never sees.

"Thought you'd like to join us," was the sailmaker's greeting to my curious head as I poked it in the doorway. He was seated on one of the alpine inn type of long benches that bordered the scrubbed deal table. In a corner glowered the satanic looking donkeyman. He glanced up for a moment with his rhinoceros eyes, then lowered them, seeming to draw out of the table black thoughts about the happenings on Aland long ago. But what they were, he hid behind his long fingers covering his mouth and massaging his grizzly chin. His other hand reached for a glass filled with wine on the table. Beside him sat our stolid carpenter.

"What'll it be, Yackie?" The sailmaker lifted a bottle. I hesitated, figuring how best to get my feet over the bench without disturbing this company of august mariners.

"Why, err ... make mine plunk. Every time, please." I sat down. As the sailmaker glugged plunk into a glass for me, my eyes followed the hypnotic gyrations of a balloon-shaped spot of sunshine from the round porthole which danced up and down the white bulkhead in time to the motion of the ship. It seemed that *L'Avenir* was joining in the fun. But I wondered. Surely a company of mariners don't call a break like this in the day without reason. Perhaps this is some fantastic Finnish holiday? Independence Day? No, we had that on the voyage out. Maria Knulla Day? That was still to come, my shipmates had enjoyed informing me. Most likely it must be the sailmaker's "*namdag*," the day of the saint for which he was named. Anyway, I thought, here's "*skol*" to him. Why question the rare acceptance into this company of ancient mariners, who could each count up more years on the seven seas than the master and mates combined. As for my boyish shipmates, "Boo" to them; a callow lot.

The carpenter's features were sharp as a woodcut, yet they had a relaxed quality. I wondered about his life. "Why will you never tell me anything about the years you spent in America?" I asked, but he only smiled his usual mysterious grin. I tried to tease him. "Bet you won't tell what you did there because you were in Sing Sing the whole time!" He just twirled his glass, then drank it in one swallow.

The sailmaker left and returned with his photo album. He opened it and pointed out a picture of a man in dark clothes. "See, this is my brother. He is a missionary in China." I gasped, somehow shocked to find that this hoary old King Neptune was not pure pagan, but the brother to someone as tame as a missionary. Possibly he was even a prosaic churchgoer himself. This Neptune might even attend services, staid, conventional, in a drab churchgoing suit, his front heavy with a gold watch chain, creaking along in tight, shiny boots.

"Your family doesn't believe in staying at home," I remarked, making what romance I could of the sailmaker's disconcerting background.

"Well," he said, there are quite a few of my ten children left at home still. Like this little girl in the picture here. My favourite daughter, she is only twelve years old but by God, you ought to see the greeting she'll give her old daddy when I come home. Yes, that's the one, in the white dress in the garden." I thought of the dichotomy between the two — the lone, old bull moose of a sailmaker, unique aboard the barque, and his other world, full and populated by himself in far off Finland. His enjoyment in reassuring himself of their existence through the medium of the photo album, here in the southern ocean was almost pathetic, it seemed to me.

"It's a bit rough, going to sea, a long voyage, leaving your family at home, you hardly know your daughters." Perhaps I reminded him of his own older daughters, touching a tender spot in the old barnacle, responded to on my part, by gentle, admiring remarks. The carpenter and the donkeyman leaned forward around the deal table, with its ring of glasses filled with sweet wine, but the faraway thoughts of home which smoothed their faces were soon exploded by a volcanic roar from the mate.

"Gott in heaven! What de hell *you* do in heer, Yackie!"

I shot up from the bench like a cat whose tail has been stepped on. The mate shoved me into the alleyway. "Get out here. On with work, uppa deck, for Christ sake." Through the pattern of light surrounding the mate's dark form, filling the doorway of the mess room, I glimpsed the sailmaker, slanting his eyes away with that sheepish, innocent, yet shifty look of a reprobate. The donkeyman sat, as unruffled as iron; the carpenter was not visible; while Johansson nodded, indicating everything was all right.

Whether the mate approved or not, the little company continued their carousing for hours. They started a discussion which grew into a difference of opinion, rose to an argument and culminated in a fight. Finally the donkeyman had the sailmaker in flight, pursuing him in a high rage, lusting for the satisfaction of opening his enemy's scalp in a mess of glass, blood, and wine. The sailmaker took refuge in the famous muscular arms of the burly second mate, who slung him into a locked and barred cabin aft, rescuing him from the blood and wine aftermath. By now the donkeyman was as befuddled as the ogre fumbling for Jack gone down the beanstalk. This Jacky felt fortunate to have been levered, even so abruptly, out of that pretty party by the vigilant first mate, wise in the outcome of a crew's party, despite the initial bonhomie.

The Australian sun had dried out the deck seams so that they warped open in large cracks. Miss Kronig emerged on deck to complain. "Everything I have is sopping. Water is just dripping everywhere in my cabin." But until the rain, which poured down in torrents, swelled the wood again, the drips would continue.

Our watch, as a punishment for responding too slowly to an officer's whistle summons, had to spend all the night watches standing by round the foremast. Most of us drooped like wet cab horses awaiting a call. Only Ceysen rejoiced in the discomfort. He delighted in recalling his suffering on other voyages. "*Le premier lieutenant sur le dernier voilier etait un sadique. Il nous tenait sous sa férule. En pleine tempête de neige, quelles que soient les intempéries, sur le pont toujours.*" [The first lieutenant on the last voyage was a sadist. He held us under an iron rule. In a full gale with snow, however bad the weather was, (we were) on the bridge, always]. Then he recounted the saga of his shoes. "*Mes souliers se sont mis à voyager dans ma cabine, remplis d'eau, touchant port à chaque banquette, causant des bruits insolites.*" [My shoes began to travel inside my cabin on the voyage, they were filled with water, docking at each bench, causing unwonted (unusual) squeaks]. At least he had life in him, to find amusement in those hardships.

Above us, the barque's stays trembled and tautened with the forces acting on them. We kept clear of the foresail, with the sheets of water spilling down its acreage. I stood gazing aloft at the angles of the stays, which, in navigation school, had just been lines on a sheet of paper, with strain to be calculated by trigonometry, now in heroic proportions. No time for musing, though, as we were soon ordered to take in the t'gallants. The glass continued to fall, so it was "Topsails in too!" But the wind tore at the fore topsail until the buntlines snapped like little cotton threads, instead of half-inch-thick wire. The great sail spread out as though stretching a sheeted arm, making the mast bend like a straw in the wind. Through the shrieking gale we heard faintly the bull bellows of the sailmaker. His months of sewing were about to be liquidated. Orders to save the topsail, roared by the master, reached us like faraway squeaks. How could $250 worth of sail be saved in such a wind? How could the captain explain to Erikson, the owner, how and why he had lost it? In a trice all hands had joined in laying out along the fore topsail yard. The board-like sail sometimes soared high above us, then descended, flying back across the yard with a whack. We huddled low on the footrope, while the sail tore at us, threatening to wipe us from our mean little perch. I surveyed the twenty men on the yard with me, calculating how many of us might drop into the sea if our combined weight and the pull of the sail should break the footrope.

It was not the footrope though, but the parrel that sprung, with a noise that seemed to shatter the whole ship. That loosened the yard from the mast, and it whanged like a note on a xylophone struck with a sledgehammer. The remains of the parrel still held the cavorting yard to the mast, mercifully giving us time for a block and spilling line to be rigged and passed around the bunt of the wildly flailing sail. Then the sail could be hauled in to the yard, making the rest of the furling more or less routine. From the whipping yard, I looked out on the ocean, admiring the foam flecked verdancy of it as the delicate tints of dawn began to creep over the still raging sea. All the stress we had undergone was followed by a feeling of oneness with the speed of the barque, a rare, dreamlike sensation of flying freely through the mysterious air that precedes daylight. "Looks grand!" I said to Dane Doctor, beside me as we reef-knotted the gaskets. "What does?" he replied.

Below decks again, we found that Frasne's mate, Josephine, had produced kittens in the midst of the storm, and in the second mate's bunk too. That good-hearted man, coming off watch, nevertheless smiled to see his bunk already occupied. He tenderly gave the little family into the care of the sailmaker in the sailroom. When I went to work there, the sailmaker was just coming in from deck. He had been drowning some of Josephine's too numerous family. Did he seem almost ready to wipe away a tear? After flinging those helpless kittens into the sea, he tried to conceal his emotions by slamming the door shut with a great bang. He took extra care with the fastenings.

"Seas are coming over heavy still, on deck up there. I'm making sure this door's fast. So you don't go up on deck no more Jack."

I looked at him, "No need to, I hope, with everything pretty snug on the yards at last, eh?" I answered, but was startled when the sailmaker roared "Christ Jesus, Jack, while you was up on that topsail yard, Skipper and Mate was fair busting their lungs out ahollerin' away up at you!" I looked at him, wondering vaguely, what he was talking about.

"What For? Wasn't I laying my weight around up there properly?"

"Hell! They was ahollerin' for you to come down out of all that."

Surprised, I answered, "Why that's my job up there. Anyway the wind was so loud, I didn't hear a peep out of the skipper or the mate. Now I couldn't disobey orders I didn't hear, could I?"

Chapter 14

Airman Has Something to Say

Coming off watch one evening, I was turning to my cabin when the airman called me. "Come here, woman," he ordered. I came up, curious. He shoved a basin into my hands. "Take this to Miss Kronig. She is sick. Look after her." I was about to retort that I was not hired as a stewardess, but on peering into the cabin and seeing a sighing, prostrate Miss Kronig, humanity got the better of my pride. But what to do about her? Nursing was certainly not my metier. She indicated that she needed the basin, so I held it under her chin. Miss Kronig gave a few gasps, retched, then fell back and soon slid into a deep sleep.

When I left her the airman beckoned me to his cabin. "I've got something to say to you," he said. He so rarely talked to me that at times I even forgot his existence on board. I leaned my oil-skinned shoulder against the door post as he went on. "Why don't you become an airwoman, instead of trying to stay at sea as a sailor?"

"For the simple reason that aeroplanes don't interest me in the least."

"But here at sea, you will have lives in your hands! Eventually you might be in full charge of people's lives."

"And why should I not?"

"Such a situation is preposterous. You don't seem to realize. Imagine, say, if a ship ran into danger, they would all be entirely dependent on you. No woman must ever be allowed to be in control of such an important post. You ... you just haven't the brain power necessary for such responsibility. No woman has. These circumstances cannot be permitted with so much at stake."

"Telephone operators, doctors, lawyers, all have life at stake at times under their care, to name a few at random."

"Ah yes, but those are all under the orders of some body. They are not allowed to make big decisions involving risks to many passengers as a ship's master sometimes is. Now as I have suggested, in the air, flying solo, you have only your own life to look after."

This small-minded bickering, even if kindly meant, was harder to take than the murderous threats and coarse arguments of the crowd forrard. Finally I burst into tears with a great wail. At this, the airman, spoiled darling of London society, reached into some nook in his cabin and brought out a hoarded bottle of champagne. My sobs choked off any protests of not wasting that on me, and soon he had thrust a glass into my shaking hand. My tears fell into the bubbles. I squatted on the floor, leaning against the bulkhead and sipped the drink, my sadness contrasting with the festive joy of bubbling champagne. The airman stood at the porthole, hand on hip, cigarette between his fingers. "Another thing," he began haughtily, eying me critically, "the way you act towards these foreigners, as though they were equals. We are British. We must show them we are superior. Where is your loyalty to the British Empire? These foreigners should be shown where they belong and be taught their place or they will try to put it over on us."

"Foreigners?"

I was genuinely puzzled, wondering what he meant. Perhaps the Scots lighterman and his "much of a muchness, meanest crowd ..."

"Oh. My shipmates."

"Yes. Obviously. Don't be stupid and pretend you don't know. Never let them think they are equal to a Britisher. Remember *that* my girl!"

He was a well-read man, but he was right out of the days of

Kipling. My amazed eyes had now dried, and I dove into an argument with the figure standing there, so assured in his tattersall check jacket. "The kind of man who wears horse's heads on his tie," Barbara had described him succinctly on her first acquaintance with him. I explained that having travelled since I was a child, I hoped for some sort of International Europe eventually. He winced.

"Deplorable ... shameful really."

And so on and on, till eight bells struck. At muster I approached one of the midnight-muffled bundles that was Jumbo, and told him that poor Miss Kronig was sick.

"Yah, sick," he mocked, "She iss flirting. She drinking wit dat airman. This I find terrible."

Next day Miss Kronig wobbled to the saloon. She began to pick daintily at the lobscouse, saying, "Oh yes, I am a little better thank you. It was just a touch of malaria."

The commanders smiled to themselves. Malaria? Around Cape Horn? I defended her for some reason, "Cape Horn fever. You've heard of that surely?" Miss Kronig joined in their chuckles with a smile. Her deafness kept her unhurt.

Chapter 15

Barrett, the airman, caught an albatross. Its hooked beak had been held in the usual sailors' contraption of wire, board and salthorse bait. On deck, with its huge beak released, it snapped angrily at its harassers. The commanders took photos. Commander Fisher looked up albatross in his book of marine nature study and found that there are many different kinds of albatrosses. Everyone examined the ten-foot wing span of the great bird, its dull brown and white plumage and its wide, fin-like feet. It took waddling steps across the deck. The book said that an albatross will become violently seasick if placed on a deck. But this dethroned king of the sea stood for an hour, wild, fierce, but not seasick. When he was finally allowed to fall back into the sea, he sat there for a moment, heaving and bobbing as though overcome by his frightening experience. Then he rose up out of the sea and flew off to join some others of his kind.

He may have undergone some indignities in being hauled aboard *L'Avenir* but he had a much happier time in providing some entertainment than the other live boredom-breakers in the well deck. There, live baby rats were thrown to the cat. Just before that cat would have put the poor creature out of its misery, it was snatched from his paws, and the performance repeated. I could have squeaked in anguish with the terror-stricken baby, rat or no rat, but a mere girl chiming in would only sharpen the pleasure of the rat's tormenters. I noticed the smile on Jumbo's broad flat features as his chubby hands snatched at the scuttering little scrap of fur that the cat was scrabbling after too. An insight, irrational perhaps, shot through me. Suppose I were that rat? Was this a warning from my intuition?

The *hya* (shark) written up in the log book by Tredge had a rough time of it too. As soon as it had been caught, the shark's tail was cut off, while it still quivered with life. I was haunted by the groans of the fish as its backbone was being sawn through. I remembered the Nova Scotian fisherman who told me that they enjoyed the "aaaaghhhh" sound a shark made when live coals were stuffed down its throat. I told him that I saw no sense in such cruelty. The Bluenose replied, "Well by the Lord Harry, now what kind of mercy do you figure such a creature is going to show you if you was in the water?" That showed the unchanging attitude that sailors have to sharks. *L'Avenir's* young vikings happily ripped up the shark, tearing out the guts, their arms red to the elbows in blood. But their joy overflowed when we caught a dolphin. Its red life flowed like lava over the deck into the scuppers, and they went mad as savages at a feast, while remaining solemn silent Norsemen. They tore open the belly, and murmured in wonder at the queer portions of the animal falling to the deck. Dane Doctor bore away a lung and crouched apart by himself, scraping and dissecting it. The guts disposed of, the dolphin became dozens of meatballs in *Koken's* hands, and the blood was hosed away as part of the general cleaning process going on throughout the ship.

As part of the house cleaning, all the wooden tables and cupboards in the galley were ordered to be broken up. Danska and I, assigned to this task, soon found the reason for the extravagant rending of the fittings. Cockroaches. "Watch this, Yackie," called Danska, as he thrust a red hot poker into a crack in the wood. Such myriads of cockroaches swarmed onto the boards that the table was hidden by their mass.

Other small creatures had to have their homes ravaged and be burned alive too. Loads of "B flats" infested the "donkey's breakfast" as they called the fo'castle mattresses. A fire was built in the well deck, and the mattresses were held over it one by one until their "tenants" dropped into it. I can't say that I sympathized with these vermin to the extent that I did with the fish. At least those were within human understanding as fellow creatures. I was classed as sentimental about animal life. Does a bed bug feel as keenly as a fish or rat?

One day in the doldrums, sent scurrying aloft by the whistle summoning all hands, I panted "God, what's the rush?" The weather was calm and grey. All hands were too intent, hauling buntlines and clewlines with desperate speed to bother answering. Then I saw a waterspout swaying lazily on the horizon, as though making up its funnel mind whether it would whiz over athwart *L'Avenir* and slam down tons of water on her and blow out her sails. We were lucky that day, as it disappeared over the horizon.

That threat was nerve-wracking, but more grating in the doldrums was the constant rain, rain, rain, day after day, night after night. Shoes grew deep mould like moss. It was too hot to wear oilskins and too wet not to. All that water might have been the silver in the mines of Mexico and Tredge a Spanish grandee, he rejoiced so in collecting it. "You must be getting bucket now," he ordered me, his feet sloshing on the shiny deck. He urged us all on, through entire night watches, scraping up buckets in niches he had scouted out. When the deep freshwater tanks, which held tons, the giant barrels on deck, the baths, the tanks abaft the galley, the officers bath and even the tanks for the toilets were all filled to overflowing, Tredge still looked for more receptacles. He eyed the scuppers and sought to plug them. They had been freshly painted during the few sunny spells, and the mate refused to allow them to scraped with buckets any more. "Goddamn good thing!" swore Mac, wringing out his gob hat and wiping his streaming forelock. We all echoed this, precious as fresh water is aboard a sailing ship in hot seas.

Scraping teak occupied many days in the westerlies. Our hands, already chapped by salt and stiff ropes in the bitter cold, were eroded by the caustic soda used to burn off the bits of varnish which had not been completely scraped off the teak by our knives. Caustic soda, if not used with caution, can eat through skin and flesh too, right to the bone. No safety equipment was used in those days, although we used a sort of dish mop, made of sticks, rags, and string, to apply it. Inevitably, the wind blew it onto our skin, and even into an eye or two, but prompt washing prevented serious damage. Worse even than the sessions with caustic soda, though, were the many days of washing paintwork with "*Soda Vatten*" into which the hands were constantly dipped. I lifted a layer of skin right off my hands, and everyone's nails turned black as we "soogeed" all the white paintwork. Tredge had mixed this burning cleanser unusually strong. In his zeal, he had thrown all the soda on board into the solution, however, we had the consolation that as all the soda was used, no more soda washing could be done.

During this period of painful toil, Commander Butlin had loaned me a book on the sea. In it was a poem eulogizing the magic of sea life. A sailor, done with voyaging, forgets the hardships and remembers only the curve of the sails, the stars in the tropic night, and so on. I stared cynically at that effusion. What utter trash, scribbling such crazy myths. I thought I would never forget the sores on my hands, fighting off sleep when both watches were called out, close calls aloft, being wet day and night in the icy westerlies, the faintness coming over me under the heavy weight of changing sails in the tropic heat. How could that fool of a poet imagine that any sailor could forget all that? Yet today, I have to try hard to recall those physical miseries. It is the glorious side of sail that shines out so clearly in my memories.

After the soogeeing, I was assigned to the sailroom to help the sailmaker, doing chores for him such as ripping up the old sails and taking out the stitches so that the sails could be reused as buntline clothes. "Tell me Jack," he said one day, "the postmistress in Germein, didn't she give you a stack of newspapers? I've read about all there is aboard here. Let me have a look at them for a change." I ran to retrieve the papers and shoved them into his hands.

Shortly afterwards, the sailmaker rejected the lot and returned them, declaring, "I can't get on with all that stuff about how many cows come to be sold in Adelaide market last week and all about how many turnips was growed somewhere, and what the rabbits are doing to the crops and the blowflies in the sheep. I'm no farmer."

I grinned at him, "So you wouldn't sell the sea and go to a farm?" (a reversal of the sailors' old saw about farms and the sea).

"I'm glad to have the papers back," I continued, "because they stop a draft that comes whistling into my bunk fit to cut me in two."

"Much better to find a nice young man to keep you warm." I laughed. "Heck no, I much prefer these. A lot less trouble." The sailmaker scoffed, "Well you could be worse off than you are, maybe. You might have been such a one as Barbara. Olav fooled that poor girl. I know Olav. He never earned any money in his life. How is he going to keep a wife?"

"I dunno."

At work in the sailroom, we were sometimes joined by Otto, who crept in and did the odd bit of stitching. He had spent the time in port in hospital in Port Pirie, because of having contracted tuberculosis. He was likely to die on the voyage home, and lived like a pariah in a solitary cabin, and was even given separate eating utensils. With little or no work to do, it left him with plenty of time to mull over his misfortune. After four years service at sea, he now had no chance of getting his officer's papers, even if he should survive to try. If he couldn't breathe out his infection on the rest of the crew, he found in me a victim on whom he could expend his distress.

As we worked, the sailmaker and I discussed books we had read. Otto broke in, "If I had been your parents, I'd never let you read all those sea books. I'd have forced you to learn how to cook, sew, and look after a house instead. You ought to have been taught things a girl needs to know. Make sure you'd be some good to a man in bed too." He licked his thin lips.

Stung, I retorted, "What good is all that *hausfrau* stuff if one is not alive doing it? You would have robbed me of all thoughts, ideas, dreams." He waved his arm.

"A gurl doesn't need anything else. It's the best thing for her to be able to please a man. Bloody bitches ... should be kept in their places. They know they got a cunt, too, and it ain't just to piss with."

I took a deep breath to fill my jerseyed chest, I hoped, to the bull-like proportions of the sailmaker. "You're just full of that muck because you see me here, strong and well. You are jealous of me, with a sea career ahead. That's why you do the mean ..." I held back. If I let on that he upset me, he would only enjoy even more his vile trick of slipping into my cabin when it was my watch on deck and filling my tooth glass with turds and his tuburcular spit. I continued, "that's why you detest yourself. That's why you can't bear to see a girl given a chance to use her brain the way she wants, when you, yourself have no future at sea. Hell! Maybe you're going to *die* soon. Then where will all your hate get you?"

The old sailmaker's thick neck pushed his head up and he paused in his stitching to stare at us, then admonished severely, "Hey there. You young ones. Don't you go saying such things."

Otto trembled and I shook, frightened by my capacity for cruelty. We stayed silent for the rest of the watch.

How did I come to be so callous that I could kick a man when he was down? Was this the "Brock" turning sour and vengeful under the constant badgering? Brock, my surname, means badger, and I had taken on the aggressive biting and snarling of that animal when teased. Perhaps now that Otto was weak as a girl, he was in the same boat as I, in a way. Therefore, we were enough alike to irritate each other, as do an Englishman and an American. A foreigner, being completely different, can be excused his faults. Still, provoked, I had spat venom. To my surprise however, I discovered at the end of the voyage that I had not been the only one to be exasperated by this tragic yet irritating invalid. When we were being paid off in Glasgow, the other Germans, Ceysen, and I were in the office. The Germans, who had been called back to their country by Hitler, repelled each other, as I noted earlier, like magnets of the same polarity. Ceysen was not inclined to think kindly of Germans either with his memories of Germans in Belgium during his childhood in World War I. The consul was taking each seaman singly to his inner office. When I entered it a Bible was held out to me and I was asked to put my hand on it. The consul began to question me.

"You will swear to tell the truth and nothing but the truth, so help you God?"

"I do."

"There was a German seaman on board the barque *L'Avenir*?"

"There were several Germans on board."

I thought perhaps for some reason the consul wanted to question me about Jumbo. I remembered the banter about spying for Hitler.

"But this one was ill. He did no work?"

"Oh yes, Otto. He did no work, but he used to sew sails sometimes."

Seated in a chair beside the consul, our captain shifted uneasily and then waved his arm in a nervous gesture. "This man, he was sewing sails just when he want to, only to pass the time, you understand? But he not doing any hard verk, you see." The consul nodded briskly.

I chimed in with the master. "Oh yes, just for occupation, not real work."

"You never saw the captain threaten to strike this man?"

The consul questioned me cooly, looking me hard in the eyes. "No."

He leaned forward and said "This German seaman claims that the captain, in an argument, gave him a blow with his fist and knocked him out. Did you ever see or hear this?"

My heart beating fast, I replied "No," firmly, but my salt-hardened thoughts rejoiced. I cheered, inside. Hurrah for our staunch good Old Man! I hoped he really gave that rat a right good wallop!

My face must have revealed my thoughts because the consul looked at me sharply and proceeded, "You have not even heard any rumours of such an attack by the master on this seaman?"

"No."

I maintained my position stalwartly and was released from the office. Over the low division of the little room where I had been interrogated, I could hear Chesus, Jumbo, and the others give the same negative evidence about the fight between the captain and Otto, which, it was obvious, must actually have taken place. Despite Otto's pitiful state, no one testified on his behalf.

L'Avenir began to pick up the northeast trade winds. With Tredge as officer of the watch, and with stowaway George and I taking continuous turns at the wheel, we were allowed less sleep than the rest of the watch. With the first mate they all worked as daymen. During one spell at the wheel, towards dawn but still dark enough for me to steer by a star, I was amazed to find that this star had suddenly zipped to the other side of the ship. Dazed, and trying to figure out how the star had moved so weirdly, I heard the stowaway's voice floating up to the steering platform.

"Kerrrisst! Look at the siles!"

George was whisper-shouting as he rushed aft from his post up forward as lookout. "The bloody siles!" he repeated in his hoarse Aussie accent, making me lift my eyes aloft to look at the canvas. "Wot the 'ell's the matter wiv 'em?" he demanded. *L'Avenir* hung in stays, everything aback. It was the ship that had swung about, not the star, while I had dropped asleep on my feet, like an old horse!

"I guess you had better find Tredge and haul the headsails out to windward," I advised George, thinking fearfully of the master stomping out to view the mess, rather than thinking what it might do in dismasting the ship. George raced off to find Tredge snoozing deeply on the skylight bench. He thrummed on Tredge's back, which straightened as his head swung up to see the sails flat against the masts. Tredge and George floated like wraiths about the deck, bringing the staysails and jib out to windward while I put the helm up. Gently, with leisurely grace, the barque swung onto her course again as the sails filled, just as if she had not had a little jaunt on her own while I slept on my feet and Tredge nodded off dreaming of heroic deeds in faraway ports.

At breakfast, Commander Butlin observed, "Strange thing last night, did the wind change? It doesn't usually in these parts. But we noticed the moon shining out of the port in one position and then it suddenly disappeared. Couldn't see it out of the port at all. Also we felt the ship right herself for a while and go on the other tack and then heel steadily on course again." Tredge occupied himself crumbling his bread. I felt some explanation was owing those keen minds. "Odd," I agreed. "The moon set extra early here, maybe."

"Nooo, that couldn't be. We have been noting the moon's rising and setting particularly, because we are having fun working out the old "lunars" that used to be employed in navigation."

This lunacy of *L'Avenir* waltzing about in the steady trades left the commanders more than suspicious. I felt that Tredge and I, as watch dozers, must have committed an unusual and extreme crime of the sea. Later I heard from an old ship master. "Very common, such weariness in sail," he reassured me. "We used to place buckets of water right in our paths pacing the poop. If we slept while still walking, well ..."

With only two of us standing watch I had more responsible jobs assigned me, such as sounding deep tanks, overhauling the ship's charts, and tarring a winch. While I was warming the tar for this job on the galley stove, *Koken* even informed me, "I hearing de boys dey say your work much better now, you go fast." Even the raucous Bergman, after I had heaved up buckets of water to him for four hours through the galley skylight hoarsely praised me. "Oho Yackie are stark! Beeg muscle in arm." I even began to dream of the day when those same muscles could flick the spiky wash-down hose over *his* feet and make *him* dance to my tune.

But pride goeth before a fall. When changing sail a number of daymen and George and the commanders and the master were engaged in hoisting a topsail yard. The halliard was not long enough to reach a particular capstan and a line needed to be bent to the halliard. Alert, I stepped forward and began throwing it in a double sheet bend using an unusual, quick method of crossing the lines, instead of first making a bight. Perhaps not being familiar with this method, the seamen chorused "She's doing it wrong, the goddam gurl. She can't make that knot. Don't let her." My hands went nerveless. Suppose my sheet bend didn't hold? The tons of the yard crashing down, crushing, killing ... Meekly I handed the halliard to Redbeard, whose pimply face seemed almost to burst with triumph. He flourished the halliard into the very bend I had been making. I had it right, but like a ninny, I had just weakened. I was cross with myself. Taunts of "Yackie can't make a sheet bend" brought rage rolling in my gut. I wanted to sing out "Call me a tart, that's absurd. But insult my seamanship, NO!"

I held my tongue though, with the authoritative captain and the highly trained naval commanders about. Stupid to make a scene in front of all. Perhaps from cowardice, or perhaps with discipline, I leaned over my capstan bar, arms trembling. The steady heaving smoothed my frustrations. Reason said it was no use railing; I had been at fault. But it was hard to master the constant brainwashing. Take any boy in the crew, single him out as not fit to be a member. Tell him over and over that he has not the aptitude for anything worthwhile. Tell that boy that God, even, did not intend him for this work and you will build up an enormous handicap against him doing even an ordinary job. My answer to the ambassadors from God used to be, "If God had intended me to sit at home all day, a regular baby factory, why didn't he make me so dumb, like a queen bee, so that I would be content with no other life but that? Why has He given me the urge to understand the way of a ship at sea? Why can I solve problems in navigation? Why have I got hands just like yours, able to turn in an eye splice or rust chip, and eyes that can read a compass card as well as yours can, and ears to listen for a foghorn like yours do? Why did He put it into my heart to come to sea and help me to get here too?

Instinctively, I knew that this sentimental reasoning was more effective than throwing a bucket of coal at them. Chesus retreated to standing by the fore shrouds, picking his teeth while gazing out to sea. Dennis, seated on the fore bitts, looked down at his big square bare feet, shuffling them about. Letonen, half understanding, rejoicing in his newly learned English, kept up hoarse giggles of "oh yes oh yes," and Jumbo's black beret slid away into the shadows behind the ventilator from his listening post there.

Chapter 17

Murder and Rape?

Jumbo was really having a bad time. One day he detained me in an arm grip. "The mate, he been much angry wit you dat you vas drinking wit *segal* maker and donkeyman," he hissed.

"Guess I must have been a darn fool. Hadn't looked at it that way, you know. I suppose, come to think of it though, we were drinking."

A vision of my half-finished glass of wine rose up from its obscure corner of a picture in which I bathed in the bright glory of the company of the elect.

"Dat ben no place for a lady of goot familee," Jumbo chided me.

"Who ever told you I was such an idiotic thing?"

Jumbo's face flickered, nonplussed. I added softly "still, the 'liner she's a lady,'" trying to bring the lady into a seagoing line at least.

"Vas dis?" said Jumbo, not comprehending at all.

"Oh nothing," I smiled vaguely, "it is just a little poem from England you brought to mind, which mentions ladies."

Jumbo shook his fist in a gesture of impatience. "You never listening to me. You so ... so ..." He could find no English word to fit his exasperation.

"Stubborn?" I suggested.

"*Ach*, I know not. You making boys mat alzo. You all times saying you be an officer at sea some day. They not liking dis from girl." He tried to instill some European ideas of discretion into a blunt Canadian. "It been different if you had been Finnish girl."

"Like the *Viking* girl?"

"Well yes, she only helping steward. But *you*! You vant to be good as man. You not lissen me. You drive me overbort! You not doing vat I saying. But too late it is! When I coming, falling down from up in rigging. Down dead on deck. At your feet, *then* you sorry!"

"Humpf." I shrugged my shoulders with outer calm, but with an anxious stomach inwardly. "Well you bloody ought to take care," I told him. "Hold tight up there, so as to make sure you don't land in a mess on deck."

Jumbo plopped down into the fore bitts and burst into tears. "You not caring for me. You care nothing ..."

I looked at him, dumbfounded, at a loss how to calm that stout box of a chest emitting heavy, quiet sobs. Ringing through my mind I heard "'I weep for you,'" the Walrus said." Barbara's voice also echoed in my mind. "Ever see a man cry? It's terrible."

I bargained, "If only you'll stop crying, I'll do anything to please you, only just don't cry. I'll act the prim prissy girl, not chum up with the sailmaker or join in with the boys when they laugh at the cats '*twa block*' [copulating] on the hatch." Jumbo's eyes turned towards me, and I thought of a crocodile gloomily glancing up from a muddy creek, with its baleful but acute look.

"You only saying dis. You must be wearing hat and hendbeg like real lady ashore, alzo."

I listened as Jumbo dictated these extra terms. Jesus! A hat! A handbag! I'd lose it for sure, and all my shore going money in it too. A hat! I moaned, thinking of my desperate clawing at a massive creation of lace, ribbons, and frills I had been forced to wear as a four-year-old going for a fashionable carriage ride in St. Andrews, New Brunswick. I would suck and bite at the chin elastic of such a contraption, venting my rage at the uncomfortable headgear. Now, however, I searched through my trouser pockets.

"Gee, if only I could find you a handkerchief."

"Vas dis you looking for?"

"*Naselduk*," I translated into Swedish, the esperanto of *L'Avenir*. I thought it ridiculous to use the Swedish "*duk*" which implied heavy canvas duck to an English mind, for wiping away tears. "Mine sleeve, that I must use then," sniffed Jumbo. Looking at Jumbo sitting there, revolt seized me.

"No, I won't!"

"You won't?"

I stamped my foot. "I refuse to be a priggish girl for you or anyone else. I know you may be right saying I'd get on better aboard here if I didn't fraternise and be straightforward and honest with the boys, but why pretend that I don't want to follow a sea career? Why shrivel up at their stupid swear words? The kind of girl who puts on a big pretence that she is so proper, she's up to real mischief, for sure. After all, I *am* a girl, so I ought to know, more than you do, about that."

I swung about and stamped aft, leaving Jumbo humped over in lugubrious thought to figure all that out. Nevertheless, the dice rolled later in a storm, resulting in a victory for Jumbo and a perplexity for me. With the watch I had headed for the shrouds to scramble aloft and take in the t'gallants. Jumbo stopped me, and stripping off his Prussian military greatcoat, which he prized, he tossed it into my arms and ordered, "Vait. You be holding dis for me while I go up in rigging." Then he leapt after the others and swarmed aloft. There was plenty of wind blowing, but he had taken it out of my sails. He had taken me completely aback with this insult. I swore as I scouted about for some niche into which I could stuff this unwanted burden, and free my hands to mount into the shrouds with the others. Hang it on a belaying pin rail? It would tangle with the purchase. Leave it on the hatch? The wind would carry it off, and besides, the seas were coming right over. Drop it in the flushing scuppers? I hadn't the heart to stoop so low. By the time I had fumbled with how to rid myself of this "old coat of the sea," it was too late to be of use going aloft, and I joined the small deck party letting go the cluelines. As my shipmates descended, I expected to be the butt of their sneers. Surprisingly, they hailed me in a friendly manner, with a sort of high-toned superiority over the girl who stayed where she belonged, on deck. It was a quirk in male psychology which Barbara had tried to interpret for me in her example of the womanly Scots girl.

These Finnish ships were run on economy rather than safety-first lines. In order to save coal oil, the ship's lights had not been lit while in the lonelier and unfrequented parts of the ocean. However, as we were now sailing through some of the shipping lanes, they had to be lit at sunset. Each member of the crew took a turn at attending to the lights. The lamplighter reached them through a small locker under one side of the fo'castle head. The port light had to be lit through what is aptly termed on the seven seas, "the shithouse." An agitated Jumbo sought me out with a warning.

"I listen and I heard the boys say ven you go take your turn to light dis lamp, dey all are taking you in the *skithus* and den overboard dey are trowing you. Dey can do dis, ven de mate he be not looking. Dey say it not law dat a woman vork in Finnish ship outside Baltic sea. You not suppose be on board here for vorking. It not be so bat ven you was Finnish girl, but you not. Day say you take job from dem. Woman take seaman's job."

I laughed.

"Dis not for laughing," Jumbo said urgently.

"It makes me smile to think the boys have paid me such a compliment."

"*Ach* so? And how be dis?"

"A lefthanded compliment maybe, but they must find I am improving as a sailor if they think I am such a menace to their future jobs they have to kill to prevent me and other women, perhaps, from taking over the ships from them. Ha ha! That sure is one hell of a compliment to a girl."

"Dis I not understand. You vill never hear, never, vat I telling you. You always laughing so. Take care! Or you been dead. Dis you must listen. Do as I telling you. Go to the mate and be telling him dat you will not lighting dis lamp ven it comes to your turn."

I could not go whining to the mate or any of the after guard with such a tale. I had to learn to face up to such difficulties alone. These situations could come up again during my future life at sea. Anyway, Jumbo's warning might only be a joke, maybe to repay me for the "Indian Chief" father joke I had played. Still, I had had to bite and kick my way free from many a semi-good-hearted struggle when corralled by the boys when no one was about and I wondered if Jumbo's rumour might be true. There would be no Queensbury rules here. Even the boys slapped each others faces when they quarrelled. I never actually saw them box. Little Danska had once seen me bothered by Ekstrom's clutching, and made a suggestion.

"Yackie, you take belaying pin and put hole in his head. Then he must go have it fixed, you see, by captain. Captain asks him 'How you get that hole in your head?' Then that man, he must say it, 'Why Yackie have put that hole in my head.' So he gets black mark on his discharge paper and he can never get certificate as mate."

"Ah, that's kind of mean."

I had done nothing until my Canadian-Irish good nature was driven too far. Ekstrom, when relieving me on lookout, tackled me. Angrily, and without good humour, I wriggled free and retreated aft. Grabbing a belaying pin, I slid silently up behind the foremast in the darkness, and like an Indian with tomahawk in hand, I contemplated cracking his skull. Ekstrom sat calmly on the forehatch, swinging his feet. I only needed to take aim, or perhaps, better to swat him with the pin. But this, this might be murder. Here I was, actually shaking with the lust to kill! You read about others having the feeling, but never believe that you yourself could be swept up by such an evil passion. "Violence begets violence," an old sailing master in a sea story had said when faced with mutiny. That thought restrained me, and if not very high-minded, at least took the form of a good angel putting a hand on my tense arm, which had been ready to commit a deed I might regret to the end of my days.

Thus, a belaying pin was not going to solve my lamp-lighting dilemma. How to stave off a number of attackers? Female cunning? I thought that was despicable, but after all, Delilah had found Samson's weakness. Where did the boys' hair grow? Certainly they were ambitious to keep their jobs, which they feared I might usurp. Dennis, the ship's premier gossip, fell in with my plan of defence unwittingly, as I engaged him in casual conversation.

"What do you think happened to Frasne? He was so clever at dodging seas and then think how he lived all these months aboard, through the westerlies and all, and now for no reason he seems to have overbalanced overboard in these fairly calm waters."

Dennis grunted, "Serves that blooming cat right if he did. Given tinned salmon, made a fuss of. An animal. While us, what do we get? Slops fit for pigs!"

"But I don't believe anyone could have been so mean as to take it out on a helpless animal by throwing him overboard. The captain misses him badly. He was almost broken-hearted. Look how he had the whole ship searched, alow and aloft. Well I don't suppose Frasne will turn up now. No one can ever find out for certain who was so cruel as to drop him overside if they did. But if like harm came to me, it would be known exactly who did it." I blurted.

No great surprise crossed Dennis's face on hearing this far-fetched assertion from me, which made me wonder if he had heard some talk of me going the same way as feline Frasne. Nevertheless, on such an extremely long voyage as L'Avenir's homeward trip, wild unreason can race through the minds of those on board. There is nothing to grasp. The horizon circles all, and is never overcome, it is a magic circle which disappears as one approaches, like the end of a rainbow. In the tropics too, the heat is so great that the head becomes dizzy. Alow, in the box-like compartments, the air is still. The ports closed tight against a sudden squall, keep the air like a heavy drug. On deck it burns. One falls into a sort of trance as the shimmering heat takes on forms. Hatreds can boil, and little events on the ship loom out of all proportion. Against the grey monotony of repetitive labour, the irritations become violent, and voyagers can be aroused to silliness and even savagery. So Otto drooled his sexy innuendos, Miss Kronig took to the bottle with the airman, and the crew plotted to murder "Yackie." I broke into tears under the strain in the airman's cabin, and the cat was lost.

Dennis's curiosity was whetted, and he wanted to know how anyone could detect what might be done in the middle of a dark and rainy night. I admitted that it might not be possible at the moment, but if I was to be shoved overboard, when my papers were collected by the master, the authorities would find my journal of the trip. In it were the names of those under suspicion of wanting my death. Easy then, with a bit of sharp questioning ..." His jaw dropped, almost with delight at having such a spicy bit of news to carry to the fo'castle, with the importance of headlines in our newspaperless community. He hurried off, to announce that the girl must be taking an interest in just who attacked her, as she had all their names in a book in her cabin. I chuckled as he disappeared, picturing his full lips jabbering all that rubbish.

The ruse seems to have worked, or maybe it was just good fortune that when my turn came to light the lamps, everyone's attention was elsewhere. I slipped alone thorough the alleyway, a grey blur like a scuttling ship's rat. I don't think the sidelights were ever lit with such alacrity. But I stopped to make sure, leaning over from the deck above, that they glowed brightly, and they could be reported as "*clare lanterne*" to the mate. Their gay colours shone, protecting *L'Avenir* and me as we ploughed through the dark seas.

Chapter 18

Doldrums

Miss Kronig's leg, injured when she jumped down into the tossing ship's boat when going ashore in Australia, had now healed. The next thing we knew, she was climbing out to the main yardarm. "By golly, she's a grand sport, isn't she?" I remarked, admiring her to the mate, as we watched her swinging out on the flemish horse. "Well over fifty years old, and so wiry and tall as she looks there."

"That ain't the way a woman should look," he scowled, "they's only good when they look like woman. Warm and fat." Redbeard, nearby, with beard pointed to the sky, squinting up at Miss Kronig's fabulous athletics, echoed the mate. "That alt woman, way up there; she is mad," he pronounced and walked away.

Miss Kronig, when she climbed down, came to sit and rest on the after hatch, where I was enmeshed in a coil of ratlin stuff, my hands fiddling fast to untangle it. The sailmaker had given it up in despair and thrown it at me with instructions to clear it. Miss Kronig addressed me confidentially.

"It's about Jumbo. He tells his troubles to me. I speak German so well. Really, it is rather a shame the way you treat Jumbo. You won't make up your mind about him."

"Carmen couldn't be worse to Jose, eh?"

I laughed, but she remained deaf to this frivolity, continuing seriously.

"He says the boys are making it hell for him in the fo'castle, on account of you. They threw cold water over him last night! He can't stand much more. Not unless he can be sure you want to be more than friends with him and get engaged."

"Well, if he can't stick a little water he's no good to me. How much backbone has he? How could he stand up to half what I have to take from the crowd up forrard? *Water!* That's nothing! They turned the deck hose full on me; kept it on a good half hour, while we washed 'undra backen,' latrines and all. Ohman held the hose, laughing enough to split his bloody face. Cold weather too. I was sopped and shivered the rest of the watch, but smiled all the time as though I were a belly dancer, like it was fun. Water, Jumbo, Huh!"

Miss Kronig began "Then you want me to tell him you don't ..." but was interrupted by the mate.

"Get below, old woman. You gabble too much with the crew. Yackie must be doing work now."

Miss Kronig jumped to her feet as though the mate had prodded her with a marlin spike. Turning to face him, her breath whistled out. "Ooooh," she gasped. "Well of all the ..." she searched for a word strong enough to express her indignation with the desperation of a fish gasping for oxygen in the bottom of a boat. Then she drew herself up and addressed the mate. She might have been an Egyptian Pharaoh rising from his sarcophagus to rebuke a rebellious subject. "You have absolutely no business speaking to me like that." Her strong short hair seemed to bristle with her fury, and her slacks shook at their bottoms as she stamped her foot. "I shall simply *not stand* for this rudeness."

The mate stood his ground. "You bothering all the crew when they working. Get below to your cabeen. Get! Or staying quiet." Turning on his heel, military style, the mate retreated before Miss Kronig might take a notion to lay about her in my belaying pin cum murderous fashion.

"He is a *NASTY nasty* man. I dislike him intensely," she hissed with utter distaste.

"Well, I'd much rather him than Jumbo. But there, that's how it is," I stated tersely, as one of Mother's north country ancestors would have done. "Guess you'd better hop off though," I warned her, not wishing to provoke more discord. Her eyes widened at my assertion of preference for the mate.

"So then, I'll have to go back to Jumbo and tell him how you feel." She set out on the warpath.

I wondered if on the way, she might be going to pursue the old sailmaker and make him frantic too. He had finally deserted his airy sailroom and taken refuge in a smelly corner of a cabin up under the fo'castle head. All his assistants had to work there as well, and sometimes me too. There he had begged, "Save me Jack! Don't you let that old scarecrow know I'm here, or I'll wring your neck, that I will! She'll come in here and *get* me, chitter chattering, driving me crazy. For *God's* sake Jack, see that she don't know about this place," he had pleaded.

I had hardly gone to take my trick at the wheel when evidence arrived that Miss Kronig had not bothered to waste her time dallying with the sailmaker. A wobbling group staggered past the wheel platform, weighted down carrying a fainting Jumbo. Did I imagine that for a second he turned his head as they passed the wheel? If so, he was not going to see any distress on this helmsman's face. Nevertheless, the whole ship was stirred into a turmoil over the awful decision that had to be made about him. Should Jumbo be operated on for appendicitis or not? The commanders advised the master against any attempt to operate. "We had a like situation in a small, doctorless vessel. When we arrived in port, we were complimented by the medico who took over the case. We thought we had done well not to interfere by using any violent measures on the patient."

In the dogwatch up forrard I asked Dane Doctor about Jumbo's condition.

"A man that has enough life in him to be watching who comes and goes out the fo'castle door? Such a one is not gravely ill." So Jumbo was thrown to the tender mercy of that old lion, Tredge, who rejoiced in this glorious opportunity to win medical fame. He fumbled about among his numerous dusty bottles in the medicine chest, while mumbling their Latin names, and selected one. That one must have had all the punch and power Tredge had in his fist when he knocked out the "six beeg Sout Americans," for subsequently I saw Jumbo, pale and pasty, as Dennis described him, stumbling out frequently and miserably to the foul *skithus*, now the scene of a murderous attack on his bowels, rather than the one he had anticipated the boys might give me.

Quite a number of the boys had been entered as "*sjuk*" (sick) in the logbook. Some, no doubt, were *sjuk* as a means of getting a little break in the routine. The steward asked me, one morning, as I sat with the galley staff at five a.m. coffee, "Why you never sick, Yackie?" *Koken* stopped chewing to hear my recipe for unfailing buoyancy.

"Why should I be sick? Good life. Good air and food." I waved my cup in hearty salutation towards *Koken*. He had been sipping his coffee, but his eyes, peering over the rim of his cup, popped with pleasure, instead of fear, as when they had threatened to cut his throat in Australia. He even blushed at being complimented. What with Jumbo and the number who were *sjuk*, our thoughts turned to health.

"I heard a number of the boys got hernias doing all the pully hauly there is to do aboard," I said to the steward. With his keyhole-peeking mind he would have the details of goings on that were kept dark from me. The steward nodded. "I beat those boys to the hernia," I declared, patting my belly. "I don't belong to the belly button society any more. Lost my badge." The cook steward and their ragamuffin helpers stiffened with curiosity, like a row of listening rabbit ears. "Sure I did," I continued, "When I was two years old. The surgeon who stitched me up told my mother 'I hate to cut up a little baby like this, but there is no other way out.' However the poor doctor was the one who should have been pitied. Dr. Macrae, he died shortly afterwards on the battlefields of France. He wrote a very beautiful swan song. I don't suppose you Swedish fellows know it though; 'In Flander's fields the poppies grow ...'" The galley staff shook their heads, muttering "*Yevla, Tsk tsk.*" Such far-fetched, half understood tales in English reached beyond the border of the hard-working monotony of their lives.

Like other sea cooks in Finnish ships, our *Koken* knew his job, having been at school for a year to learn it. This was a change from ancient days, when the stupidest of the ordinary seamen, or perhaps a mere ship's boy, was shoved into the galley to make out as best he could. *Koken* baked the most delectable bread I have ever tasted, even on shore. Perhaps it was exercise and sea air, but I dreamt of food all day, craving sweetness. Sometimes I emerged from the steward's pantry victorious, ballooned as though I were pregnant, with a pile of stolen sugar buns stowed away inside my shirt. Chesus was also an expert thief from the galley. Often while I heated a can of washing water there, when the cook was briefly absent, I would see a gawky shadow swing by, like an oversized Burmese puppet. Levitation seemed to take possession of some of the sugared raisin breads that were cooling on the table, and they deftly floated away. With those loaves, cheers of "welcome" greeted Chesus in the fo'castle. Under the spell of his heady successes, Chesus grew bolder. One day the skipper flung open an empty cabin door, from which emanated suspicious sounds and smells. Inside, he found a tableau: Chesus and an alcohol stove, a can of sea water containing (oh whisper it) *eggs snitched from the chicken coop.* It's a wonder that Chesus lived!

We led them a life, that galley staff, who spent their days sliding about on a greasy floor, holding sloshing cauldrons in a seaway, and who dripped beads of sweat into the food as they bent over preparing it when the galley was hellish hot in the tropics. They had to keep a constant stream of meals coming out. One watch would spring up ungratefully on deck after devouring their victuals, and then the other would take its place, clamouring for lobscouse or pea soup and pancakes, or what have you. Aboard ship, the cook, steward and their boy helpers are the despised butts of the deck sailors. If the food doesn't satisfy their lusty appetites, a cook might have the whole contents of the slushy "kid" (pot) dumped over his head. I may have been scared aloft, and exhausted hauling lines, but I never envied the days of that ghetto of galley slaves with their dawn-to-dusk peeling of potatoes, chopping meat, pounding the iron-hard stockfish, boiling beef, roasting meat, baking bread, simmering fruit soup, frying blood pancakes, emptying ashes, filling their coal-hoppers, and swilling garbage. The steward washed and scrubbed and folded linens, dusted and polished, and waited on the passengers.

Our creeping passage and the lack of fresh food resulted in many rebellious stomachs. One evening while I stood steering on the wheel platform, the captain and steward lounged on the main hatch, below me. Though I was unable to see their features in the dusk, from the few words of Swedish I had picked up and the tone of their voices, I sensed the furrows of worry creasing their brows. They discussed starvation. "*Mat ... brod ... icke potatis. Sistonkorfs inte bra, Hur myket?*" (meat, bread, no potatoes. Not good, how much?) How best to string out the provisions after so many days, now going on to 120, so far at sea. And goodness knows, how many yet to come. I took comfort in the holds replete with tons of wheat. Captain Jeffreys, head of the Limehouse navigation school, had recounted the case of one of the grain ships. Her hungry crew had ground their own wheat. "Healthy," Captain Jeffreys stated. "At least such things in a sailing ship are a lot healthier than cleaning deep tanks in the poisonous air in the bowels of a steamer."

The porpoise breathing humanly, and playing about the bow, and the albacore laughing their rainbow colours as they leaped high out of the sunlit water were destined to be threatened by a spear which the donkeyman had forged in the well deck on his anvil. The skipper, dreaming of fried fish, spent hours face down in the net under the bowsprit, his round bum in the air, and beside him the donkey man, with his sinewy arm upraised with spear poised as they scanned for porpoise and albacore. How I hoped they would miss! But this was how the dolphin had become their victim and was made into those dozens of meatballs by "*Koken.*"

Chapter 19

Spellbinding Trade
Winds

The sense of isolation, grandeur, and space engendered by the succession of long days and nights passed in the open ocean brought on a magical spell. Miss Kronig expressed its effect well one day as she leant on the rail, looking out to the horizon: "I feel as if I could go on like this for ever and ever. Somehow I just don't look forward to reaching land." From where I was scraping paint spots off the deck nearby I grunted "Nor do I," in reply. But the ocean was not ours alone. A steamer hove into sight and headed for us, breaking that circle of aloofness that had surrounded us for so many weeks. We began to imagine that all sorts of portentous events must have taken place during our months isolated at sea. What if war had broken out? Perhaps the Depression was over. The British commanders' thoughts flew to King George V and his very serious illness. Had he survived? The master prepared to check his chronometers. By signalling in semaphore, the British commanders obtained the check for him. As the steamer approached, we could see that her name was *Mopan* out of Liverpool. After five months at sea we called across the eternal cry from sailing ships, "What news?" by megaphone. "Max Baer beat Primo Carnera," came back; an anticlimax perhaps, but reassuring, after five months at sea.

This forerunner of the end of our voyage set me to wondering. Our little steel box, blown hither and yon over the seas, would soon finally fetch land. Aboard, absorbed in the daily life and work, I had drifted, oblivious to my distant home, relatives, sweetheart, and friends, as though they belonged to some far off, unearthly existence. But soon the spiritual cohesion of our narrow community would burst like a bubble when *L'Avenir* warped alongside a dock in Britain. I tried to imagine that moment as I chipped away at the anchor, a monotonous job I had been allotted which gave me plenty of time to ponder my future. On my next voyage I would be a year ahead of the new apprentices. I would be able to show them such skills as how to pass a weather earring, sound deep tanks, or reeve a three-fold tackle, with the standing part coming out of the middle sheave. With muscles hardened by so many months of tough regime, I was able to make my weight felt on the end of a brace. I almost felt myself to be a Swede, and resolved to hold my tongue with Scandinavian silence and act with more aplomb on my next voyage. As to my initial trepidation about my ability to handle the men successfully, I believed that the discipline of sea life was fitting me to meet even that with ease. In spite of the hostility shown me at times, I remembered most the happier occasions when good humour brought laughs right up from the bottom of my lungs. I could not forget how we had laughed at Danska's "nice kisses," when the shark was brought aboard with a remora attached, and the sucker head of the parasite fish was pulled off the shark, or Chesus's drawling description of how he cooked eggs in a cabin. How infectious was Lehtonen's hearty laugh at the antics of big waves slopping aboard and his humour as he described the wet ships *Grace Hawar* and being *Undra Vatten* (underwater) in heavy weather. My chats with the gentle-mannered Ceysen, even the coarse jokes of the little cabin boy and his hoarse chuckles — insidiously I had become at home aboard with these unpretentious folk. Good and bad, I was attached to them all as though they, whom the airman derided as "foreigners," had become my family. Now, if I were to join a new ship, how awkward to have to become acquainted with the foibles, names, and natures of an entirely different crowd.

I glanced up at *L'Avenir's* foremast and her gracious sails. My hands had touched nearly every inch of them, and her spars, deck, and hull as well. My first ship; but "different ships, different ways" as the Dutchman remarked as he went aft to furl the jib. To sign off at the end of the voyage meant disorientation and becoming a stranger in a new ship. Ships and mates would come and go, washed back and forth, meeting and parting on the tides of the oceans. In the bars of many ports, sailors would yarn over their glasses of liquor. Perhaps in the years ahead, some time in Algiers or in Antwerp, one might remark to another, "Do you know that seawoman, Captain Brock?"

"She sails with the X line, doesn't she?"

"That's the one."

Wot's she like?"

"Oh, not too bad," or perhaps "confounded bitch!" in sailors' eternal grumble when something offended their idea of propriety. All these thoughts reverberated through my head. Maybe, after all, I would get married and stay ashore as the airman thought right and proper for me, and the mate had forcefully advised me to do. Probably the commanders thought so too, and then Jumbo had declared that was an idea beyond his loveliest dreams. Well, it could be a cosy, friendly, safe life. But how boring! No, no, not for me! My shipmates may have declared "sea not for gurl," but I was sure that land was not for girl.

As I chipped away at the rusty anchor in the pleasant trade winds, I saw that I wanted was to have the sea and a home too. Why not get married, but take my husband to sea with me? Husbands had taken wives to sea, so why not a wife? I smiled to myself, chipping away more briskly at the anchor, which must have good ground to hold well. It appeared to me to be a symbol of the possibilities before me.

Contact with *Mopan*, the harbinger of land, had begun the disintegration of the unity of *L'Avenir's* crew. Ceysen began to dream of Belgium, Jumbo of the food awaiting him in Hamburg, Dennis of his home on Finsbury Road in London, and the steward wondered if his Greta had remained true to him in Mariehamn. One day a gull flew in our wake, plaintively calling. It was the first of those that would come out to circle us from the wild rocks of the Scilly Isles off Land's End.

"Land Ho!" came the cry at last. I dreaded to hear it and yet sped aloft with George and Chesus to get a better glimpse of the forbidding rocks of the Scillies which loomed in the evening gloaming. Soon we slid by Land's End, and the wind changed to a headwind which sent us to work on the braces. Danska called "Yackie, *Foc brace*," (fore brace) making a childish pun which roused the watch to roars of laughter. Then came Tredge's groaning chantey, "*Ooooo Eeeeer, Englond, Englond, Loooong Haul*," which sobered them up. Outside Falmouth Harbour the pilot climbed aboard and conned us into the roadstead. There we let go the anchor in a smoking roar which announced *L'Avenir's* arrival, 138 days out from Port Germein, Australia.

We laid aloft and soon had the sails in their final furl, then broke out with lusty cheers which rang across the harbour. Deep from the bottom of our hearts they came. Just for this instant, these "peoples of all countries" were cemented together in rejoicing over our victory in the tussle with the hungry sea.

A reporter swung aboard and I directed him to the master's quarters. He returned, saying it was me he wanted for a recital of the adventures I must have had on this voyage. I now felt so much a part of the ordinary crew, and we had encountered so few spectacular happenings on what for a sailor was an uneventful voyage, that I could not conjure up any hurricanes, cargo shifting, or dismasting to relate to him, beyond the normal storms of any passage. Long hours of toil hardly seemed good copy. How could one describe to a strange reporter the inner excitement of being at sea, the bewitchery of the sea in all its faces, or the mighty battle for shipmates' respect? "We caught a shark, but it wasn't a very big one," I offered feebly.

"Perhaps you wouldn't mind if we took some pictures. I wish I could get some exciting angle. Can you suggest something?"

"What about from aloft?"

He responded "That might be very good" and clambered bravely into the fore shrouds after me, thumping up them, his camera swaying and bumping until he reached the futtocks. "I know just how you feel," I called down from the foretop, "nearly everyone has trouble getting over the futtocks." He tried the lubber's hole, but his camera blocked him. I leaned over to take it from his fluttering hand. "If it helps you any, I can take your camera for you," I said. He still hesitated and when his mackintosh caught in the shrouds, he struggled feebly. Below the upturned face of the reporter, I glimpsed the grinning faces of my shipmates on deck. They were finding novel amusement in their flimsy girl apprentice holding out a hand to help a terrified male up into the rigging. With their sniggers I perceived glances of respect for me. Suddenly they made me realize what training I had been given in all the months aboard. The struggles of the anxious fellow whose camera I now held seemed to represent the sort of chrysalid stage from which I had wriggled. There were no more drenched, crumpled sea wings for me. I had emerged on the voyage, and could now spread my sea wings and go anywhere as a fully fledged butterfly of a mariner. "I'm afraid I just can't do it," he panted. "We'll have to give up on taking any pictures here." He backed down humbly.

Thus the master and officers of *L'Avenir*, in addition to driving that old barque, with her twisted main deck safely around the world and back again, had also achieved a miracle of sea training by licking a Raggedy Ann into shape, into the makings of a sailor. Used as these hardy seamen were to dealing with tinkers and tailors and soldiers and stowaways and all kinds of rubbishy young men who were sent to sea because their parents couldn't control them, converting motley and unpromising dross into alert sailor material, the captain had completed a harder task and had made good on his Copenhagen promise, "So we are going to make a sailor of you, eh?"

Dennis stopped beside me. "So, I hear you had a letter from Barbara in your mail."

"Yes, and she says a little Olav is on the way."

Dennis evinced great interest in this piece of news, so I told him more. "They are in Tahiti, and Olav loves all the hula girls. Poor Barbara is often left alone and she is quite ill, I believe."

"So that's the way it goes. Well, I'm sorry. She was a nice girl."

From his manner, I wondered if he hadn't been a great admirer of her too. Then newspapers were brought aboard, and the seamen fluttered open the pages in a fever to get news of their own countries. The two Belgians, Ceysen and Albert, tsked "*Ooh la las*" of dismay on hearing the news of the death of their beloved King Albert. Dennis speculated over the mystery of the "trunk murder" which convulsed England, while Danska consulted me on the significance of a report of gold discoveries in Canada. Even the Finns were prodded out of their stoic taciturnity by a photo of a corset advertisement in my *Montreal Sunday Standard*, and babbled zestfully over it. When the papers had all been scanned, glances went shoreward to the green of the fields above Falmouth. The land wafted a fragrance to nostrils that were delicately sensitive after months of pure sea air. We sniffed the pungency of sun-dried hay, finding it sweeter than scent from a bottle.

Chapter 20

Anchored for Good

Otto stood apart from the rejoicing. He drooped sadly, contrasting with the upright lines of his seabag, standing packed beside him. It was now only a reminder of his brief sea career, and awaited the boat which was to take them both ashore with the passengers. I had an impulse to hold out my hand to him and offer him the sailor's valedictory "So long!" or even "Good luck!"

I might have added "Things may turn out for the best after all," but that was a false platitude, almost an indecent offering I felt, to make to that unfortunate sailor. I remained silent after all, hesitating, as I noticed his eyes seemed to dart hatred around the deck. His body slumped like a half-empty potato sack with despair. But for the grace of God, that might be me too, cast on shore, if Erikson refused to sign me on again.

Merry laughter surged from the fo'castle head, as Stowaway George, leaning on the capstan, discussed his predicament with English officials in neat uniforms. They had marched up to George with glum hostility and sharp questions. His hearty charm had melted them, as though they were icebergs put into the Australian desert. Did he persuade them to let him go? Or did they deport him back to Australia, or hold him in England behind bars? Perhaps the commanders, who thought him of good stuff, not to be wasted, pleaded his case for a job at sea. Whatever his fate, he surely kicked it loose, laughing, and hopped on with kangaroo vitality.

Finally orders came for *L'Avenir* to proceed to Glasgow to unload. The Finns greeted this announcement with hails of *Saaatan* (the Devil!), as they had hoped to go to Hull. This was a popular port with them, because many Finns lived there. Even London and Charlie Brown's would have been more favoured. "No chance for you to see woman give little baby beer in Charley Brown's," I teased Sonny, as we hauled on the falls of the ship's boat, which had returned with the news from shore. Sonny even smiled, albeit faintly.

A tug was sent to tow *L'Avenir* all the way around to Glasgow, because she had arrived late for her wheat cargo to enter the market. Under tow, after breasting the ripping tides off Land's End, it did not seem long until *L'Avenir* glided up the lovely Clyde, past weird Ailsa Crag. During this coastwise journey, the boys whooped and whistled when they saw railways, girls, dogs, houses, and cattle again. We passed the vast skeleton of the *Queen Mary* under construction in the stocks. Her size filled us with wonder as we slid by. Her workmen gave *L'Avenir* a cheer of British encouragement, a sound to remember, when they saw this little sailer passing the great giant they were building.

Skimming along beside such placid scenes, sweat and toil seemed out of the picture; however, as we approached Glasgow, we were turned to, to cockbill the yards ready for unloading. The large lower yards had to be swung down on one side to the rail and lashed there heavily to clear space for the cargo to be unloaded on the other side. We had just succeeded in making a smart job of tautening the enormous lashings, when it was found that the pilot had mistaken the side on which *L'Avenir* was to berth. The whole procedure had to be reversed in double quick time too. It was harder than a day of sail changing. The pilot was called some names in swear words that were new even to me.

L'Avenir had a charter for a summer schedule of sailing the Baltic on short cruises with full cabins of good-time passengers, and there was no room for me aboard. Also, hearing in letters from my family that they were anxious to see me before I might enter upon another venturesome voyage, I signed off in Glasgow.

My last glimpse of *L'Avenir* tied up in dock left a sad impression. She looked fettered and dishevelled with her yards sticking out at queer angles. Her hull appeared to have shrunk, and seemed almost to be cowering against the background of dingy buildings that overshadowed her. Somehow she seemed threatened. But with relief that hard toil and the generally good-natured bullying from my shipmates had ceased for a short spell, I shouldered my sea bag and stepped ashore briskly.

I was shocked by the white faces of the land people. Sympathy for them, that they have not known the freshness of the sea, overwhelmed me. I waited too long before attempting to cross the road in the face of whizzing traffic. It was more fearsome than big seas.

As a sailor signed on in a Finnish ship, I possessed no British seaman's discharge book. Instead, the master's good recommendation and certificate of my service on board, stamped by the consul on my being paid off, legally entitled me to claim the amount of sea time I had put in aboard *L'Avenir*. Thus I had nearly a year to my credit of the four required for my certificate as second mate.

Before we left *L'Avenir* and signed off, Jumbo had told me that he had received news that his mother was gravely ill and that he would go straight back to Hamburg. The sailmaker had joked that Jumbo was really talking about a baroness he knew and would see in Germany. Despite this, I listened to Jumbo's declarations and plans for the future. "You will not come more to work for dis bloody Erikson and you can find place some governess wit my auntie; she haf a little girl and you can teach English. Den I will do all I can so you be happy. Dat is all I vish. I haf now place waiting for me in Hamburg East African Line."

It all sounded very regulated and secure. My mind was in a whirl as it seemed that so many voices were shouting advice at me — the mate, Miss Kronig, the sailmaker, Danska. Then, too, I thought about what I perceived as my failures. Had I not thought about marriage while chipping at the anchor? Why did I have to choose either a career *or* marriage? As a woman I wanted to experience all the world. Perhaps Ben would have forgotten me after my year away. I thought about beginning anew and living with Jumbo in Germany. What would it be like to live again in a cultured household, to be stowed safely away for the rest of my life in green, quiet hills, with flowers and a farm with fat, generous, and jovial people to attend to? It almost looked good at that point in those Depression times when I was not sure of having a berth aboard another ship. Jumbo wanted me to see him off on the train as he left for Hamburg. I was not ready to give him any answer, and so bade him farewell with promises to talk further about the future. Then I caught an overnight bus to London.

To my astonishment, Ben, his sister, and her fiancé were there to meet me when I arrived. Ben had signed off the *Bendigo* with wages from a three month voyage, so was able to stay in London for a while. His sister was well-established in quarters in Kensal Rise and I went off to the YMCA. Ben and I never ceased talking; there was so much to tell about my wondrous voyage, my shipmates, and the characters aboard. They were a great contrast to Ben's quiet and courtly manner and his understanding of how I felt about the sea. We also liked the same things, music and museums, and I saw how greatly he differed from Jumbo's dictatorial manner and my raucous shipmates. Yet with the unsureness of my position at that point, I could also see that there was some attraction in Jumbo's secure, practical plans. I confessed this to Ben, who was dumbfounded and left. Next morning, causing a great stir among the intrigue-loving elderly ladies there, a bunch of roses arrived at the YWCA, followed shortly after by Ben. We talked over our situation, and in the end, he suggested that I write to Jumbo, saying that I did not want to see him again. He even dictated the letter, which I found rather harsher than I would have written, but I mailed it, which shows where my heart really lay, even if at that point I was feeling torn in several directions. I never heard from Jumbo again, but occasionally I wondered if he took up with the baroness whom he had talked about to the sailmaker.

Then orders arrived from Erikson through his agents in London. Erikson offered to sign me up to sail as ordinary seaman in *Viking*. That great barque, 4000 tons to *L'Avenir's* 3650, was scheduled to sail for Australia in a couple of months. By signing me on again, the shipowner had granted me a signal honour. According to our original contract, Erikson had in no way obliged himself to sign me on his vessels again if I proved unsuitable as a sailor. My anxiety about being re-engaged was ended; I was to be an ordinary seaman at thirty shillings a month. That was a wonderful moment; the future, *L'Avenir* for Amazon Annette, was all A-One. But there is a Greek fable about Atalanta, just about to win a race, who lost by stopping to pick up a golden apple thrown in her path by her rival. This Atalanta picked up an apple too.

Ben and I talked over the whole question of my rebellion against the role expected of me and my committment to a life at sea, and how we might accommodate both our careers and marriage. We planned to continue with our sea careers until we had each obtained our tickets. Then we planned to sail together, perhaps eventually as owner managers of a small cargo vessel.

Meanwhile, my parents were very anxious that I come home at least for a visit before *Viking* sailed in the fall. I looked for a passage to Montreal, and Ben applied to the registrar for a marriage licence so that we could be married before I sailed to Canada. Ben's sister Ethel and her fiancé were our witnesses along with the Wolffs, two sisters with whom I had been in Girl Guides in Montreal, now living in London. These dear souls worked in London as a dental assistant and a dietician. They even made a wedding cake and provided a feast for our wedding breakfast. Ethel presented me with a bridal bouquet, and I, remembering Barbara and Alan's wedding in Australia, the first I had seen, when I had to be instructed on what to do with my bridesmaid's bouquet, asked Ethel how I was to handle the bride's bouquet. Ben and I began our life together in the attic of the rooming house where the Wolffs stayed before I returned for a brief visit to reassure my parents that their daughter had not only survived her year as apprentice seaman, but had flourished. For the moment Ben and I determined to keep our marriage a secret so as not to impede my forthcoming voyage in *Viking*.

I found a cheap passage for only fifty dollars aboard *Hazlewood*, a collier bound from Swansea to Montreal. The trip was as pleasant a ten days as one could expect for a bride without her new husband, except that the several other passengers and I were always ravenous as the food was meagre. Finally we went in a delegation to the captain and informed him that we were hungry. The upshot was that bread was made available for us to take at any time; however, shades of Marie

Antoinette, I was carrying a piece of my wedding cake for my sister, but only the ribbons were left when we arrived in Montreal.

The ten days at home with my parents were a happy time, but reinforced my conviction that it would be sheer career suicide to tell them of my marriage, so overpowering was their sense of responsibility and of what was fitting. My sister Ruth was equally high-minded, but we had always shared confidences, and I told her of my marriage because I thought someone should know in the event that anything happened to me on the forthcoming voyage in *Viking*. She had met Ben, and despite her qualms, agreed to keep our secret. I could not forget how much I had resented the women at my aunt's home in Taunton who had asked "who did she marry?" about a young woman, not "what does she do?" If society made it almost impossible for a woman to combine a career and marriage, then I felt justified in maintaining secrecy until I had proved by my voyage in *Viking* that both could be compatible. Then I heard from the owners that *Viking* would likely be ready to sail sooner than expected and the visit with my family was cut short. My dear father kindly gave me a passage on the *Empress of Britain* so that I could be on time, and I returned to London and Ben to await my sailing orders.

Ben had a berth as quartermaster on *Jervis Bay*, a steamer that would become famous in World War II, and soon there were only a few days left before he would sail to Australia on a three-month voyage and I would go to Copenhagen to join *Viking*. I received another letter from Erikson's agents that underlined the surge of confidence I had felt when Erikson agreed to sign me on *Viking*. Erikson advised that *Viking* would carry a young girl as passenger to Australia. She was seventeen years old, and her parents had only allowed her to travel on the ship because I was to be aboard.

Meanwhile, my aunt in Taunton had written several times asking me to stay, and I suggested to Ben that I should go at least for a day, or she would wonder why I did not come. Ben agreed to accompany me as far as the station, but when we arrived, to be met by my aunt's chauffeured car, we suddenly both agreed that we should go together and confide our secret to my aunt. My brother had just written to say "I hope you will see fit to look up

Aunt Frances if you can spare the time. She is a most thoroughly sensible and solid sort of person; you can confide in her, if you wish with no fear of untactful little tales." After all, Aunt Frances had survived my youthful prank of riding a horse through the front door of her great house, but perhaps I should have remembered that when I had asked her about the secret passages and tunnel in the house, from the days when it had been a monastery, she had replied firmly that I didn't want to go down there; it was much too dirty and overgrown and was no place for a girl. Perhaps, too, I was fearful of not being able to carry off the deception, and in any event, I was at heart unhappy about having to deceive. So it was that we found ourselves confiding in my aunt. My aunt was horrified as I was now due to sail in *Viking* in a few days, and turned all her formidable guns on me. Aunt Frances was the very same aunt I had mentioned to Dennis as we had approached *L'Avenir* in the boat tossing out from Copenhagen harbour as I began my career, and now she became the *deus ex machina* that ended it. She immediately sent a letter to my mother which I think sums up the implacable beliefs of her generation and class and their uncompromising confidence in them.

Monday   Nynehead Court,
23.9.34   Taunton

Dearest Doreen,

Annette arrived here on Saturday morning at 10 AM for the day and bringing with her a young fellow aged 23. Ben Davis, who she told me was her husband.

They were married at a Registry Office early in July. He is the son of a policeman and is a sailor in the Merchant Service. They did not intend to tell you till A had returned from her next voyage thinking thereby to save you the shock and worry which added to the anxiety you already have at her being at sea. They thought would [sic] be too much for you, but I emphatically told them that they must write at once and tell you as it was the cruellest thing they could do to you to hide it from you a whole year. The young fellow as far as I could judge seemed thoroughly straight forward, clean living and clean minded, serious with a love of books and music and a passion for the sea equal to A's. He had no intention of marrying A until he was in a position to keep her, but apparently she fell under bad influences on *L'Avenir* and it was to save her from further annoyances that he decided he must marry her so as to protect her. They seem to have been fond of each other six years. I have tried my best to persuade Annette to give up going on this new ship and hope I may have succeeded. It is not suitable for a girl to be cooped up nine months with a crew of foreigners and only perhaps two women on board. I suggested that she takes a cargo boat to Montreal and stays a month with you and that the young fellow works his passage out on some boat and there you can thrash out the whole matter. I liked the young fellow and I think you must just be thankful that she has not got tied up to some very undesirable foreigner. He seems almost to worship Annette and has told me he never looked at any other girl. I think poor children that they were worried to death about keeping it secret and really felt it a relief when I insisted on their writing to you. I feel very very sorry for you, but at the same time I think it will work out all right and that they will make a happy life of it and be great companions to each other.

If you feel like it cable Annette to come out to you. It might settle the matter of her not going on this ship which I think is most important. If there is anything further I can do to help you or tell you just write me.

Your loving sister
Frances

Inexorable Aunt Frances forced me to write to the shipowner and reveal my marriage. "It's not suitable, you being cooped up with foreigners for so long," she argued. This brought me utter dismay, because I discovered that marriage cancelled contracts. Mine for my cherished next voyage in *Viking* was vetoed by the owner at once in a blunt statement that "owing to the altered circumstance he cannot now take you." No more chance for me aboard vessels of other lines either, because of course they would want to know, "Why did you leave your last ship?"

I faced a blank wall, which perhaps is hard to understand today, when so many wives continue their careers after marriage, but in those years, even stenographers had to hide the awful secret if they wished to be allowed to continue in their employment after their wedding day. As for a woman in so unconventional a job as a seaman, well, it was just unheard of; the walls were high and not about to come down. In June 1935, when I inquired again of Erikson about the possibility of employment, I was brusquely informed by Gustave Erikson himself that he had given my situation "due consideration, but I can only offer you a berth on usual passenger terms."

My Edwardian aunt, so full of unyielding ideas of propriety and honour, was unable to realize what a loss it was to me, what a waste of valuable human skill and attainment. Now all my years of study were made futile. Now all the intense effort it had cost me to find a berth at sea was useless. She could not even begin to understand the deep joys and sorrows of the vigorous contest that constituted life aboard *L'Avenir* when it was totally beyond her imagination or experience. To her, my life was all whim and adventuring. She was convinced that I must certainly be better off "safely out" of all this, at all costs. Still, to console me for clipping my sea wings, and shoving closed the cage door of domesticity behind me, she suggested cheerily, as one might to a small child after removing a dangerous plaything, "You will be able to voyage with your husband when he becomes a shipmaster." She knew nothing about the sea. Owners did not allow masters to take their wives to sea anymore as had been done in the old days.

Suppose though, by some fluke, this proposition of my aunt's proved possible, and I became an exception to the rule. This brought a vision of me in the future, old and grey, sitting in the wing of the bridge, bending over my knitting, a captain's wife, having no position on board to justify my taking part in the running of the steamer, or daring to interfere in navigational routine, allowed on board only on sufferance. However comfortable such a future might appear to my aunt, it brought no rapture of battling canvas aloft, or joining in the muscular rhythmical camaraderie of hauling in braces. And more important, being already rather old to attain perfection in my craft, as I already was, this blow of my aunt's killed any possibility of learning my trade while pliably young enough to do so. "Oh no! Oh no!" I cried, like someone who was being tortured to force her to recant, "that wouldn't be the same at all. Besides such a life hasn't any meaning when one is old." My aunt, well advanced in years, took this remark amiss and retorted indignantly, "Of course life has just as much meaning when one is old!"

Putting forward such a protest showed that I was wiser than my years. Youth is the time for high adventure; to shiver in dreams at the sight of the ruby and emerald sidelights of a *Kiloran*, or burst out into merry laughter after a sweating night of taking in sail in a storm. I had youth and I had had good prospects, but now I had missed the boat in which to ride the flood tide. "There is a tide in the affairs of men, which, taken at the flood, leads on to ..." The mastery of the ocean? Wrack and ruin? Who could say? That future remained forever a foreign land, one to which I never sailed — the land of *might have been*.

As things were, my husband went to sea on a three-month voyage to Australia, leaving me alone in England. I was sunk as far as seafaring was concerned. So too was my counterpart *L'Avenir*. She was bought by the Hamburg American Line and completely refitted, including wireless. Breaking seagoing tradition, always believed unlucky, her name was changed to *Admiral Karpfanger*. Her last message was an "all's well" as she sailed south of New Zealand in March 1938. Some time later she foundered with all hands. It was never discovered how or where, beyond the recovery of her tailboard at Tristan da Cunha. Could it have been in that area of empty ocean where I had been seized with such unreasoning panic as I stood on lookout in the Wild Westerlies on the fo'castle head, four years before? While I drowned in the overwhelming waves of population in London, my counterpart *L'Avenir* went down to the bottom of the ocean, after having mastered the winds of the world for thirty years.

Epilogue

Farewell to *L'Avenir* in Glasgow, my marriage, and the forced end of my career at sea did not break the ties to *L'Avenir* and my shipmates entirely. Over the years I was in contact with some of them and heard news of others. As I had sailed round the Horn, I became a member of the world wide International Association of Cape Horners. After the war I attended a number of the annual congresses in which members get together to renew acquaintances, to read the names of their comrades who had departed life in the previous year, and to evoke for a moment the sound of sail over water, the occasional melancholy, and the unique comradeship of a long voyage under sail. Perhaps, too, reliving some of those singular, glorious, funny, unearthly, and sometimes terrifying moments under sail at sea brought back their youth, so clear cut in memory despite the turmoil of later voyages and dealings with a multitude of crews since. The 1972 congress in Copenhagen and 1974 at Stockholm brought reunions with a larger number of my *L'Avenir* shipmates. Forty years dissolved in an instant as once more I heard myself called Yackie. The mate took me affectionately by the shoulders to introduce as "Yackie, my apprentice in *L'Avenir*. I taught her all she knows about to be a sailor!"

In Copenhagen the congress toured Kronberg Castle, Hamlet's Elsinore, which I had seen dripping and mysterious in the fog as *L'Avenir* slipped by forty years earlier when we set sail. The castle has a fabulous collection of ship models which I wanted to see, but hardly had I entered when I heard "Yackie!" and MacDowall stepped up to me. I had no difficulty recognizing him. We rattled on ninety to the dozen with memories.

"You had a hell of a time aboard! They made it tough for you, *Tough!*"

"Perhaps I deserved it," I suggested, remembering how spoilt I must have seemed to men used to working sometimes for three days at a stretch in a storm.

"Do you remember my pal Segerstedt, the tall Swede?"

"Oh yes, he worked very hard, and was very quiet."

"He is an engineer now, but he was very sick for years and it was a long time before they found out it was a chip from the enamel plates we used aboard *L'Avenir*, which hurt his stomach all that time.

"Poor Segerstedt! I have heard of this, and never used enamel pots on that account."

"What was the second mate's name?"

"I can't remember, but I should because I have heard of him from time to time from Captain Koivistoinen, who is a 'pure Finn' like him."

I had met Eino Koivistoinen, at the time a member of the crew on *Winterhude*, at Port Germein, when the two ships were berthed alongside each other. In the intervening forty years we had corresponded, exchanging news of our families, and I looked forward to meeting him and his wife at Copenhagen, but he arrived back too late from a long voyage to the Pacific to attend. MacDowall continued,

"And the big lanky German-American fellow, Groth, he used to steal eggs from the chicken coop and cook them in a cabin and the captain caught him! Erikson's son gave me our captain's report of each of the crew. He listed Groth as a thief!"

"I liked Groth, even if he was a thief. I called him 'Chesus' because he said it all the time. Not like that little dwarf of a German, Jumbo, who I'm mighty glad I didn't marry, who said he was a relative of the Kaiser."

"That fellow was a mean teller of tales," said MacDowall.

Out in the courtyard of the castle, a girl's band played *"Vive la Canadienne"* in honour of Apprentice Yackie from so long ago. We walked through the rooms, talking and catching glimpses of the marvellous ship models, and carved seventeenth-century ship's lanterns, until we came to the great model of *Viking*, a beauty at one-half inch scale to the foot. When I looked at her, for a moment I was back in London, feeling again the shattering moment when my voyage in her, and my career, were cancelled. I never did see all the models, as we were summoned to return to the buses which were to take us to the coast for lunch.

Later, as I walked with the Cape Horners at Tivoli Gardens, where a special concert was being given for the Cape Horners, I heard a voice say "Mees Broke?" I turned, and there was the mate, his once near skeletal frame now blown to slightly Santa Claus proportions. Doubtless he was making the same observations of me. Joyfully we all shook hands. The steward was there too, and a beer at a nearby table seemed to be the order of the day. I still didn't drink beer, and asked for tea.

"Chocolate Sailor," teased the mate, as he had once done on *L'Avenir*. I couldn't call the mate "Hugo" as MacDowall and the others were doing, for even after forty years, from the old rule of respect on board, he was always "the mate" to an apprentice.

"Forty years, and no one has changed much!" enthused MacDowall. Well, the mate had a beer paunch, the steward had sprouted bushy eyebrows, and MacDowall was now grizzled. Mercifully, my stern was hidden under the table.

On my own for a few hours in Copenhagen I walked down to the port to look for the offices of Shierbeck, the ship's agent, from where my voyage began. I found the building, still under the same name, and remembered Shierbeck himself, blocking the doorway with his huge frame, his eyes slithering over me and his voice rasping as he told me that I must await the arrival of Captain Erikson. The building was closed for noon hour, so I did not see whether the office was still there, with "faded paintings of square riggers in dark seas rolling in neatly permed waves" as I had seen forty years earlier. Peering in the window, I saw that the coils of rope and blocks hanging from the beams were gone. The office had been modernized and the beams painted over. Turning away, I walked up the street looking out across the harbour to the "Little Mermaid" as I had done so many years earlier, my excited young heart beating as I had waited to join my ship. I thought again of *L'Avenir* and the friendships made and still enduring after forty years.

[1] *Flying Cloud* was purchased by the Navy Officers' Club in Montreal, where it remained on display until after WW II when thebuilding was sold and the contents auctioned. I tried to buy it back at that point, but it had been bought in the auction by an American. Many years later I retrieved it from the buyer's family.

[2] Not surprising! Percy Grainger had a major career as a pianist as well as a composer. He was considered *the performer* of the Tchaikovsky Piano Concerto No. 1, and especially of the Grieg Piano Concerto and Grieg's solo piano music. Having heard Grainger play, Grieg invited him to Norway in 1906 to study with him.

[3] Mother Carey's chickens are small sea birds which fly over cold waters. See also Rudyard Kipling, *Anchor Song*.

Appendix

L'Avenir: Crew, Officers, and Passengers

CREW

A. Arho: Redbeard. Captain Eino Koivistoinen told me in one letter "I met Arho the other day and we were talking about you, and he conceded 'Yackie was a pretty good sailor.'"

Ceysen: John Ceysen a Belgian. In 1936, Ben's ship was sent to Antwerp and I joined him there. We looked up Ceysen's address, and found him. We had a happy reunion talking about our days in *L'Avenir*, and he and his girlfriend took us around Antwerp. Ceysen was about to go for his compulsory military service. After the war I lost track of him.

Englond: Allan Englond, "Frankenstein." Ella Grainger spoke of him on one occasion when I was staying with her and Percy. She said that, surprisingly, Englond turned out to be very clever and became a well-known church dignitary, although I never found any confirmation of this.

Dane Doctor: Jurgen Jurgensen. I had a letter from him in the summer of 1934 in which he enclosed the photo of me on the royal yard of *L'Avenir*, at Christmas, 1932.

Danska: Harry Johansen. He must have made his next voyage in *Herzogen Cecilie*, which was wrecked off the Devon coast. I made the trip down from London to see her, and as we came alongside her, I glimpsed Danska, but saw no more of him. Later a shipmate of his sent me Danska's greetings, but I never saw him again.

Ekstrom: Karl Ekstrom passed for Master before the war, and when it broke out was put in charge of some extensive docking manoeuvres. Not having had enough experience, he found this appointment a great strain, and, as he was very conscientous, worked himself into a breakdown and spent a year ashore. He then went back to sea, spending twenty-five years there, before retiring to become a tax collector. He build a beautiful model of *L'Avenir*, and after Ben's death, my daughter Gale and I were entertained in his home. His wife and I corresponded, in Swedish, for many years. He did much work on the sails of *Pomern*, which was berthed in Mariehamn. Karl was appointed president of a later Congress of Cape Horners at Aland, but tragically, died a couple of days before the Congress.

Chesus: Eric Groth. I liked him and his dour wit. I never saw him again.

MacDowall: William "Bill" MacDowall became a Hansa Marine Insurance expert, and was sent all over the world investigating claims. On one occasion in Japan, he had struggled with the greatest patience over a difficult case, when the Japanese announced that he was rude, had hurt their feelings and they could not do business with him. MacDowall thereupon struck his own chest and announced "What about *my* feelings! You have not considered them." The Japanese were so shocked they settled at once, and MacDowall was treated with the greatest courtesy thereafter on all his trips to Japan. At the Stockholm Cape Horner's Congress in 1974, Bill found a table next to the Swedish King's for me and my daughter. In his last years Bill was an invalid, but I had news of him through Segerstedt, and shortly before he died, spoke to him on the telephone. Both Bill and his pal Segerstedt, were kind, not "kicky" to me on *L'Avenir*.

Segerstedt: Captain Evert Segerstedt became a naval architect, and with his wife Dagmar, who was a graduate in chemical science, built up a marina in Uddevalla, Sweden, where I visited them in 1977. Their home was full of marine treasures, including a magnificent scale model Evert had made of a four-masted barque. He died in 1997, leaving many grandchildren.

Dennis: Dennis Wilen, our "slavedriver." His name came up at a banquet in Aland, and I was told that he had joined the Royal Air Force during the war, and was killed.

Jumbo: Herbert Zublke. I never heard anything more of him, but as he was German, I wondered if he had been aboard *L'Avenir*, rechristened *Admiral Karpfanger*, when she foundered in 1938.

Koivistoinen: Sailmaker in *Winterhude*, when she was berthed alongside *L'Avenir* in Port Germein. He became Captain Eino Koivestoinen, and we corresponded for forty years. We met again at later Congresses. With his wife he had travelled on cargo ships all over the world while he wrote many books and articles, including a life of Captain Gustaf Erikson, the shipowner. Shortly before he died, Eino sent me his last book, *Billowing Sails*, in English, which had a chapter on our meeting in Port Germein in 1933. He became Harbour Master at Kotka, Finland, and I visited with him and his wife Salme at the Helsinki Congress in 1977.

OFFICERS

Captain Nils Erikson: In later years he worked on ice breakers. In a letter to me, Captain Gole Sundberg, Director of the Aland Nautical Museum, who wrote a book on *L'Avenir*, sent me remarks from Captain Gustaf Erikson (*L'Avenir's* owner) he had found in a series of Erikson's letters. The owner remarked after he agreed to take me, but before I actually signed on, that

L'*Avenir* was to get "an American Miss who wishes to sign on as an apprentice. I don't know if she can work on deck at all, but maybe she will be able to attend the women passengers." Then in a letter from Australia during the voyage, Captain Nils Erikson wrote that Gustaf Erikson was really wrong in his judgement about me. "I am pleased with the woman apprentice. She is in full work as the others. She is not any flirt, who mingles with the crew. She is mostly by her self during her freewatches."

First Mate: Captain Hugo Karlson. After leaving L'*Avenir* he had gone up for his master's ticket. During the war he was four years in New York, where he organized a company with three other Finns, calling themselves the Hudson Rope Company. They made cargo nets, and did splicing work and so on. He was separated from wife for the entire war. Later, when Captain Karlson was in oil tankers, and she could have sailed with him, she could not because of her ailing mother. I was entertained in their home in Aland with a party of L'*Avenir* survivors and Barbara Strachey. They tried to persuade me to sing chanties as I had done at sea, but the magic of the sea had been replaced by shyness.

Second Mate: Charles Nyman. We met at both the Helsinki and Aland Congresses. I do not know what his career was after leaving L'*Avenir*, but he was a very genial host in Helsinki, taking me to see the artwork there and introducing me to friends as "my seaman apprentice in L'*Avenir*." He was selfless in his letters, being more concerned with my latest art shows than any accomplishment of his own.

Third Mate: "Tredge," Captain Helge Heikkinen, obtained his master's certificate and continued sailing. In 1982 he wrote to me, "Last year I get at last from Ostende, Medaille '*Hommage des Capitaines Cap-Horniers*.' 4 times Cape Horn rounded and seven Cape Horn books written." One of these books was on our voyage in L'*Avenir*, titled in Swedish *Onskeskeppet*, which the second mate Charles Nyman found and gave me when I was in Helsinki, or I would not have known of it. Captain Heikkinen was wounded in the war and suffered from ill health for some time after.

My comment on L'*Avenir* that his mouth revealed a certain

sweetness, despite his bombast, came back to me in 1983, when he wrote me a card saying "I am laden with sorrow because my beloved friend in weal and woe, Airdale terrier King is dead at the age of 8 years. Seven years ago he saved my life with some rowdy assault, purpose of killing. He is buried in our rose garden."

Steward: Rudolph Johanson found me at the Copenhagen Congress and recounted his life and how his son married a Canadian girl who had come to Mariehamn as a tourist. When Johanson arrived in Montreal, he set out to visit his son in Bathurst, New Brunswick, and despite all his travels, could not conceive of the vastness of Canada. He set out by bus and was amazed at the time it took. He boasted of the money he made as a barman aboard the Mariehamn ferry, selling tax-free liquor. "Two, tree tousand dollar a mont I make!" At the Aland Congress I visited the steward's home in Mariehamn. It was full of seagoing souvenirs, and he had made a remarkable rock garden. He told me of meeting the dissipated Finnish passenger Olav Hultin, who had married Barbara Strachey. "Very bad this man, now. All sick, he do so many bad tings."

Sailmaker: John Sommarstrom never came to any of the congresses, but his son did. In the Aland Nautical Club book of Aland's sea history, Sommarstrom is described as the "legendary sailmaker." He served solely in sailing ships for almost fifty years. He made his last voyage in *Passat* in 1949–50 before retiring to Mariehamn, where he enjoyed walking about the town and became a familiar figure there until incapacitated by a stroke. MacDowall went to see him, and to the old sailmaker's great delight, smuggled in a bottle of whisky, as he was allowed no drink. I made a watercolour of Sommarstrom sewing sails on the deck of *L'Avenir* in the tropics with his assistant Johansson Ragner. This painting is in the Alands Seafaring Museum in Mariehamn.

PASSENGERS

Dutch Lady: Mrs. Van Andel settled in Australia with her daughter. When my husband's ship was there during the war, the crew was given a dance by a team of local nurses, one of whom was Mrs. Van Andel's daughter. They got talking of ships, and she mentioned her mother's voyage to Australia in *L'Avenir*. Thus I got in touch again. Mrs. Van Andel wrote me saying what a nice young man Ben was and she was happy that I was married. I remembered the conventional future she had wished me as we strolled the deck of *L'Avenir*.

Commander Claude Butlin wrote a book on his trip in *L'Avenir*, illustrated with some very good photographs. He and his wife attended the Ostende and Oslo congresses and we renewed acquaintances. I visited them in Winchester in 1981. In 1934 on *L'Avenir* they had bought a painting of the barque done by Tredge, using only scraps of ship's paint and large brushes. We all looked at the painting, so full of action, with admiration for the fine job Tredge had done. Commander Butlin died in New Zealand where they had gone to live with their son. He told me that his friend aboard *L'Avenir*, Commander Fisher, had been promoted to the rank of admiral.

Percy and Ella Grainger: I stayed with them for a few days about 1936 while Ben was at sea, in their cottage near Hastings in England. Ella and I especially had a wonderful time recalling the incidents and people on the voyage. Later, after the war, with my son and daughter, I spent a day with them at Cromwell Place in White Plains. Ella made beautiful tiles, an art she had learned in Paris in her youth. Percy was not in good health, but he took great joy in developing his "free music" machine, which could realize intervals of tones, and describing its elaborate construction to me. We attended a band concert featuring Percy's music in Central Park in New York.

Miss Kronig: She was always "Miss Kronig" to me. I lost touch with her after a time, but we exchanged photos of the voyage. She came all the way out to suburbia to visit Ben and me in our house near Harrow, which we named "The Fo'castle."

Barbara Strachey Halpern: She worked for thirty years as a radio producer for the BBC and as a program planner for the BBC World Service. She continued to travel as much as was compatible with her work. Her brother became a computer programmer in Oxford, where she eventually settled. After divorcing Olav Hultin, she married Wolff Halpern, about whom she had told me aboard *L'Avenir*. They had a son, and her husband was killed in the air force in World War II. After my many attendances at congresses, she invited me to stay in Oxford, and we had many happy times. She wrote several books, including *Remarkable Relations, Mary Berenson*, and *The Strachey Line*. She would sometimes test out the clarity of her descriptions on me. In her last letter she said that she "was reduced to writing my own memoirs, which is at any rate fun for me."

Glossary

ABACK: Backward against the mast, said of a square-rigged vessel, or of her sails when the wind is acting on the forward side of the sails, flattening them against the mast and tending to drive the vessel astern.

ABAFT: Toward the stern.

ABEAM: Running at right angles to the longitudinal line of a vessel.

ACCOMMODATION LADDER: A portable flight of steps slung at a gangway, leading down a ship's side for access to or from a quay or boat alongside.

ACOCKBILL: Said of a ship's yards when they are tipped up at an angle with the deck.

AFT: At or near the stern.

ALBATROSS: A web-footed bird of the petrel family, largest of the sea birds and capable of very long sustained flight.

ALLEYWAY: Corridor in the crew or passenger accommodation.

ALOFT: Any place in the rigging, on the yards or on the masts.

ALOW: Opposite of ALOFT; low down or near the deck.

ALTITUDE: Height or extent upward; angle of elevation of a heavenly body above the horizon measured as an arc of a vertical circle intercepted by the body and the horizon.

ANCHOR: A weighty hooked instrument, which when lowered to the sea floor holds a vessel in place by its connecting cable; Anchor-shank: the vertical main part.

ANCHOR-CRANE: A machine to lift, lower, and horizontally transfer an anchor.

APPRENTICE: In British merchant ships, a youth bound by legal agreement, or indentures, to serve for a period of four years at sea in order to qualify for his Certificate of Competence.

ASTROLABE: An ancient astronomical instrument of various forms used for observing altitudes and for solution of problems involving celestial angular distances.

ATHWART: Across, from side to side, at right angles from the fore-aft line; across a vessel's course.

AWEIGH: Said of the anchor when its flukes are just clear of the bottom, as in "the anchor's aweigh."

BACKSTAY: A rope or stay, or one of a set of stays leading from the upper part of any mast above a lower mast to the ship's side abaft her lower rigging.

BALLAST: Weight carried either for proper stability or to secure the greatest possible economy of propelling power.

BARQUE: A three, four. or five-masted vessel having her after mast fore and aft rigged, and the others square rigged. Also BARK.

BATTEN: Narrow strip of wood for "fairing in" lines; strips of wood or steel used in securing tarpaulins in place, as in over hatches.

BATTEN CLEATS: Right-angle shaped brackets fixed to hatch coamings for holding and wedging tarpaulin battens in position

BEAT: In sailing, to work to windward by alternate tacks.

BELAY: To make fast; to fasten a rope by winding in figure-eight fashion over a belaying pin, cleat, kevel, bitt, etc.

BELAYING PIN: Short bar of brass, iron, or wood used to secure a rope and particularly to belay the running rigging.

BEND: To make fast or connect, as ends of a rope or hawser or a sail to a boom, gaff, stay, or yard. SHEET BEND: A hitch used to make fast a tackle's standing end to a becket on a block.

BERTH: Bed or cot, commonly called a bunk. Room or space required for a ship in riding at anchor or in which to turn around.

BILGE: Part of the ship's hull extending outward from her keel to a point where her sides rise vertically.

BILGE-KEEL: A fin or line of timbers or plating set perpendicular to a vessel's shell along her bilges for about two-thirds of her length as a brake against rolling, fitted on each side and usually called "rolling chocks."

BITTS: Strong post of wood or iron, usually fastened to a deck in pairs and named according to their use, as in riding-bitts, towing-bitts, mooring-bitts, etc.

BLACKBIRD: A ship carrying slaves as a business.

BLOCK: A mechanical device for moving an object by means of a rope or chain leading over its contained sheave or sheaves.

BOAT: Usual term given to small craft.

BOATSWAIN: (Bosun) A subordinate officer in a merchantman in general charge of the ship's deck force, rigging, boats, cargo gear, deck stores, and deck maintenance work.

BOOM: Spar used to spread a fore-and-aft-sail, especially its foot.

BOW: Forward end of a vessel.

BOSUN'S CHAIR: A standard piece of gear in all ships consisting of a short board slung by a four-legged bridle and used for sitting in while working aloft or on the ship's side, lowering a man into a hold, etc.

BRAIL: A rope used to truss up a sail.

BREAK: Point where a vessel's deck terminates and ascent or descent to the next deck begins.

BREAK OF POOP: The extreme forward end of a poop deck.

BRIDGE: A high transverse platform, often an extension of a deckhouse top, running from side to side of a vessel and from which a complete, all round view is least interfered with.

BRIG: A two-masted square-rigged vessel, her mainmast having a fore-and-aft mainsail or SPANKER in addition to, or without, a square mainsail. HERMAPHRODITE BRIG Two-masted vessel square rigged on her foremast and schooner rigged on her mainmast.

BULWARK: The raised side of a ship, above the upper deck.

BUNT: Bulky middle part of those square sails which are clewed up to the middle of a yard before being furled.

BUNTLINE: One of several roped attached to a square sail's foot, led to a masthead and thence to deck, and used to spill and gather a sail up to its yard when taking it in.

CABLE: A heavy rope or chain used to hold a vessel at anchor.

CAPE HORN: The southernmost of the group of islands lying below the island of Tierra del Fuego, its cape is the southernmost extremity of South America, called "the Horn" by sailors.

CAPSTAN: A vertical drum revolving on a spindle used for exerting power required in heaving on a rope or anchor cable.

CAPSTAN BAR: A pole inserted into holes around the capstan head and supplying the necessary leverage to turn the capstan.

CAST: To throw, to cause to fall, to let down, to toss.

CAST OFF: To throw off, put off, or let go a rope, boat, etc., as to cast off from the ship's side.

CHANTEY: A song used by sailors in chorus during the work of hoisting a yard, heaving an anchor, or any operation requiring united effort.

CHART: A map, especially a draft or projection on paper of the whole or portion of an ocean, sea, lake, or river, or of coastal waters, showing details such as land elevations, lighthouses, signal stations, towns, and conspicuous marks, depths of water, nature of bottom, outlying rocks, shoals, sunken wrecks, tidal information, set of currents, variation of compass, and other data for use of mariners.

CHART-HOUSE: Space provided for stowage of ship's charts, nautical books, ship's chronometres, and other navigational equipment.

CHIPPING: Removing thick scale of rust from iron or steel surfaces, or dressing edges of metal plates etc.

CLEAT: A strip of wood or metal fastened to other material to strengthen, keep in place, prevent slipping etc. A piece of wood, iron or other metal shaped as a short, stout bar with projecting ends on which ropes are belayed. BATTEN CLEATS: Right-angle shaped brackets fixed to hatch coamings for holding and wedging tarpaulin battens in position.

CLEW: Either of the lower corners of a square sail or lower aftermost extremity of a fore-and-aft sail.

CLEW LINE: A purchase or single rope leading to the deck for hauling up to the yards the clews of topsails, top-gallant sails, and royals.

COASTER: A coasting vessel which sails from port to port along a coast, not across the sea; a person or vessel engaged in the coasting trade.

COIL: A length of cordage stowed or gathered in rings or spirals so as to form a compact mass.

COMPANIONWAY: A stairway leading from a vessel's deckto a cabin or other accommodation below; generally the space occupied by such a stairway.

CONSUL: An agent commissioned by a sovereign state to reside in a foreign city or port for the purpose of caring for and protecting commercial interests of its citizens and its seamen's rights and welfare.

CORDAGE: Ropes, lines, etc. In a collective sense ropes constituting hawsers and running rigging of a ship.

COURSE: Point of the compass to which a vessel's path is directed. Direction in which a ship is steered.

CRANSE: Old name for an iron band or ring fitted to steady or secure a spar. Also CRANSE IRON.

CRINGLE: An iron or rope stop or grommet on the bolt rope of a sail to which a sheet, tack, earring, leech-line, reef-tackle etc. is secured.

CROSSTREES: Two pieces of wood or metal laid athwartship on the trestle trees and forming a foundation for the top, or platform at lower masthead, also a means of spreading and securing topmast shrouds. They are also fitted at a topmasthead to spread top-gallant shrouds.

CROW'S NEST: A small observation platform near the top of a ship's mast.

DARN THE WATER: Tack back and forth many times.

DAVIT: A light curved or straight-armed crane for lifting and lowering boats, anchors, accommodation ladders, or other permanent equipment. Usually in pairs when fitted for boats.

DAYMEN: Workers not standing watch.

DECK: Plating or planking secured to and covering all or part of any tier of beams. The floor of any compartment.

DISCHARGE: Certificate given to a seaman upon completing a voyage or leaving a vessel. Nickname for a ship's cook, also legendary figure taking part in the ceremony of crossing the line (equator).

DOLDRUMS: That equatorial region or belt of low barometric pressure and calm winds, lying between the northeast and southeast trade winds in the Atlantic and Pacific oceans.

DONKEY: Short for donkey-engine, donkey boiler, donkey-pump.

DONKEYMAN: The engineer who attends such equipment.

DUNGAREE: Blue cotton trousers.

DUNNAGE: Pieces of cordwood, slats, boards, etc., placed under and around cargo in a ship's hold for protection against contact with bilge water, leakage from other cargo, contact with ship's sides or structural parts, and condensation therefrom.

FAKE: One of the circular parts or loops in a coil of rope or wire.

FELUCCA: Class of small sailing vessels once common in Mediterranean, Portuguese, and Spanish coastal waters.

FENDER: A buffer, bumper protective placed between a vessel's side and a pier or another vessel such as a spar, bundle of old rope or a pudding of matting.

FIGUREHEAD: Ornamental forward curbing termination of the outwater, immediately below the bowsprit, usually a statue or bust of a mythological personage, or a noted admiral.

FLAMFEW: An ancient word for moonlight reflected on water.

FLEMISH COIL: A rope spirally coiled about its end and all turns lying flat and snug on deck.

FLEMISH HORSE: A short footrope on a topsail or lower yardarm for the convenience of the man who passes the earing in reefing.

FOOT BRACE: One of the two purchases by which the fore yard is braced and trimmed.

FOOT: Lower edge of any sail, which in a jib or staysail is the side extending from tack (lower forward corner) to clew (after corner).

FOOT ROPE: Called a horse, a stout hemp or wire rope heavily served, extending along and suspended from a yard, on which men stand when furling, reefing, bending, or unbending sails.

FORE PEAK: Extreme forward part of a fore hold.

FORECASTLE: The *forwearde castel* on European ships of the middle ages, a raised, fortified platform at the bows which gave command of an enemy's decks in battle; in modern sailing ships, a deck house used as seamen's quarters, immediately abaft the foremast, called the FO'CASTLE.

FORWARD: In or pertaining to the fore part of a ship, as forward scuttle, forward locker.

FURL: To roll up or gather a square sail to its yard and secure it with gaskets (small ropes kept in readiness on each yard).

FUTTOCK SHROUDS: Usually of iron rods, are downward extensions of topmast shrouds leading from the rim of the top to futtock band.

FUTTOCK: In wooden shipbuilding, curved parts or sections of transverse frames extending from floor timbers at turn of bilge to top timbers.

GAFF: Pole with a hook on the end used to retrieve something from the surface of the water.

GLASS: Any of several instruments in which glass is an important feature, as in hour-glass, log-glass, night-glass, weather-glass (barometer).

GO BELOW: To proceed to a lower deck or hold, to leave the deck watch or work and repair to one's quarters.

GROMMET: Ring or strop of rope made by laying up a single strand round itself to build the usual three strands as in stropping a block. A metal (usually brass) eyelet set in a sail or edge of a canvas cover to receive a strop or lacing.

HALYARD: Usually in plural form as Halyards or Halliards or Haulyards, single rope purchase by which a sail is hoisted or set.

HAND IN STAYS: Hesitation in a vessel's coming about.

HANDY: Said of a vessel possessing qualities of being easily managed or manoeuvred through being obedient to helm or turning action of the screw, or adapted to easily handling, as in tacking, shortening, or setting sail.

HANDY BILLY: Small tackle for general use about the deck, as in setting up on halyards, taking in slack of mooring lines, where steam or other power is not available.

HATCH: Covering and protective arrangement, including hatch-covers and hatch-coaming, over and around an opening on deck.

HAUL: To pull, tug, drag, as on a rope.

HAWSER: Any lengthy, heavy fibre or wire rope used for warping, mooring or towing.

HAZING: Practice of keeping a man or crew hard at work unnecessarily, petty tyranny of superiors which makes life on board unbearable.

HEADWAY: Motion ahead in a ship.

HEADWIND: Wind blowing directly against the head of a ship, against which the ship must tack.

HEAVE: To draw, haul, or pull on a rope.

HEAVE AWAY: To push, as on a capstan bar.

HEEL: To incline laterally or list.

HELM: The instrument or entire apparatus by which a vessel is steered; usually a steering wheel or tiller alone. Angle through which the rudder is turned from amidship position; as in 20° helm.

HERMAPHRODITE BRIG: Two-masted vessel square rigged on her foremast and schooner rigged on her mainmast.

HITCH: One of many different kinds of knots, nooses, or loops by which a rope is made fast to an object and may readily be loosed therefrom.

HOLD: Entire cargo space below deck, often applied to space below a lowermost deck only.

HOLIDAY: A day of exemption from work. A neglected portion or spot on a surface being painted, varnished, or tarred, etc.

HORN: One of the crosstrees' ends; arms of a cleat; jaws of a boom or gaff or other protruding or extended part of anything.

HULL: Body of a vessel, exclusive of deck houses, all spars and rigging, boilers, machinery, and equipment.

HURRAH'S NEST: Sailor's term for a tangle of cordage, blocks, spars, etc; rubbish, wreckage, especially a mass of carried away rigging. Also called a RAFFLE.

JACKSTAY: Iron rod or wooden batten fitted along a yard, gaff, or boom as a means of bending sail to a spar.

JACOB'S LADDER: A handy rope-sided ladder having wooden rungs which are set between strands of and are seized to the rope, used for passage to or from an overside stage, boat-boom, etc.

JONAH: Person on board ship to whose presence the cause of misfortunes is attributed.

LANYARD: A rope used for setting up rigging, fastening or stretching sails or for convenience in handling articles. Also LANIARD.

LASHING: Fastening made by a piece of cordage, chain, or wire securing a movable object or uniting two or more parts or objects together; the rope, chain, etc., forming such fastening.

LEE: Sheltered side or area, or that protected from wind or sea, as under the lee of a cliff; or, another ship in the lee of a vessel.

LEECH: One of the outer vertical edges of a square sail, or the after edge of a fore and aft sail. Also LEACH.

LIGHT TOWER: Erect construction holding the sidelights on a vessel.

LIGHTER: A large boat, scow, or barge, usually man- or sail-powered, for conveying cargo to and from vessels in harbour, transporting coal, construction materials, garbage, etc.

LINE: General term for a length of cordage; the particular size of which is understood by its use with a combining word, as in HEAVING LINE, LEAD LINE, MOORING LINE, etc.

LINE, THE: The equator; first crossing for passengers and crew is the opportunity for traditional hijinks.

LINER: Merchant vessel on a regular run or belonging to a line of vessels. Often used for passenger ships.

LOBSCOUSE: A sailor's stew of salt meat, vegetables, and hard tack.

LOG BOOK: Ship's journal or day by day record of events, observations, distance, courses steered, weather experienced, etc.

LOG: Any of several different devices for measuring a vessel's speed through the water.

LOOKOUT: A seaman stationed on the fo'castle or in the crow's nest for the purpose of maintaining a watchful eye for any lights, land, or floating objects that might heave into sight, and reporting such to the officer of the watch.

LUBBER'S HOLE: In larger square-rigged ships, hole in a top-platform next to lower masthead, through which a man may crawl instead of climbing over the outer edge of the top platform when going aloft.

LUFF: Sailing a ship close to the wind; the foremost, rounded, and fullest part of a ship's bow; the foremost edge of a fore and aft sail; to bring the head of a vessel into the wind, with the sails shaking.

LUNAR: Short for lunar observation.

MAKE: To arrive at or sight a place or position steered for.

MAKE FAST: To secure by belaying or hitching, as a rope to fasten in place as a sail by its gaskets; to secure a ship at a pier.

MAKE SAIL: To unfurl a sail or sails.

MARC ST. HILAIRE METHOD: First introduced by Commandant Marc St. Hilaire of the French navy about 1885; an important improvement in determination of the line of position, called New Navigation for a probationary period of about thirty years. Its marked departure from prevailing practice lay in a short cut offered by the solution of spherical trigonometrical problems involved for value of a heavenly body's altitude at a ship's estimated position at an instant corresponding to an altitude of some body observed by sextant, and in using the difference between such calculated and observed altitudes, called the intercept, for laying off the position line on a chart.

MARLIN SPIKE: Iron pin, about sixteen inches long and tapered to a point that is either fine or wedge-shaped; used to pen and separate strands of a rope when splicing. It has a hole at the opposite end for a lanyard.

MAST: A pole or spar, usually of round timber or tubular metal, set upright in a vessel to sustain the sails or equipment, such as radio and radar antennas.

In a four-masted barque, the masts, aft from the bow, are the *fore mast, main mast, mizzen mast*, and *jigger mast*. Protruding ahead from the bow is the *bowsprit*. Extending aft from the jigger mast, from the deck aloft, are the *spanker boom* and the *gaff boom*. From the deck aloft, the sections of the mast are lowermast, topmast, topgallant mast and royal mast. The bowsprit carries triangular jib sails; the fore, main, and mizzen masts carry square rigged sails, and forward triangular staysails; the jigger carries both fore and aft triangular sails. See SAILS for the names and order of the sails.

MASTER: Officer in command of a merchant or a fishing vessel, usually given the courtesy title of Captain.

MATE: Officer next in command and assistant to the master of a merchant vessel. One of a number of officers, from two to eight or more, depending of the size and type of vessel, who assist in navigation and operation of the ship.

MIDSHIP: At the middle of the ship, viewed either transversely or longitudinally.

MIDSHIPS: Amidships, the middle part of a vessel.

MISS STAYS: To fail in the manoeuvre of coming about, or placing vessel on a new tack, usually because of losing headway in the attempt.

MOORING: Act of securing a vessel by means of her anchors or hawsers.

MOORING LINE: Any rope or hawser used to secure a vessel in berth.

MOTHER CAREY: Among sailors, the traditional owner of certain birds of the petrel family, especially of the stormy petrels of the North Atlantic, called by sailors *Mother Carey's chickens*.

MUSTER: An assembling of the ship's company, passengers, or special detachments thereof.

NOON: Middle of the day, twelve o'clock in the day by standard local time; time of the sun's upper transit. It is customary at sea to reckon the day's run, fuel consumption, and work done by engines from noon to noon.

Glossary

PALM: Flat or inside surface of the fluke of an old-fashioned anchor. A sailmaker's instrument for driving the needle in sewing canvas, whipping ropes, etc., consisting of a stiff rawhide or leather band which fits around the hand, with a hole for the thumb, for the purpose of holding in the proper position a thimble next to the palm of the sewer's hand. The needle is held between thumb and forefinger with its eye end in the thimble, thus it is pushed by the palm through the canvas.

PAMPARO: A cold, dry wind from the Argentine pampas, which causes violent sudden storms at sea when it meets the heavy unstable tropical air of the South Atlantic off the coasts of Argentina and Uruguay.

PARREL: A fitting which holds a hoisting yard to its mast.

PITCH: To plunge or heave, as in the alternate lift and fall of each end of a vessel in a head sea. See ROLL.

PLATING: Arrangement of plates or plates collectively, forming a deck, or a vessel's outer surface or skin, a bulkhead, etc.

POOP: Space below an enclosed superstructure at the extreme after end of a vessel. Also POOPDECK extending over such an erection. BREAK OF POOP: the extreme forward end of a poop deck.

PORT: Formerly LARBOARD, the left side of a vessel looking forward; belonging or pertaining to the port side.

PORT: Any harbour, haven, roadstead, inlet, cove, etc. in which vessels may find shelter.

PURCHASE: Mechanism, such as a tackle, windlass, capstan, screw or handspike, by which a mechanical advantage is gained in order to move heavy bodies or extend the ship's rigging.

QUARTERMASTER: In merchant vessels, particularly of the liner type, one of a number from four to eight, depending of the size and class of ship, of able seamen who steer, keep navigation, bridge and equipment, wheelhouse, chartroom, etc. clear and in order, stand gangway watch in port, attend to flags displayed, and generally assist in matters pertaining directly to the safe navigation of the vessel.

QUAY: A wharf or other waterside construction at which vessels are berthed.

RAIL: The heavy plank, timber or plate, forming the top of a vessel's bulwarks.

RATLINE: Small three-stranded, right-hand laid, tarred hemp line, varying in size from 15 to 21 thread (1 1/4 to 1 1/2 inch circumference), named from its original use for ratlines, small ropes strung across a vessel's shrouds, forming the series of steps or runs in a ladder-like arrangement which provides the means of climbing aloft.

RECKONING: Calculated or estimated position of a vessel, especially that arrived at according to course and distance made good from a reliable fix, as that obtained from celestial observations or from the bearing of shore objects.

REEVE: To pass the end of a rope, chain, etc. through a hope or opening, as in a block, dead-eye, ring bolt, or the like.

REGULATIONS FOR PREVENTING COLLISIONS AT SEA: The present international rules consisting of 32 Articles (31 at the time of L'Avenir) dating from 1885, when the articles adopted by Great Britain in 1884 were adopted and amended by an act of the U.S. Congress.

RELIEF: Act of relieving or being released from a post or duty. One who takes his turn or relieves another, as a helmsman, lookout man, watchman, etc.

RIGGING: Tackle, the system of cordage which supports the ship's masts and extends the sails; includes shrouds, stays, backstays, and halliards, used with the yards, spreaders and braces, bowsprit, boom, and gaff.

RIGGING SCREW: A turnbuckle fixed at the lower or inboard end of a shroud, backstay, etc. for setting up such pieces of standing rigging, instead of using the deadeye and lanyard system.

ROBAND: A short piece of rope-yard, spunyarn, sennit, or the like, used for seizing each eyelet in the head of luff of a sail to a band, hoop, or jackstay, as in bending various sails.

ROPE: General term for cordage composed of strand, as a rule larger than one inch in circumference. RIGHT LAID ROPE: cordage in which the strands advance in a left to right slope. LEFT LAID ROPE: the opposite.

ROUNDING THE HORN: Moving from the south Atlantic to Pacific oceans (or the reverse) via Cape Horn or the Straits of Magellan separating Tierra del Fuego from the mainland, or Beagle Channel, separating Tierra del Fuego from Cape Horn. Traditionally exceptionally difficult for sailing vessels, the passage could take many weeks, even months, because of adverse winds, storms, waves, and currents where the two great oceans are compressed into narrow straits

ROVING: See ROBAND.

RUDDER: The vertical flat piece or structure of wood or metal which is fitted at the after end of a vessel's immersed body as the means by which she is steered.

RUDDERHEAD: The upper or inboard end of the rudder stock to which the tiller or the quadrant is fitted.

SAIL: A piece of canvas or other material attached to a mast and spread to the wind, by which a vessel is propelled. See MAST, above.

The six square sails carried are, from the deck aloft:

Foremast: 1] foresail or fore course; 2] fore lower topsail; 3] fore upper topsail; 4] fore lower top gallant; 5] fore upper top gallant; 6] fore royal.

Mainmast: 1] mainsail or main course; 2] main lower topsail; 3] main upper topsail; 4] main lower topgallant; 5] main upper topgallant; 6] main royal.

Mizzenmast: 1] crossjack mizzen course; 2] mizzen lower topsail; 3] mizzen upper topsail; 4] mizzen lower topgallant; 5] mizzen upper topgallant; 6] mizzen royal.

The triangular sails:

Bowsprit and foremast, from the bow forward, 1] fore topmast staysail; 2] inner jib; 3] outer jib; 4] flying jib.

Mainmast, carried forward of the mast; 1] main topmast staysail; 2] main topgallant staysail; 3] main royal staysail.

Mizzenmast, carried forward; 1] mizzen topmast staysail; 2] mizzen topgallant staysail; 3] mizzen royal staysail

Jigger mast, carried forward; 1]jigger staysail; 2] jigger topmast staysail; 3] jigger topgallant staysail

Jigger mast, carried aft; 1] lower spanker; 2] upper spanker; 3] gaff topsail

SAILMAKER: One whose occupation is the making of sails, one engaged and skilled in sailmaking. A petty officer in a sailing ship who has charge of the upkeep of sails and all canvas work, such as boat covers, windsails, and tarpaulins.

SALT HORSE: Sailors' term for salt meat, formerly pickled in casks for long voyages.

SARGASSO SEA: Extensive area of comparatively still water in the North Atlantic that has inspired many tales and legends, so named from *sargassum* or Gulf weed that abounds on the surface throughout the region.

SCUPPER: Any opening for carrying off water from a deck, either directly or through a scupper pipe.

SCUTTLE: A small opening in a deck or elsewhere, usually fitted with a cover or lid, or a door, as for access to a compartment or hatchway.

SEIZING: The turns of a marline, spunyarn, wire, or special cordage used to seize one object to another; the act of fastening with turns of small cordage or seizing stuff.

SENNIT: Small cordage made by braiding ropeyarn, spunyarn, or other small stuff, used for chafing-service, lanyards, lashings, robands, etc.

SERVE; To wind marline, spunyarn, or other small stuff around a rope, keeping the turns close together, as a protection against weather or wear.

SEXTANT: Optical instrument for measuring angular distances; especially altitudes of heavenly bodies at sea.

SHACKLE: Originally a circular or oval-shaped ring fitted on the inside of a gun port or a scuttle for securing such at sea. Any of several metal fittings, commonly U-shaped, with a removable pin or bolt across its mouth, for connecting chain, making fast a pendant, stay, guy, etc.

SHEER: Upward curvature of a vessel's upper lines from about midships towards each end.

SHEET BEND: Hitch used in forming meshing in a fishing net; used to make fast a tackle's standing end to a becket on a block.

SHELL: Outside covering of planking or plating forming the surface of a vessel's hull. Also SKIN.

SHELTER DECK: A continuous deck above the principal or strength deck of the hull.

SHROUDS: A set of ropes from the masthead to the ship's sides, supporting the masts.

SIDELIGHT: One of the lights required to be shown on each side of the vessel underway, to indicate the general direction in which the vessel is heading; a green light on the starboard side, and red light on the port.

SIGHT: Sextant observation of a heavenly body, as a sight of the sun, in determining position at sea.

SKID: One of two or more parallel pieces of timber, structural iron, etc., supporting a heavy object, as a spar or water tank on deck. BOAT SKIDS: a pair of athwartship timbers or beams of structural iron, often extending from side to side of, and supported by, stanchions above a weather deck, primarily for raising boats clear of the deck.

SKYLIGHT: A deck erection fitted with framed glass covers or windows for admission of light and often serving as a ventilator, as above a cabin, crew's quarters, engine room, etc.

SLACK: Loose, not taut or tense.

SLEIGH RIDE: Whalemen's term for the first wild dash of the open boat behind a freshly harpooned whale.

SLING: A rope strop or special chain that is secured to and takes the weight of a draft or piece of cargo, machinery, etc., when connected to a hoisting fall or tackle.

SOOGEE: A solution of washing soda, soap powder, soft soap, and the like for washing paint. To wash or scrub paintwork or decks with soogee.

SPILLING LINE: Any line used for gathering in a sail or a brail, especially such a rope on a square sail.

SPAR: General term for a boom, mast, yard, stout pole, etc.

SPLICE: A joining of two rope ends, or an end with any part of the same or another rope, by interweaving the strands. To unite pieces of cordage, a rope to a chain, etc.

SPUN YARN: Soft right or left hand laid hemp small stuff, of two, three or four yarns. Used for seizing and service.

SQUALL: A suddenly rising strong wind, or sudden increase of wind, or short duration, usually followed immediately by rain or snow; a gust of wind.

SQUARE: At right angles with the fore and aft line and with the masts; sail of a vessel's yards when so braced or squared.

SQUARE RIGGED: Having some principal sails of a square shape and spread on yards; said of a brig, brigantine, barque, barquentine, or ship.

STANDING: Fixed, not moveable, established, as a standing gaff, standing block, standing orders.

STARBOARD: Pertaining to or situated on or toward the right-hand side of a vessel, looking forward.

STEAMER: General term for a vessel propelled by steam power, as distinguished from a sailing vessel.

STERN: Extreme after end of vessel; that portion above the counter and abaft the stern post.

STERN SHEETS: Space in a boat between the stern and the thwarts.

STEVEDORE: One whose occupation is unloading or loading vessels; a longshoreman.

STEWARD: Member of crew whose duty is catering to the domestic requirements of passengers and/or officers.

STOW: To pack away, lash in place, or otherwise secure something in position aboard ship; to place compactly and without loss of space, as a cargo in a vessel's hold.

STOWAWAY: One who conceals himself in a vessel for the purpose of obtaining a free or unauthorized passage.

STRAND: In cordage, one of several twisted yarns or threads or groups of such, which are laid up or twisted together to form a rope.

SUMNER LINE: The line of position resulting from an altitude observation of a heavenly body; chief feature of which is that the ship's position lies at some point on such a line. Named for its discoverer, Thomas H. Sumner, as American shipmaster.

TACKING: To change from one tack to another by coming about or turning the vessel into the wind and bringing the wind onto the other side, the sail being trimmed or hauled about accordingly.

TACKLE: A purchase, or set of blocks; usually two in which a rope or chain is rove for obtaining a mechanical advantage in hoisting or pulling.

TARPAULIN: A sheet of stout, waterproof canvas, jute, or hemp, for covering a hatch, cargo, etc.

TAUT: Hauled tight, tensely stretched; not slacked, as a rope or sail, cable, chain, etc.

TOP: In square-rigged vessels, a platform at a lower masthead, usually semicircular in shape with curved sides forward, fixed on the trestle trees, at approximately the same height as the eyes of the shrouds.

TRADE WINDS: Commonly called the Trades; those blowing from an approximately constant direction toward the thermal equator and deflected by the rotation of the earth. The band of these winds, one above and one below the equator.

TRAIL BOARD: In older sailing vessels, an ornamented plank on either side of the cutwater, serving as a brace or stiffener for the figurehead.

TRAMP: Short for tramp steamer, a powered cargo vessel that engages in picking up and carrying cargo at whatever port it can be found, as distinguished from a cargo liner, or vessel plying a regular run.

TURNBUCKLE: Mechanical device for setting up shrouds, stays, deck-load lashing, steering chains, etc.

UNBEND: To detach or remove from a secured position, as an anchor from its cable; a rope that is hitched or knotted to something, a sail from its yard, stay, mast, etc.

VENTILATOR: Any opening, conduit, pipe, or the like, through which fresh air is introduced and vitiated air, gasses, etc., escape.

VERNIER: An auxiliary scale fitted to slide along the measuring scale of an instrument, as on the side of a sextant.

VIKING: Member of a crew of the hardy Norsemen or Scandinavians who, as freebooters, rovers, or pirates, plundered the coasts of Europe from the eighth to tenth centuries.

WAIST: Midship, or widest part of the upper deck.

WAKE: Disturbed water following, or the track left by, a moving ship, iceberg, storm, etc.

WARP: A rope or hawser used in mooring or shifting a vessel, as by making its end fast to a post, buoy, stanchion, or other fixed object. To warp ship; to haul or heave a vessel by a warp.

WATCH: A period of duty, usually four hours, to which a division of ship's crew, or a specified number of men, is assigned. Any group having this duty is referred to as the Watch.

WATERSPOUT: One of the most remarkable phenomena observed at sea. A sea-borne tornado, it first appears as a whirling inverted cone-shaped mass of water reaching downwards, as if alive, with an elongated trunk or column to meet a corresponding, whirling disturbance on the surface. Unpredictable and fast-moving, exceptionally dangerous to a sailing vessel.

WEATHER SIDE: The side towards the wind, opposed to the lee side.

WEIGH: To raise or lift a vessel's anchor from the bottom, especially in the act of departing from an anchorage.

YARD: A long, slendering spar set crosswise on a mast used to support the sails.

List of Erikson sailing ships with size and tonnage

Moshula	4 mast barque	5,300	
Passat	" "		4,700
Lawhill	" "	4,600	
Pamir	" "		4,500
Olivebank	" "	4,400	
Herzogin Cecilie	" "	4,350	
Pommern	" "	4,050	
Viking	" "	4,000	
Archibald Russel	" "	3.950	
L'Avenir	" "	3,650	
Ponape	" "	3,500	
Penang	3 "	3.250	
Winterhude	" "		3,250
Killoran	" "	3,050	
Grace Hawar	3 f.s.		3,950
Kylemore	3 barque		1,900
Lingard	" "	1.600	
Pestalozzi	" "	1,600	
Elakoon	" "	1,400	
Warma	" "	1,400	
Dione	4 sch		1,000
Estonia	3 sch	800	
Baltic	4 sch		750

Bibliography

Butlin, Commander C. M. *White Sails Crowding.* London: Jonathan Cape, 1935. "Voyage of *L'Avenir*" includes story of Annette Brock Davis and photograph of her aloft on yard.

Kahre, George., ed. Greenhill. *The Last Tall Ships: Gustav Erikson and the Aland Sailing Fleets 1872–1947.* Greenwich: Conway Maritime Press, 1848, 1978.

Koivistoinen, Eino. *Billowing Sails.* Hameenlinna: Karesto Oyankayapaino. 1988.

Harland, John. *Seamanship in the Age of Sail.* London: Conway Maritime Press, 1985.

Underhill, Harold. *Sailing Ship Rigs and Rigging.* Glasgow: Brown, Son and Ferguson, 1955.

——. *Sail Training and Cadet Ships.* Glasgow: Brown, Son and Ferguson, 1956.

About the Author

Annette Brock Davis challenged the definition of men's and women's roles, and became the first woman in the British Empire to serve as a crew member aboard a four-masted merchant sailing vessel.

Landlocked in Montreal during World War II, Davis studied painting with Arthur Lismer, one of Canada's famed Group of Seven. After the war, as an artist, she cared for her husband, invalided from the merchant service, and their two children. In the last four decades, she has exhibited at Place des Arts, Montreal, the World's Fair, New York, and in galleries in New York, Montego Bay, Jamaica, and in Massachusetts and Florida. She has been awarded prizes from the University of New Brunswick and the Art Association of Nantucket. As she sailed around Cape Horn, she is a full-fledged member of the *Association Internationale Cap Horniers de St. Malo.*

In her ninetieth year, Annette Brock Davis maintains a serious writing and painting schedule. She still sleeps in a bunk bed, and continues to navigate her bicycle on errands in Bridgenorth, the town where she lives in southern Ontario.